DIGGING
FOR
RICHARD III

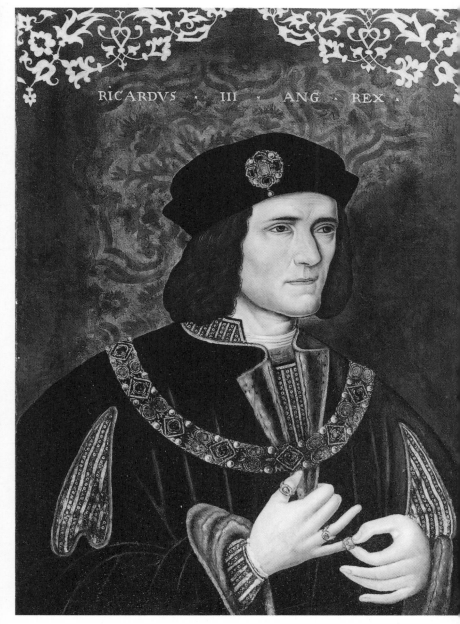

RICARDVS · III · ANG · REX ·

Portrait of Richard III in the National Portrait Gallery, by an unknown artist; thought to date from 1580 to 1600, it is close to a portrait in the Royal Collection that may have been the prototype for nearly 20 known paintings.

MIKE PITTS

DIGGING
FOR
RICHARD III

The Search for the Lost King

43 illustrations

 **Thames & Hudson**

CONTENTS

Act III

EXCAVATION IN 2012

Scene 1. Greyfriars. A car park

In which an excavation is launched in a car park, and archaeologists
find a friary, a church and a human skeleton

Scene 2. The same. A grave

In which a skeleton is excavated

Act IV

AN AUTOPSY

In which various scientific studies are conducted on a skeleton
to establish age, gender, height and build of the individual, details of diet,
health and pathology, and approximate date of death

Act V

AN INQUEST

In which scientific, historical and artistic research together establish
the cause of death and the identity of a person represented by a skeleton

Epilogue. Battlefields and burials

In which we consider why finding a king's remains matters, follow
what happened after the revelation, and describe how the site was found
where the Battle of Bosworth was fought

PROLOGUE

For Nicky

'For there is nothing lost, that may be found, if sought.'

Edmund Spenser, The Faerie Queene

'What we are about to tell you is truly astonishing.'

On 4 February 2013, a team from the University of Leicester delivered its verdict to a mesmerized press room, watched by media studios around the world: they had found the remains of Richard III, one of the most disputed monarchs in British history.

This is the story of how that happened.

The discovery, as Richard Buckley, the lead archaeologist behind the project, said, was an astonishing achievement.

Richard III is both a historical figure at the centre of dark and bloody events signalling the end of the Middle Ages, and an enduring mythical ogre, captured by Shakespeare as the archetypal villain. He is a man whose almost psychotic ambition holds a fearful fascination. Or, it may be, he is a maligned king whose noble progress was cut short and then concealed by those who would distort history for personal gain.

His very life embodies terror and conspiracy. It demands precise analysis, the uncovering of truth and the exposure of falsities. How appropriate, then, that the most forensic of historical practitioners, scruffy, mud-spattered archaeologists in league with futuristic scientists, should uncover the physical remains of the protagonist himself. Fragile, delicate and intimate, Richard III's bones are hard evidence that few had expected ever to see.

Yet improbable as the discovery was, this success was not the only remarkable thing about the project. In my career as an archaeologist and writer, I have seen, studied and reported on more excavations than I can remember; I have worked on many myself, and even directed a few. But never have I witnessed an excavation like the one that found Richard III.

It was well planned, as all good excavations are. It had precise goals, again a sign of a field project likely to deliver results. But here events parted with normality.

The dig began on a Saturday in August 2012. The team had five objectives, and two weeks in which to achieve them. What typically happens in such situations is that discoveries are made that go some way towards solving the problems the archaeologists have set themselves. But other finds, as you might expect, raise new questions. At the end of the dig, the archaeologists pack up their things and anticipate the long process of analysis – always much longer (and more expensive) than the actual dig – and feel already they now know more than they did. But they also know there are new things they don't understand. There is a sort of balance, with old, partly solved questions on one hand, and new questions to answer on the other. If funding bodies will permit, they will have to come back and dig again – in its way, of course, an achievement in itself. They enjoy digging.

The excavation in Leicester was not like that. The archaeologists achieved their first objective on the first day. This had been considered in advance to be 'a reasonable expectation', though no one would have bet on pulling it off on day one. It took a little longer to achieve objective two ('a probability') – nearly a week. They ticked off objective three ('a possibility') on the eighth day, four ('an outside chance') on the twelfth, and five ('not seriously considered possible', with Richard Buckley having promised to eat his hat if it happened) on the same day as four. Two objectives in one day! And they still had two days of digging left.

The excavation had been commissioned by Philippa Langley. Philippa is not an archaeologist, but a writer with an interest in history and a passion for Richard III. Before they began, the team had warned her not to be too hopeful. There was only one thing she really wanted from the project: to find the remains of Richard III. This was the objective the archaeologists judged, in plain speaking, to be impossible. Yet when the digging began, it seemed, anything might happen.

'People would find things', Philippa told me, 'not just every day but really almost every hour. Every moment, we would hear a shout saying, "Look at this!" And we'd all be running to see what it was, and then we'd be running to the other side to see something else that had been found.'

This was fun. They were sitting down in the tent having lunch, and Philippa said to the diggers, 'God, I love your job. No wonder you're archaeologists!'

A ring of bemused faces looked up from their sandwiches.

'This is just the best job in the world!' Philippa repeated. 'If I'd known it was like this, I might have been an archaeologist!'

And they all looked at her, and said no, Philippa, no. Archaeology is being out in the rain and cold, moving dirt, hurting your back and bruising your hands. The pay is poor. Most of the time you're lucky if you find a small piece of broken pot you'd have difficulty selling on eBay. Stick with something easy and well paid, like being a writer.

'This dig', said the archaeologists, 'is NOT normal.'[1]

Act I

ENGLAND,
1452–85

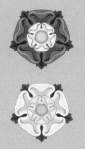

A man stands alone, centre stage. He hears a door shut behind us, and turns to look. Leaning into a limp in his left leg and swivelling his raised right shoulder, he ambles towards us, eyeing us with an expression of curiosity and disdain, a hint of teasing humour, perhaps fear. He closes in and pauses, bent like a tree grown in constant wind.

We then hear one of Shakespeare's most famous soliloquies. In this 1955 movie Richard III is played by Sir Laurence Olivier. The actor, the direction and the words – 'Now is the winter of our discontent' – together make an extraordinarily compelling scene.[1]

Shakespeare's Richard is an embodiment of evil, crippled physically and mentally by birth. Yet his intelligence and charisma fascinate us, as he schemes and murders his way to the power soon to be taken from him by his savage death in battle.

Shakespeare is one reason for Richard III's enduring presence, but not the only one. Richard lived in turbulent, changing times. The Battle of Bosworth, at which he died in 1485, was a watershed in British history. It effectively ended the thirty-year Wars of the Roses, replacing the Plantagenet dynasty, source of more English kings than any other, with the Tudor dynasty, opening the way for Henry VIII and Elizabeth I.

The Plantagenets are not forgotten: the current British monarch still receives significant income from their former estates; the Duke of Lancaster's Regiment toasts the Queen as the duke, and displays a red rose. But their power died with the Middle Ages. For the English, Bosworth symbolizes the medieval world's end, and the start of the early modern era – a bloody, explosive event to mark the late arrival of the Renaissance.[2]

Richard was born in 1452, a century after the Black Death, which killed up to half or more of the entire population of Europe and profoundly challenged its economy, politics and culture, with effects continuing during his lifetime. He was barely a year old when the Hundred Years' War ended. This era of conflict between England and France was a struggle among ruling families that spread power through

Shakespeare's Richard III played by Mark Rylance, English actor and former Artistic Director of Shakespeare's Globe Theatre, in London in 2012/13 and New York in 2013/14.

the wider population. It encouraged the centralization of states – and the national sentiments that these engendered – while draining English resources. The royal household was effectively put out of business. A failing economy and frustration with government inspired protest, and brutalized society. The wars also affected military technology and thinking, resulting in evidence at Bosworth that, centuries later, could be used by archaeologists to revise the conventional history of the battle's course.

Richard was 21 when the London merchant William Caxton, then working in Belgium, printed the first book in English. Within a decade of his death, Christopher Columbus had made landfall in America, the first English-speaking university to teach medicine had opened (in Aberdeen), and Leonardo da Vinci – born in the same year as Richard – was working on one of his most famous paintings, *The Last Supper*. It was no accident that Shakespeare devoted so much of his talent to these extraordinary times – eight of his ten history plays cover the century and a half that culminated on Bosworth field.[3]

Richard was king of England for just over two years, but in that short reign enough happened to inspire generations of writers. He began controversially by seizing the throne, brutally and illegally. His two young nephews, rightful heirs, disappeared – the 'princes in the Tower' – though even at the time what happened to them was largely a mystery. And he ended his rule in unforgettable style, fighting bravely even when he knew he was doomed. When Richard died, he became the only English monarch to lose his life in battle since the accession of the Norman dynasty in 1066, a record that remains unbroken.

Just over a century later, Shakespeare described a monster. He was writing fiction, inspired by texts from nearer Richard's time that exaggerated the king's faults. Yet that does not necessarily mean Richard did not have any. And if he was no saint, he certainly experienced as good as he gave. While he grew up, his family stole, tortured and murdered in pursuit of power, or just survival – as did others around them. His family suffered too. His paternal grandfather had been beheaded before Richard was born. He was eight years old when his father and an older brother were killed in battle. Later, another brother – Edward IV – executed their brother George, an act, say some historians, in which Richard was complicit.

We would be cautious today about making judgments in an atmosphere of intrigue and fear, so how much more care must we bring to what we read about events that occurred over five centuries ago. As a modern historian has said, Richard's times were 'a period of struggle for power, carried on in an atmosphere of rumour, suspicion, propaganda, plot and counter-plot. Only those at the centre could be fully aware of what was going on.'[4] And even if they knew, almost none of those at that dark place felt the need to tell us.

Yet there are sufficient records of the times through which Richard lived to more than engage our interest. Events were both striking and rapid, even if occasionally they seem to play out in slow motion. Journeys, by ship or horse, or often on foot, took time. A simple message had to be physically conveyed, so that when action awaited critical intelligence, it could be more efficient to travel to the news source than to rely on messengers. Even as plots were secretly reshaped and counterattacks mustered in affairs that changed daily, there was time enough for gossip and confusion to build, and for decision-makers to reflect.

So we too ponder. Through the prism of history we see a life of corruption and terror as a king struggles to retain power, breaking the law, killing as he sees fit, yet at other times showing empathy for ordinary people or enjoying a play or concert. We also see a man forced into decisions – sometimes by circumstances, sometimes by his own actions – which he understands will change his life but whose outcomes he cannot foresee. This is a human being expressing fear and courage, hatred and affection, judgment on the past and hopes for the future. The scene was thus set for dispute, conspiracy theories and reinvention long before Shakespeare. The search for the real Richard III began with his birth.

*

That event occurred on 2 October 1452, a Monday, in Fotheringhay Castle in Northamptonshire. We owe this detail to a charming artifact, an illuminated prayer book owned by Richard.[5] We are firmly in the Middle Ages. The castle, built 50 years after the Norman Conquest, became English royal property in the late 13th century. The prayer book, known as a Book of Hours, had been illustrated and written by hand in the medieval international language of Latin. Some 50 years after it was made, it was acquired by a king. And against 2 October that king added, in fine flowing script, the above details of his own birth.

The pretty little book was said to have been found in Richard's tent after the Battle of Bosworth. Its next owner was the new king Henry VII's mother. Almost exactly a century after Bosworth, the first printed Book of Common Prayer was issued, in English, and 50 years after that Fotheringhay Castle was a ruin. The Middle Ages were no more.

Frontispiece from Richard III's Book of Hours (*c.* 1440); the angel Gabriel tells the Virgin Mary that she will bear Jesus. Richard's birth is recorded on 2 October 1452.

There is another curious pivotal feature of Richard's birth: its location. Fotheringhay is just 65 km (40 miles) from a farm in Leicestershire now deemed to be the centre of England.[6] And that is less than 5 km (3 miles) from the field where Richard died. A life of mythic significance in English history began and ended at its geographical heart.

Like those of all of his class, it was also a life marked by genealogy. Many of us today take an active interest in our family histories, helped by magazines, websites and blogs. We find stories of poverty and loss, of menial employment, early deaths and even criminal activities. The lives of our ancestors highlight their determination to survive, and the wider changes that have made possible our own relatively comfortable existence. Five centuries ago, for members of the aristocracy, genealogy had a harder reality. It defined their power.

In the 1949 movie *Kind Hearts and Coronets*, Louis Mazzini, deprived of his birthright by his mother's unconventional marriage, seeks revenge through the simple process of murdering all those who come between him and a dukedom. As he advances on his goal, he marks his accomplishments on a family tree hidden behind a picture hanging over his mantelpiece.[7] Fifteenth-century members of the House of Plantagenet would have understood what Mazzini was doing. But their trees were less like neatly branching diagrams than thickets. (Indeed, to combat the genealogical complexities of this period, all occurrences of Richard III's name in the following text are capitalized, so that he may be distinguished from other Richards. The family tree overleaf should also be helpful.)

Parents sometimes had so many children that only those who mattered in the power game would appear in their lists. We remain complicit in such editing. How many published trees show RICHARD III's full complement of four sisters and seven brothers?[8] Death could come at any time, from disease, by accident, through axe or sword, arrow or bullet. Few lived to become elderly and infirm.

Men and women of quite differing ages might outlive their wives and husbands, enabling them to marry more than once into different families, and their former or future spouses might do (or have done) likewise. A wedding was a way to reshape a family's tree, and potentially its fortunes, acquiring titles that could bring huge assets in the form of estates and rents. Yet little could be taken for granted.

Consider Isabel Neville, daughter of an immensely wealthy earl, another Richard, later known as Warwick the Kingmaker. Isabel's father needed her both to preserve his riches and to bolster them. She was 17 when in 1469 she married George, Duke of Clarence. The duke was the younger brother of the then king – Edward IV – a match that, if things went well, should have assured dynastic income and safety, as well as offering the promise of power. But things did not go well.

Isabel had four children. The first was stillborn in a ship off Calais. Another survived for less than three months. A third did better: he

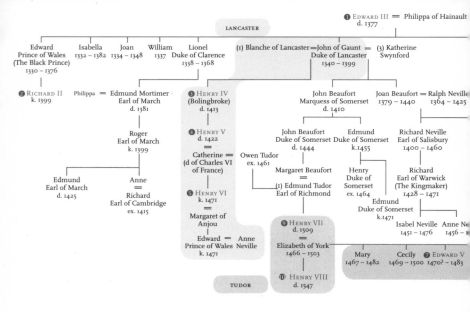

For two centuries England was ruled by the male descendants of one man, Edward III (1327–77), and fought over by the inter-marrying factions of Lancaster and York; the Tudor Henry VIII (1509–47) could trace ancestry to Edward through both houses.

was 24 when Henry VII had him beheaded, extinguishing the legitimate male line of the House of Plantagenet. Isabel's daughter lived longest, only to face execution by Henry VIII.

Isabel herself, however, never knew of the violent demise of her two longest-living children, having died shortly after bearing her last. Though her cause of death is now thought to have been natural, her husband George convinced himself she had been poisoned, and arranged for the brutal arrest and hanging of one of his late wife's ladies-in-waiting. Like marriage, the courts could be used for personal ends by those with authority.

This was the world known to RICHARD Plantagenet, Duke of Gloucester, Constable of England and then KING RICHARD III – to list a few of the successive names and titles of the eighth son of the Duke of York. The Lancastrians and the Yorkists supplied the dynastic backbone for the Wars of the Roses, as individuals exploited family and political

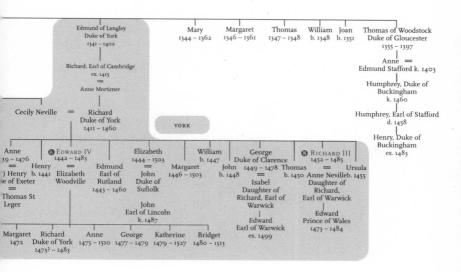

loyalties to further their ends. RICHARD was born a Yorkist. His eldest brother would become king Edward IV, but the three preceding kings, Henry VI, V and IV, were Lancastrians. Though RICHARD's father, Richard Duke of York, sought to overthrow Henry VI, it was his sons who succeeded in ascending the throne. Ultimately, however, the feud between the two families ended at Bosworth, when the new House of Tudor left both Lancastrians and Yorkists behind.

Yet these Lancastrians and Yorkists were all descended from Edward III, who had died only 75 years before RICHARD was born. And it was this shared lineage, and shared claim to the throne, that was the cause of their animosity. So too were other families caught up in the feuding, marrying into whichever dynasty they saw fit. Isabel Neville and her sister Anne, for example, were descended from a daughter of John of Gaunt (founder of the Lancastrian dynasty), herself a half-sister of the Lancastrian Henry IV. Anne's first husband would be his direct descendant Edward Prince of Wales, Henry VI's son, later killed in battle. A year later, Anne would marry the future RICHARD III, giving up the title Princess of Wales but in time becoming Queen of England.

Act I

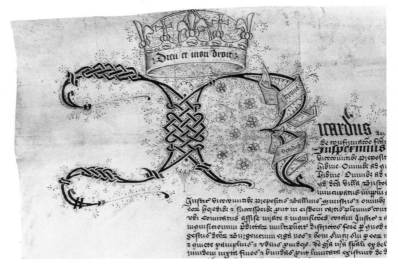

A fine initial R (for *Ricardus*, Latin for Richard) with roses, crown and royal motto, illuminated on animal skin in 1484 at the top of a legal document prepared at the king's court.

And the Tudors were not so different. Like Anne Neville, Henry VII (first king of the Tudor line) was descended from Henry IV's father, John of Gaunt. But the wife who bore his successor Henry VIII would be a Yorkist – Edward IV's eldest child. The Tudors might as well have been known as a Lancastrian-Yorkist alliance (indeed this union was what their combined red and white rose emblem symbolized): or, in a word, Plantagenets, the house from which both families anyway derived.

If history tends to simplify the record to make a clearer story, it was a mess genealogically. This tangle was easily exploited by warring factions. And in 1452, Richard Duke of York, soon to be father to the future RICHARD III, set out to see what he could achieve by doing exactly that.

The Duke of York was descended from Edward III's fifth son, Edmund. Other things being equal, this put his claim to the throne behind that of descendants of the four sons born earlier. One of these had conveniently died before his first birthday (as Louis Mazzini put it, looking at a newspaper, 'Sometimes the deaths column brought good news, sometimes the births column brought bad'). The oldest son had fathered Richard II, who, childless, was usurped by his cousin Henry IV, heir of Edward III's fourth son, John of Gaunt. That left in the way Henry IV's (Lancastrian) descendants – currently represented by the king, Henry VI – along with other descendants of the fourth son, and family descended from the third son.

But York had other advantages: he was not in fact descended only from Edward III's fifth son. His father had married into the third son's family, so that through his mother, the duke could claim royal ancestry through Edward III's third son, trumping the Lancastrian line (descended from the fourth son) and outpaced by none. The young duke himself had been married to the ten-year-old Cecily Neville, descended from Edward III's fourth son, like the Lancastrians. This meant that the Duke of York's children could claim descent from all the sons of Edward III who had any effective claim to the throne.

And finally, York's hereditary claim was fuelled by a desire for revenge. His father had joined a conspiracy to seize power from Henry V. It failed. After a trial in Southampton, the conspirators were beheaded, notwithstanding his father's impassioned pleas. The orphaned duke – his mother had died the day after he was born – was then four.

So in 1452, emboldened by Henry VI's 'manifest incompetence',[9] York made public his ambitions and marched on London – to no great effect. Outmanoeuvred by the Duke of Somerset, a Lancastrian supporter and another descendant of Edward III's fourth son, the Duke and his wife moved to Fotheringhay, where two months later RICHARD was born.

In 1891, Henry Wheatley described the Temple Gardens, set in an old legal district in the City of London, as a 'fine, open space, fronting the Thames'; a private space, walled and gated. Such it is when, according to Shakespeare in *Henry VI, Part 1*, the Duke of York and five other men – among them the Duke of Somerset – leave the busy halls for the quiet privacy of the garden to discuss delicate matters. It is an apocryphal but poignant scene.

'Admit it', says York. 'You know I'm right.'

His friends equivocate. Exasperated, York lays down a challenge. 'Look at these roses,' he says. 'If you are with me, pick a white flower.' Somerset takes the offensive: pick a red rose, he says, and support me.

Warwick plucks a white rose, Suffolk a red. Vernon, when pushed, picks a 'pale and maiden blossom', dismissing Somerset's jest that should he prick his finger his blood would redden the flower and divert his allegiance.

There remains only a lawyer. 'The argument you held was wrong in you', he says, addressing Somerset. He too plucks a white rose.

Confident in victory, York taunts Somerset. 'Where is your case now?'

'In my scabbard,' snaps Somerset, 'ready to soak your rose in blood.'

The two men exchange escalating insults. When Somerset has stomped off, Warwick makes a prophecy. This garden brawl, he says, 'Shall send between the red rose and the white, A thousand souls to death and deadly night'.

If only so few. York was ready for battle. The Wars of the Roses, into which the people of England were dragged and slaughtered and during which the aristocracy found the old chivalric ways would no longer offer personal safety, had begun.

In 1891, Wheatley surveyed the Temple Gardens. 'Such is the smoke and foul air of London', he wrote, 'that the commonest and hardiest kind of rose has long ceased to put forth a bud.' Perhaps they died in 1452.[10]

*

The atmosphere among the English aristocracy, already disturbed by York's rebellion and fears that their king Henry VI lacked the strength to maintain peace, was further troubled by events in France. In July 1453 an English army was defeated at the Battle of Castillon. The rout finally drained the capital won by earlier generations at Crécy (1346) and Agincourt (1415). It marked the loss for England not just of hopes for control of France – ending the Hundred Years' War – but of confidence at home. Henry VI was reported to have gone mad.

With only an infant son and a wife who was a niece of the king of France, the ailing king saw support for himself and his Lancastrian dynasty fall away. Despite his recent failure to seize power, York rapidly strengthened his position, rewarding promises of loyalty with political appointments as he was himself granted the power of protector, responsible for the crown – now in the person of a five-month-old heir, Prince Edward – and kingdom.

Then, bizarrely, Henry appeared suddenly to regain his senses. Somerset, released from the Tower of London where York had contained him, plotted retribution. York was dismissed. Diplomacy had lost its force.

In May 1455 the king set out for Leicester. York intercepted him at St Albans. Battle was met.[11] But this was no Agincourt, with army pitched against army in open field. Earls hunted down fellow aristocrats in the city streets. The wounded king cowered in a cottage, absorbing the reek of piss from tanning pits. Somerset was found hiding in a pub and murdered, his red blood staining the yard. Other dukes and earls were hurt or killed, racking up the score of those seeking revenge. Henry's miraculous recovery had 'turned a tragedy into a national disaster'.[12] The round of killing would not end until Bosworth was done.

York again became Henry VI's protector, but within months he had lost the privilege. As the king wavered in and out of reality, the queen, Margaret of Anjou, focused on bolstering the Lancastrian power that her young son would inherit. So York too needed to look to his supporters. Yet both sides had cause to fear the Scots to the north and the French to the south, while English government struggled to have any control in Wales. And it was there that another descendent of Edward III (through his fourth son), the young Margaret Beaufort, contrived to launch a third dynastic contender for power: early in 1457, three months after the death of her husband Edmund Tudor, she gave birth to their only son in the safety of Pembroke Castle. She named him Henry. York's son RICHARD

A heraldic – rather than lifelike – representation of Richard III and his queen, Anne Neville, in the Salisbury Roll, perhaps intended to show them at their coronation in July 1483.

was then four. In a little under 30 years Henry and RICHARD would meet at Bosworth, the one to gain a throne and become Henry VII, first Tudor monarch, the other to lose it.

The queen's present concern, however, was not Margaret Beaufort and the Tudors, but the Yorks. In 1459 she summoned a council that found the Duke of York outside the law, and both parties prepared for conflict. York's supporters set out to join the duke at his castle in Ludlow, bringing men across the Channel from Calais, and down from Middleham Castle in Yorkshire. Queen Margaret arranged to ambush the Middleham contingent at Blore Heath, near the border between Staffordshire and Shropshire. The Lancastrian forces greatly outnumbered the Yorkist, but the latter were forewarned by spies. Using the marshy landscape to tactical advantage, they escaped with a clear victory, leaving 2,000 Lancastrian dead.[13]

As news reached Ludlow of this defeat and Yorkist supporters arrived from north and east, the duke might have felt a moment of confidence. If so, it soon passed. Setting out for London, he met the king's full army, twice the size of his. He returned to Ludlow, where his men built defences out of earthworks and wagons, near Ludford Bridge. Darkness came early on an October night. The Calais wing, having seen the royal flag that marked the presence of Henry VI himself, defected to the Lancastrians. Around midnight York and his teenage sons, Edward and Edmund, and his two supporting earls left camp to cross the bridge into town in search of a pub. They never went back: York fled to Ireland with Edmund, and the earls moved south with Edward, borrowed a boat and left for Calais.[14]

The next morning the king and queen pardoned the abandoned soldiers and allowed their own troops to loot Ludlow and abuse its citizens. York's wife Cecily had apparently been left to look after herself and their three younger children, Margaret, George and RICHARD; the last had celebrated his seventh birthday less than a fortnight before.[15] They were taken into royal care.

Parliament was summoned, and the rebels were 'attainted' – stripped of their titles and property, enriching those loyal to the crown and further embittering the Yorkist cause. By the following June, in 1460, they were ready to strike back. They invaded England.

To the Lancastrians' alarm, the attack came not from Ireland led by the Duke of York, but from his supporters and eldest son, Edward, sailing over from France and marching on London through Kent. Leaving the Tower under siege, they continued the journey northeast. The armies met in fields beside the River Nene, just south of Northampton.[16]

The king's forces, feeling secure, perhaps, behind their newly dug fort despite being heavily outnumbered, rebuffed negotiations. The Yorkists attacked. One of the king's lords betrayed him and let in the opponents. The summer afternoon was marked by unseasonably heavy rain, such that 'the [king's] guns lay deep in the water, and so were quenched and might not be shot'. Fleeing Lancastrians drowned in the swollen river. By some accounts it was all over in half an hour. Casualties may have been relatively low, but they included several lords. Henry, sheltering in his tent, was seized by an archer.

The queen fled first to Wales, and then Scotland. Cecily and her children moved to a mansion in London. When the Duke of York finally made his way over from Ireland, he marched under the arms of Edward III's third son, a clear threat to the legitimacy of Henry VI, whose claim was only through the fourth son. To further make the point, York strode into the palace of Westminster through the king's entrance, apparently expecting to be hailed as the new monarch: but Parliament wasn't ready for that, and he fumed out, snubbed. York's subsequent more diplomatic approach went better (and enriched the fortunate lawyers), and he was granted the right to inherit the throne after the king's natural death in place of Henry and Margaret's son. In the meantime he could draw a comfortable salary befitting a royal heir.

War was now inevitable. The king's sanity may have been in doubt, but he otherwise seemed healthy, and he was ten years younger than York. Queen Margaret cared less about her husband's prospects than her son Edward's, who had been disinherited. Drawing on considerable Lancastrian support, she prepared to invade England, giving York the excuse he needed to force events. Leaving Cecily with Margaret, George and RICHARD in London, the duke sent their oldest son Edward to confront the queen's allies in Wales, and set off north with Edmund.

The crown owned an old castle at Sandal, near Wakefield and 40 km (25 miles) southeast of York. The duke spent a cold, wet Christmas there with his troops, while the queen camped 16 km (ten miles) to the east. Then on 30 December 1460, for reasons that are not recorded, York left the safety of a stone fort towering over the surrounding landscape and charged ahead of his men to confront the queen's forces. He was surrounded 'like a fish in a net' and killed, along with his son Edmund and, according to varied reports, 700 to 2,500 of his army. Shakespeare has the queen and her men torture York, smearing him with his son's blood and crowning him with paper before stabbing him to death.[17]

York's strongest ally, Richard Neville, Earl of Salisbury (and grandfather of Isabel and Anne), was captured and executed the next day. His head was taken with the Duke of York's and Edmund's to the city of York, where they were displayed above Micklegate Bar. 'York', says Shakespeare's queen, 'may overlook the town of York.'[18]

Barely had he heard the news from Wakefield than York's son Edward, who was at Ludlow, learned that a Lancastrian force was marching on Hereford, 32 km (20 miles) to the north. With his father dead and himself already experienced in battle, Edward was now Henry VI's recognized successor and a prominent figure caught in the spiralling cycle of ambition and revenge, of armed conflicts and extra-judicial executions. The armies met at Mortimer's Cross. Edward secured a rapid victory, leaving 4,000 Lancastrian dead.[19]

Meanwhile, fired by success and growing aristocratic support, Queen Margaret had continued south and routed Yorkist forces in St Albans.[20] Anticipating her imminent arrival in London, York's widow Cecily sent her sons George and RICHARD to the safety of family friends in France. But Margaret in fact moved north, and it was Edward who reached the capital. On 4 March 1461, at 19 years old, he was proclaimed king.

Now needing more than ever to remove the Lancastrian threat, the new Edward IV confronted the former queen's forces in Yorkshire, at Towton. Here, in driving March sleet, tens of thousands of men on either side fought through a long day. They included a significant proportion of England's most powerful lords, though Margaret, Henry and their son Edward were safe in York. It was an overwhelming victory for the king.

Towton was the bloodiest battle ever recorded on English soil. Fleeing soldiers trod over corpses floating in a deep brook. The River Wharfe ran red. Many thousands died. Archaeologists examined the remains of 39 men packed into a shallow grave at the battlefield, after it had been accidently disturbed during building work in 1996. 'Many of the individuals', they reported, 'suffered multiple injuries ... far in excess of those necessary to cause disability and death'.[21]

A few months later, in June, RICHARD's mother Cecily recalled him and his brother George to a traumatized England. Her oldest son was king, transforming her status. But the cost was high. Her husband, her other young adult son, her brother and his son had all died at Wakefield. These were not the only losses she had to bear. Cecily had the support of three daughters aged between 15 and 21, but half her 12 children were gone – four boys and a girl had died before their first birthdays. George and RICHARD were now second and third in line to the throne, respectively. But their most formative years had been a time of pain.

*

This was not the end of the Lancastrians, however. Henry VI, his wife Margaret and their son Edward had fled to Scotland, plotting revenge. In 1464 Lancastrian attempts to raise support for their cause in the north of England, and thwart King Edward's peace negotiations with Scotland, were defeated at two battles less than a day's ride from the border.[22] Nonetheless, Margaret of Anjou sided with Scottish rebels. Lancastrian allies in France threatened England from the south. The wealthy and powerful Richard Neville, Earl of Warwick, who had fought with the Yorkists and secured the throne for Edward, dangerously felt sidelined, and in defiance of Edward, had arranged for his daughter to marry the king's brother George, now the Duke of Clarence. Edward desperately needed to secure his throne.

The project began badly. In 1469 supporters of Warwick and Edward met in Northamptonshire at Edgcote.[23] Warwick's forces won, leaving 2,000 dead on the battlefield and hunting down and beheading fleeing aristocrats. Edward was arrested, though pressure from the aristocracy forced Warwick to release him.

Eight months later Warwick attempted a second coup, and this time Edward was the victor, gaining confirmation at the battle that his own (and RICHARD's) brother Clarence was also fighting against him.[24] Warwick's next move was to invade from France, now allied with Margaret of Anjou and planning to reinstate her husband Henry as king. They had enough support to make Edward flee across the Channel. For the next six months Henry VI was back on the throne.

Then, in March 1471, it was Edward's turn to invade. After seizing a clearly confused king in London, he rode 16 km (ten miles) north with his troops to Barnet. Facing Warwick's army under cover first of darkness and then mist, he secured a victory. Fifteen hundred died – among them Warwick himself.[25] Less than three weeks later and 160 km (100 miles) to the west, battle was joined again, at Tewkesbury.[26] Here Edward defeated Margaret's army. She was arrested. The 2,000 dead included her son Edward and, along with those subsequently executed, several Lancastrian rebels. Henry VI was executed in the Tower. For Edward IV, the wars in England were over.

All this time his younger brother RICHARD – now the Duke of Gloucester – had shown great loyalty, holding order in the north on behalf of the king or joining him when asked. RICHARD saw his first military action at Barnet and Tewkesbury, at the latter perhaps in command of the royal vanguard. He was given Warwick's vast estates, and over the next decade entrenched his growing power in the north. In 1482 he was put in charge of the English army during warfare with Scotland.

GLOUCESTER's loyalty to the crown was matched by attention to his family. The bodies of his father, the Duke of York, and his brother, Edmund, had been hastily buried in Pontefract Priory after the Battle of Wakefield. In 1476 RICHARD managed their reburial at Fotheringhay with dramatic ceremony. Later he and his wife Anne had one child, a son, who died aged eight, less than a year before his mother. RICHARD seems to have felt real loss at these deaths, and he cared well for two illegitimate children born before his marriage. In contrast, his brother Clarence's increasingly erratic behaviour culminated in his execution for treason – famously being drowned in a 'butt of malmsey wine' – after being tried personally by his king and older brother, Edward IV. But up to this point, there is nothing to suggest that RICHARD was anything other than an exemplary man and lord of his time.[27]

Then, in April 1483, after a short illness, Edward IV unexpectedly died.

Prince Edward, Edward IV's oldest son, was in Ludlow. He automatically became the uncrowned king. RICHARD was in York. In London, men debated whether he alone, or as leader of a council, should care for the 12-year-old king's interests. With the unifying authority of Edward IV gone, dynastic suspicion and envy found new life.

Edward V, accompanied by his family and retinue, set out for the capital from the west, and RICHARD came down from the north. At RICHARD's suggestion, the parties met at Stony Stratford, 16km (ten miles) south of Northampton. The king, along with his mother (born Elizabeth Woodville), her brother, her older son by her first marriage and her cousin, were seemingly astonished to be subjected immediately to a dynastic coup.

RICHARD, aided by Henry Duke of Buckingham, arrested the Woodvilles, knelt before the boy-king and proclaimed himself sole protector. It seems RICHARD believed he had foiled a plot against himself, which we know as the Woodville conspiracy. For us, as with so much that is soon to come, there is little substantial evidence to explain the incident. That is not unusual for this time: extraordinary events left no better evidence than prosaic ones, such that the details of almost everything told in this chapter could be questioned or reinterpreted. The actions of the next two years, three months and 22 days have been subjected to at least as much scrutiny, retelling and making of myth and fantasy as any other period of British history. And still we often do not know what really happened.

Looking down on the bared heads of Buckingham and his uncle, Edward V apparently told them not to worry. But it was too late. RICHARD imprisoned the four seized men, including Edward's personal attendant, in Yorkshire. His request for their execution was declined, but he ordered it himself as soon as he had the prerogative. He was made official protector. He enriched Buckingham with Woodville estates and gave him considerable power in Wales and the south. The young king was made at home in the Tower of London (a fortified royal palace with a prison attached).

A few months later, in June, RICHARD charged four more lords with aiding the Woodville conspiracy. One was executed on the spot and three were retained. Elizabeth's other young son, another Richard, second in line to the throne, was taken to the Tower to join his brother. RICHARD put it about that the two princes were illegitimate, and thus ineligible to reign, and pronounced himself king. Though no one seemed to know what happened – incriminating in itself, one might think – the princes were never seen again; it was widely assumed they had been killed.[28] Whatever his motivations, it becomes easy, perhaps, to think of RICHARD as a deluded dictator. Edward IV's rule by law and authority was being replaced by one of fear. Whether, judged by the culture and the particular events of the time, that made RICHARD a good king or a bad, is debatable. It certainly made his position dangerous.

Raised to power by claiming to have thwarted an attack on royalty, RICHARD could have been expected to be immediately nervous of his own security. With spectacular ceremonies and generous gifts – cutting taxes, returning land to local communities and helping churches – he toured the country, parading the monarch's unique status and promising better times. He was particularly munificent in York, where he planned a new college in which priests would pray for him and his family (though he died too soon, and it never happened).

RICHARD's devotion to religion and concern for the poor are said to have been genuine and sincere,[29] but drawing sympathy by advertising their importance to him was a wise strategy. Almost at once traitors, real or imagined, were identified. Less than three months after RICHARD's coronation, his former ally Buckingham was known to be plotting with Henry Tudor and Edward IV's widow Elizabeth Woodville – rival interests brought together by uncertainty, fuelled by the apparent loss of the princes in the Tower.

Rebellion grew across the south, attracting not just those who feared the future, but many who had already lost property, status or people close to them, executed or killed in battle. On his way down from York to London, RICHARD wrote in his own hand in fear and dismay at Buckingham's treachery, of 'the malice of him that had best cause to be true'.[30] But luck was with the king. Open revolt began prematurely in Kent. In Wales, local lords attacked Buckingham's own castle, and stormy weather forced him to cross the River Severn into England without his troops. RICHARD tracked him down to Salisbury and had him beheaded. The storms also scattered Henry Tudor's fleet, most of which returned to Brittany without making British landfall.

The rebellion had failed. But its cause remained. And now, as the king followed the tried process of attainting suspects – over a hundred lost their estates in RICHARD's only parliament, in January 1484 – yet more had cause to fear and resent. Contacts were maintained between former backers of Edward IV in England and Henry and his allies in France. Henry had French support, too, from a monarchy fearing English hostility. RICHARD had reason to expect another invasion.

It came in August 1485. Henry landed in southwest Wales, with French mercenaries, at the entrance to an enclosed estuary; at its head was Pembroke Castle, the place where he had been born and which was now in RICHARD's control. While Henry marched through Wales towards Shrewsbury, north of the royal castle at Ludlow, RICHARD gathered men of power around him and moved to Leicester. Requests for military support were met by contingents riding from the north and east.

In four days the two forces converged 25 km (15 miles) southeast of Leicester. Henry had marched from Shrewsbury down Watling Street, the old Roman road that headed straight for London. With a larger army, RICHARD had probably taken another Roman road that met Watling Street near Atherstone, where Henry was camped.[31] RICHARD settled down in

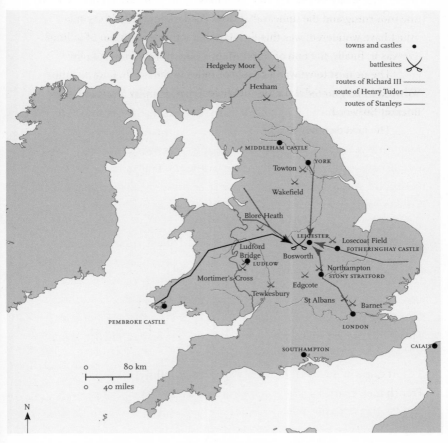

Map showing locations mentioned in the text, and the key routes by which forces reached Bosworth field in August 1485 (information from Foard and Curry, and others).

open country near Sutton Cheney, with some ten thousand soldiers.

It had been 14 years since an English king had confronted a rebel army across a battlefield. No one there could have been unfamiliar with what had happened in the 16 years before that: perhaps thirty or forty thousand men had died in a dozen battles, with many more surviving the terror, the bloodshed, the excavation of mass graves, the avenging executions, the mourning and the upheaval of lives. As darkness fell, thousands must have wondered: was this the start of another generation of killing? Or was it, finally, the end of wars? Many of them would never know.

The nearest town was a couple of miles to the north, known, since Edward I had granted it the right to hold a market every Wednesday, as Market Bosworth.

The next day they fought.

Act II

LOOKING FOR
RICHARD III

Scene 1

LEICESTER

A bridge

I'm walking from the west towards the historic core of the great, sprawling low-rise City of Leicester. Along this route, one day in August 1485, a king marched out to do battle; and on the next day, a new king marched in with his predecessor's body.

Leicester remembers the loser, which is why I am looking at a street sign that says King Richards Road. Beside it, with an arrow pointing up the quieter Tudor Road, is a warning: Humps for half mile. Even before his grave was found in a car park, Richard was truly the tarmac king.

It's an appropriate epithet, perhaps, for a man who was celebrated in this city more by myth and legend, the common gossip of inns and news sheets, than by the grandeur of official monuments – and also for a city that, at least where I am now, is apparently defined by tarmac, by corridors of traffic that cut and divide.

When King Richard finally got a public memorial here, in 1856, it was set in a factory wall by a local builder called Benjamin Broadbent, a few hundred yards on as I stand, where the road crosses the River Soar. A willow tree had done the job for those who knew, marking the site of Richard's grave, but it had been cut down. Mr Broadbent wanted something more permanent than a tree and more informative than a road

Since the mid-19th century, Leicester has been celebrating Richard III and the Wars of the Roses in street furniture.

name. The raised letters of his carved stone slab could be read as people left town over Bow Bridge or lingered at the Bow Bridge Inn opposite: 'Near this spot lie the remains of Richard III the last of the Plantagenets 1485.'[1]

Contemporary records describe how Richard was quietly buried not here, but within the city walls, in the church of Leicester Greyfriars, having first been displayed for a couple of days so the people could witness beyond doubt that the king was dead. Henry VII later paid for a monumental stone tomb. Along with everything else at the site, this seems to have disappeared when the friary was seized by Henry VIII's accountants at the Dissolution of the Monasteries in 1538.

Neither was Richard himself allowed to rest. According to tradition, an angry mob, at last able to get their hands on the hated tyrant, dug up his body, strode out of the city through the west gate with the decaying remains, and lobbed them into the river. There happened to be an old cemetery nearby. When the crowd had drifted away, 'a few pitying bystanders ... drew the corpse out of the water, and hastily placed it in consecrated ground'.[2]

Early in 1861 workmen started to take the bridge down, stone by stone, removing the very structure, it was thought, that had conveyed Richard's army to Bosworth. It was too narrow for modern traffic, just six feet across, with little niches either side for pedestrians to dodge into as carriages passed. And, it was said, its five stone arches impeded the river's flow after heavy rain, causing flooding.

Over the next two years the old Bow Bridge was replaced with a shiny new cast-iron structure, higher and wider and suspended over beams that completely cleared the water. Yet such progress brought a loss.

Along with the bridge, a favourite Leicester spot for recalling Richard III had been the Blue Boar Inn. The king was said to have stayed there before setting out to Bosworth. Supposedly it was then called the White Boar Inn, but was hastily rebranded when news reached Leicester of Henry's victory – a white boar being Richard's heraldic badge, and a blue boar, conveniently, the device of one of Henry VII's generals.

View of Bow Bridge across the River Soar, shortly before its demolition in 1861, looking west; an engraved stone (right) proclaims that Richard III's remains lie nearby.

Richard's visit not only brought fame to the hotel, but launched a small industry around the royal bed (in which the most remarkable incident was a landlady's murder and the subsequent execution of at least one man by hanging and of a woman by fire).[3]

In addition, tales of the fevered despoliation of Richard's tomb had unleashed a material counterpart to the royal bed for gossip and commerce – a royal coffin. Some 50 years in the ground before retrieval and a further 75 before first noted, the coffin could not be wood, and a stone one was duly found and proudly displayed at another inn.[4]

By 1861 the coffin had long disappeared. The old Blue Boar Inn, a fine piece of medieval architecture, had been demolished in 1836. That left the bridge as 'the only relic reminding the historical student of Richard's presence in Leicester'. Now that had gone, too. The town was entirely 'without a memorial of the king whose name lives in every man's thoughts'.[5]

Act II, Scene 1

The new Bow Bridge, completed in 1862, was cast iron; the decorated parapets, recently painted, feature red and white roses and Richard III's coat of arms detailed in blue and gold.

Well, perhaps not quite. The construction of a new bridge gave the opportunity for some inventive new commemoration. As I approach, the first thing I see is a cast-iron plate marking the name, Bow Bridge, partly obscured by the luxurious greenery and white elderflowers of a late, very wet summer. The bridge itself – strictly there are two, for two parallel lanes – is rich in historical imagery, cast in iron, newly restored, and painted in white, red, gold and black. At the centre of each parapet is Richard III's coat of arms, with a touch of blue. Two white boars hold up his crest, their hind legs standing on a motto – barely visible under layers of paint – that reads *Loyaute me Lie*, or loyalty binds me.[6] Either side, in alternating panels, are red and white roses.

As the quaint medieval bridge was swept away for industrial splendour, myth was fixed in iron. 'Upon this bridge', reads a cast plaque, 'stood a stone of some height, against which King Richard by chance struck his spur.' A wise woman noticed, and predicted that as his foot hit the stone on his way out, so on his return his head, hanging limp, would do the same. Forsooth.

The story, and the style, came from John Speed's *Historie of Great Britaine*, published in 1611. It was well known, if only from Speed's telling, but for one anonymous citizen of Leicester its representation on the new bridge was a mistake, favouring 'the puerilities and fictions of the gipsy fortune teller' – what another writer judged rather to be a 'historically interesting ... tradition' – over proper history.[7]

Yet while people argued about the relative merits of history and custom, the construction of the bridge had thrown up some solid evidence that no one was expecting. During the work, the river had been dammed so that the bed was comparatively dry. When the stone piers were taken out, wooden stakes were found, and faggots (bundles of twigs). These could have been part of the bridge's foundations, or conceivably from an earlier bridge, perhaps even a Roman one. More curious still, workmen digging on the east side of the bed unearthed an almost perfect human skeleton, close to a stone pier; the skull of a horse and an ox horn were found nearby.[8]

The men must have wondered if they'd stumbled on the king. Even as they wiped the dark mud from the bones, they could have read – or if needs be, have had read to them – Broadbent's words, looking down on the dry river bed: 'Near this spot lie the remains of Richard III'. The story spread quickly. King Dick had been found.

Meanwhile, the remains were bundled into a basket and carried off for examination. A local surgeon announced the skeleton to be that of a 20-year-old male (thus too young to be Richard III) of lower than average height. The skull was shown to a passing phrenologist – apparently the sort of visitor to be taken for granted at that time – who said it revealed a man of 'inferior intellectual development, who possessed some constructive skill, with large animal propensities', or, in plain English, an idiotic builder.

The phrenologist thought the stupid man had thrown himself into the river less than a century before. Another observer objected that the skeleton was truly ancient – not just medieval, but prehistoric, perhaps not even a modern human, and thus of immense value to science (Darwin's *On the Origin of Species* had been published less than three years before).[9]

The bones are now lost, so we cannot examine them ourselves. Lone skulls were also said to have been taken from the river, and sometimes attributed to Richard III; most of these too are lost. The completeness of the skeleton suggests a grave, and the best guess is that it was medieval. Close by, on the east side of the River Soar, there had been a friary, one of four in medieval Leicester.[10] Like the friary where, according to history, Richard had been buried, at least for the first time, this one – an Augustinian foundation known as the Austin Friars – had been demolished at the Dissolution in the 16th century. But beneath the ground, wall trenches and drains still survived, as did rubbish pits and cellars, and hundreds of graves. As the braided River Soar eroded its banks, it had probably undermined some of these burials.[11]

A century later, archaeologists were alert to the promise of this old friary site. It was in a triangle formed by two channels of the Soar, north of the road between Bow Bridge and West Bridge – the point where King Richards Road, crossing the river into Leicester, becomes St Augustine Road, the friars' road. It had never been a fashionable part of town, outside the walls, low-lying and wet. It was a place of factories, and one of the country's earliest railway terminuses – built to move coal, not people. After the Soar had been cut into a canal in 1889, drainage improved and new housing spread rapidly – this was when Tudor Road was laid out, with branch streets named Bosworth, Tewkesbury, Warwick and Vernon. But no houses were raised over the old friary.

By the 1960s, the railway had closed, the factories were running out of steam and developers were eyeing the land. It was the opportunity archaeologists had wanted. They knew there were remains of great potential interest, remains that would be destroyed if new works occurred. The threat released funds from central government, and in 1973 an excavation began, looking for the Austin Friars.

And down there, among the roads named after battles, dynasties and kings, where Richard III had marched out to Bosworth and where Henry VII had entered Leicester, where myth blended with record to create a unique memorial to momentous events and unforgettable men, came a schoolboy on his first-ever dig.

His name was Richard Buckley.

*

Half an hour's walk across town is a proper memorial. Built in the 1920s and designed by Edwin Lutyens, it is a beautiful and elegantly austere, monumental arch faced with pale Portland stone. Inspired by ancient Roman architecture and mythology, it bestrides the axis of the rising sun on Armistice Day, honouring the 12,000 Leicestershire men who died in the First World War.[12]

It is near this arch, among a group of buildings on Peace Way, that Richard Buckley today has his office – the land for the University of Leicester was a gift, another memorial to the dead of that great war. The university's School of Archaeology and Ancient History is one of the country's largest and most popular departments of its kind. It is home to the independent University of Leicester Archaeological Services (ULAS), a group of professional field archaeologists who work across the UK, turning over three quarters of a million pounds a year – over a million US dollars – in contracts to businesses and public agencies, from one-man builders to supermarket chains, airports and the BBC. ULAS has two directors: Patrick Clay and Richard Buckley.

If not on its present scale, nor by these institutions, archaeology was taught and practised in Leicester when Richard Buckley was at school. His first experience of digging, where he learned to use his first trowel, was with the predecessor of the organization he now co-directs, the Leicestershire Archaeological Unit. As we sit and talk in the university office, there's little around us – apart from the scuffed black computers

– that would have been out of place in the 1970s: tightly packed tables, piles of typed reports, bags and boxes on every surface, posters on the walls and dirt on the floor. A striped black and yellow parking ticket stuck to a desk, and Richard's well-used coffee mug bearing a portrait of Richard III, remind me why I'm here. But though the way digs are now run has changed radically – more professional, concerned with clients as well as finding things – inside this office, discussing a schoolboy's first brush with archaeology, I am transported back to another age.

It began when he was just six or seven, forcing his parents to visit castles, and collecting coins. They'd go to the Tower of London, and he'd notice the money in his mum's purse included Victorian pennies. He'd sort them all out into different heads, study the wear patterns, and feel a connection to the past. It was fascinating, and he aimed to find a century of pennies – he still has a collection.

'It's rubbish,' he says. 'I didn't care about the condition, it all came out of change, nothing bought.' These were intimate little things, intercepted as they passed from hand to hand, stamped with the year their journeys began: stories from rubbish.

When he was 12 he had an inspiring history teacher, who is now doing archaeology himself, he tells me: he got his doctorate studying prehistory. They've been in touch recently.

'Is he pleased with the way things turned out?', I ask. Richard laughs. 'I don't know,' he says. 'He may be.'

Mike Billinge, a relaxed, popular teacher who played music by Barclay James Harvest and The Who, was a classicist. That's what I'd like to do, thought Richard. He took O and A level Greek and Roman Civilization with Mr Billinge.

Richard heard there was a dig going on in Leicester. He was a bit shy, and didn't feel he could just turn up, but as luck would have it, there was a girl called Lynne who lived across the road and was a volunteer on the site. So in 1973 the 15-year-old Richard Buckley went along with Lynne, and started digging on Sundays.

He made friends and acquaintances then that would last longer than he ever imagined; archaeology was a social affair, and a small world. He met Patrick Clay, who was already working for the field unit. Lynne went on to become an archaeologist, and married another digger on the site, John Walker. While later Richard and Patrick would come to lead Leicester's archaeological field practice, John – now retired – moved first to Manchester and then north to York, where for over a decade he was Chief Executive of the York Archaeological Trust, with offices from Sheffield to Glasgow. Funny, that – the future excavation leaders in York and Leicester started off together here at a dig on a medieval friary.

Greek and Roman Civ, as Richard calls it, was mostly literature, politics and history rather than archaeology. But Mr Billinge allowed him to go to the Austin Friars dig on Wednesday afternoons, as an alternative to general studies. It was a long-running excavation – rare now, and opportunities to volunteer are even rarer – so he was able to keep up the experience for a couple of years.

He'd read archaeology books. Leonard Cottrell's *Lost Cities* had got him hooked – tales of ancient Babylon and Turkey, of Pompeii and Peru, of men driven by a love of travel and adventure.[13] But this was different. There was something here at home he hadn't found in Cottrell.

There were massive spoilheaps around the dig, which had a stone-lined medieval drain running dramatically through the middle. Because the ground was wet, there were rare waterlogged remains, including wooden bowls and scraps of decorated leather shoes. The sheer complexity of it all was amazing. How did they make sense of it?

'I'm a practical person,' says Richard. 'I like doing practical things, engineering, woodwork, that sort of thing. I really like the process of excavation, the fact that you create' – he coaxes the thought into words – 'that shapes emerge from what you're doing, pits and wells and ditches, the physical side of things.'

This was what was missing in Cottrell: the process, the organization, the puzzling out as everything changed even as you looked at it. It was tough.

'When you work on a site for the first time,' says Richard, 'you're quite shocked at what hard work it is. But it's really nice working with other people as a team, working towards a common goal.'

And while they dug out the detritus of medieval religious lives, trains rumbled over the great iron bridges crossing the river down from Central Station. Cars and buses revved and beeped along King Richards and St Augustine. The weather was hot in summer; in winter they'd sit in the hut, watching the rain pour down.

'I'd like to do this,' thought Richard. 'If I'm to become an archaeologist, I need a degree.'

So one day he went home and said he wanted to go to university and do archaeology. Neither his father, a production engineer at Rolls-Royce, nor his mother, who later worked as a secretary, had been to university. He'd be the first in the family.

He went to Durham, impressed by the sight of the floodlit cathedral and castle as he arrived by train for his interview. It was those castles again. He loved castles. Wales was full of castles, and the family had a lot of wet Welsh holidays, staying in cottages where there was at least one castle nearby – coming home to Leicester was a disappointment as there was no decent castle (so later that became a goal, to show that Leicester really had had a proper castle).

At Durham the focus was on Anglo-Saxon and Viking archaeology, and more Greek and Roman. He got to go on a training dig on a Roman fort in Wales, and he volunteered on more excavations in Leicester. One year, throughout September and October, he joined a small team of eight or nine at Sproxton – he pronounces it Sprowsun – where Patrick Clay was investigating a Bronze Age burial mound. They stayed in a derelict cottage on a private estate in the middle of nowhere. 'It was the most amazing experience,' says Richard. 'It's still my favourite excavation.'

He was about to finish his degree, and nothing seemed more natural than to ring the unit in Leicester to see if anything was going on. They offered him work on an employment scheme – more excavation. Within a year they gave him a job, and before he knew it he was a field officer. 'A bit lucky, to say the least,' he says. 'I must have had something going for me.' And then, he can't resist it, with a little laugh: 'Maybe.'

They were busy, working from temporary Portakabins on the city outskirts, at an old government decontamination training site. Much of their time was spent studying and reporting the work of earlier excavations; Richard tackled a mountain of painted Roman wall plaster. Then, in 1990, it all changed.

Hitherto, as across the country, the archaeologists had got by with a mix of grants and government support, donations, helpful developers and volunteers. But always it was a struggle to match the pace of new building and the destruction below ground that was particularly strong in a historic city seeking to renew itself, like Leicester. National legislation transformed everything. New planning instructions obliged developers to employ archaeologists if their projects were going to damage historic remains.

They had to work for businesses as a business. It gave them more to do, better conditions – although in archaeology that will always remain a relative thing (this is never a job you do for the pension) – and some spectacular digs. But it was a new world. 'Overnight', says Richard, 'we had to learn to become project managers, to cost archaeological schemes. I was quite young,' he adds. 'I'd have preferred to have carried on digging.' And five years later the council closed the unit.

Able now to support themselves, however, and with a highly skilled and experienced team, the archaeologists were welcomed by the university. In July 1995 Patrick, Richard and an administrator moved into rooms in the university's Attenborough Tower, while out in the wider world, the diggers carried on. A few years later the offices crossed over to where I am now with Richard, in the Archaeology and Ancient History Building.

There was a huge development boom early in the new millennium. When building increased, the archaeological unit grew. Patrick looked after the rural sites, and Richard the urban. The big one for Richard was

Highcross, expanding an old shopping centre – it affected an astonishing 12 per cent of the city's entire historic core. For three years they ran three big excavations, with nearly a hundred staff out on sites and 15 of them in the university. One dig had over thirteen hundred graves; another a collapsed eight-metre-high (26 ft) Roman wall and medieval town plots; a third a complete Roman townhouse beneath a medieval church and cemetery. At the latter site, managed by Richard, they found remains of the Blue Boar Inn, where Richard III is supposed to have spent two of his last three nights. There's a new Travelodge there now.[14]

In 2008 came the crash. Apartment blocks stopped going up – most of the new units remain unsold – and for the archaeologists the work plummeted. They lost a lot of staff. Now they actively sought new work.

While all this was going on, things were changing down at Bow Bridge too. Central Station closed, the tracks were ripped up and the iron spans, arching like a monster serpent over the river, were taken down. The elastic webbing factory – said in 1881 to be the busiest and most magnificent in the country – was demolished. The roads were widened. But the development anticipated as far back as 1973 never happened, not even in the boom. Now the area is mostly cheap parking (bringing new memorials in the form of a cul-de-sac called Richard III Road and its eponymous car park), a large open space surprisingly rich in grasses, flowers and trees, with blue dragonflies swarming in off the canal where lilies and reeds decorate the dark, still water.

Work on the Austin Friars dig had long been finished. In the report, published in 1981, the archaeologists – no less – noted that Richard III's grave had been despoiled after the Franciscan friary was suppressed, and his remains thrown into the river. 'According to one version of the story', they added, the bones 'were afterwards gathered up and reburied in the graveyard of the Austins' – which if true, would raise the possibility that the skeleton found in 1862 really was the king's.[15]

That's how Richard Buckley remembers it. Austin Friars, he tells me, was very close to the stone plaque by the bridge where Richard III was supposed to have gone over to Bosworth – 'Near this spot', he quotes with precision, 'lie the remains of Richard III'.

Yet though they were aware of the memorial, there was never any thought that they might look for the king. 'You don't set out to go and dig up a named individual,' he says. 'What we were really interested in was working on sites that tell us about the ordinary population. Or elucidating the plans of buildings.'

Meanwhile, between the overlooked nature reserve north of Bow Bridge, and Castle Gardens – the neatly curated park on the good side of the canal to the east – another group of historical researchers had been at work. And they had thought very hard about the message of that plaque.

The Richard III Society was founded in 1924 by a group of enthusiastic amateur historians who felt that posterity had been unjustly cruel to the king. They called themselves The Fellowship of the White Boar, adopting their current name in 1959. They now have 25 regional branches in England, one in Scotland and 16 outside the UK (four of them in Australia), with 'several thousand members worldwide'.[16]

The society had been boosted in 1951 by a novel called *The Daughter of Time*. Written by Josephine Tey, it was a critical and commercial success, and still sells well. Inspired by a copy of an early portrait of Richard III, a police inspector is convinced the king was a kind man blackened by Tudor propaganda. He investigates Richard's alleged misdemeanours and crippled appearance, and finds the case for both wanting. It is a warning to read evidence critically, and not to accept blindly all you are told. For Ricardians, aiming 'to encourage and promote a more balanced view', it was almost a manifesto, support in itself for Richard III's innocence.[17]

The society's first public move in Leicester was to commission a bronze statue, unveiled by the Duchess of Gloucester in 1980. It was made by James Butler, a sculptor of great men and nude female models (and, in 1990, The Leicester Seamstress, an 18th-century hosiery worker fixing a stocking outside the City Rooms). Richard is depicted life-size, young, fit and handsome with flowing hair, in light body armour. He wields a sword in his right hand, and in his left brandishes a crown, looking wistful and a little pained (or, perhaps, as if he is dancing a jig with a tambourine). He stands high on a cast stone block, cresting a wave.[18]

The statue was first erected in the centre of Castle Gardens, where repeated vandalism seemed to imply that at least one Leicester citizen still felt unhappy about this controversial monarch. It was moved to its present site at the garden entrance, closer to the road, and the damage stopped, though by then he had to be given a new crown and sword, the latter a shortened version of the original. When I stood at his feet at the end of my walk along King Richards Road and over Bow Bridge and West Bridge, the sun shone briefly through the cloud and humid air, and fresh scent lifted from the beds of white roses.

It is a striking figure, but perhaps most remarkable are the bronze plaques around the base. Quoting historical texts, they convey the society's message. 'A good lawmaker for the ease and solace of the common people', says one. 'Piteously slain fighting manfully in the thickest press of his enemies', reads another. Noble in sight, noble in deed.

In 1990, on a street corner in the city centre, the society unveiled a further bronze plaque: 'Near this site stood the church of the Greyfriars where the body of Richard III ... was interred after his death.' (A stone memorial slab, noting the same detail, had been set in the floor of

Life-size bronze of Richard III made for Leicester in 1980 by James Butler, whose other subjects range from Isambard Kingdom Brunel to former Kenyan president Jomo Kenyatta.

nearby Leicester Cathedral ten years before.)[19] And in 2005 they unveiled their final plaque, down at Bow Bridge, to correct the error of Benjamin Broadbent's. The latter, after the demolition of the building where it had originally hung, had been moved into a modern brick wall above the pavement on the city side of Bow Bridge. Right beside it the society placed its own, small printed green plate.

'This plaque', it says of its larger stone neighbour, 'originally erected ... on the nearby site of the Austin Friars, records the 17th-century tradition, now generally discredited, that ... the body of King Richard III was disinterred from his tomb at the Greyfriars in Leicester and thrown into the River Soar.'

The whole added up to an extremely clever, and possibly unique, propaganda exercise in public places, by a private society, about a popular historical figure. Once, Leicester had marked Richard with a random collection of street furniture that recorded his presence, but told you little

Memorial to Richard III by type designer and letter cutter David Kindersley, set in the floor of the choir of Leicester Cathedral in 1980 and photographed in 2013.

Act II, Scene 1

else. Now, there was a story. It began at the statue, where 'Richard III King of England 1483–1485' was shown proud and thoughtful, without a hint of deformity. We were told he was a good legislator, a man of the people, and that he died bravely. Across the road we were informed that the traditions that his remains were thrown into the river, or that they were buried nearby at the Austin Friars, were wrong. And in the city centre was marked the site of the friary where he was really buried.

Early in 2011 Richard Buckley was in the office doing the usual things – emails, costing jobs, thinking about the reports he needed to read – when the phone rang. It was a member of the Richard III Society, and she wished to talk about the king. But this was not to chat about his reputation or his history, or to offer ideas for another plaque. The Society wanted to give the archaeologists a job. It was, perhaps, the logical conclusion of its Leicester operation.

'Can you', asked Philippa Langley, 'dig up Richard III?'

*

Philippa Langley makes people happy.

Channel 4 television loves her: they had barely escaped having to defend dropping Time Team, the world's favourite archaeology series, when she brought them a blockbuster of a dig. Journalists love her for all the work she creates – and being so friendly – and Google must love her for all the things journalists write that get the bloggers going. The Richard III Society loves her, of course – they gave her both their Robert Hamblin Award and honorary life membership for finding their king (an indication of their faith in her, as this was four months before anyone had officially decided whether the skeleton dug up in Leicester was the right one). If you can say she is giving your lecture, or coming to your conference or your festival, you can be sure of good press coverage, and your seats will fill. People want her to sign their books, their newspapers, or anything really. They want to be photographed with her. If he's up there somewhere, I imagine Richard III's quite pleased. Internet searches for him in February 2013 were 20 times what they had been for years.[20] People care.

In 2011 all that was in the future. Philippa was as well known as any would-be screen writer with six or seven scripts seeking a producer, but none actually commissioned – she had three in development, she tells me, and then the recession hit. I imagine writing half a dozen screenplays on spec, the determination that must take, and wonder where she found the time to think about looking for a medieval king – let alone to organize the project and raise the money. So was history an obsession? I've talked to many archaeologists, and most – like Richard Buckley – date their passion back to a childhood experience. Did something inspire Philippa to pursue Richard III when she was young?

Hardly, at least as she explains it. Born in East Africa, she grew up in Hummersknott, a suburb of Darlington, a market and engineering town in northeast England. Somehow, what with moving schools and the way things were taught, she missed out entirely on Richard III in both history and English; she left knowing nothing of the historian's Richard or of Shakespeare's Richard, or what the difference between the two was, or should be. History was her favourite subject – but one minute she had a teacher who brought it all to life ('It was like watching a movie,' she says wistfully, 'listening to him'), and the next a teacher who killed it dead.

In another world she might have read history at university, and stuck with the subject. But she'd seen her brother and sister go through it, and that wasn't for her. 'I couldn't handle being the poor student,' she says. She decided to get out into the world, and earn some money.

In 1989 she moved three hours' drive north up the A1 to Edinburgh, her Scottish boyfriend's home city. She entered marketing and advertising, and ended up with The Scotsman Publications, working as sponsorship manager across all its newspaper titles. It was going well. Then she became ill, and had to stop. She began to read more, which seems curious to her. Before the illness she liked to keep fit, be active and physical.

Suddenly that was no longer an option, and reading became fundamental. 'When you get seriously ill,' she tells me, 'your view of the world and what's important changes.'

It was then she picked up the book that transformed her life. It was 1998, and she was in her mid-30s. She was going on holiday. Usually this would be an active affair, water-skiing, swimming and walking. But she was exhausted, physically and mentally. She just wanted a book, to sit round a pool and do nothing else.

So she went into Waterstone's on Edinburgh's Princes Street. It was the first store of its kind to open outside London, a warehouse of books on several floors linked by a huge, antique-style staircase hidden unexpectedly behind the classical stone façade of a 19th-century club. There were books from floor to ceiling. 'You walk in', she tells me, 'and it's just packed. And the weird thing was, I went straight to this particular shelf.'

And to a particular book – not the one in front of her, but down at the bottom. She picked it up, looked at it, thought, 'Oh, that'll do', paid for it and left. 'I mean', she says laughing, 'it must have taken me less than a minute.'

This was unusual poolside reading: a heavy, unillustrated work of non-fiction, first published in 1955 and written by an American academic named Paul Murray Kendall, who died in 1973. The book was a biography. Its subject was Richard III.

Kendall's account is a good read. It conjures scenes you might have thought beyond the reach of history. As the king and his army swept out of Leicester, the Ohio University English Literature professor tells us, Richard 'was mounted on a white courser, a slight figure even in the casing of full armour ... without fear or hope, his general's eye scanning the country, noting the bearing of soldiers, and picturing, as scouts brought their reports, the possible movements of the enemy.'[21]

Yet it was not just his style that the critics liked. 'Kendall writes well,' opined the *New York Times Book Review*, 'with the result that when the sun goes down on Bosworth field, the reader is full of wrath at the treacherous Stanleys and the calculating Northumberland.' For Kendall had a captivating agenda. His book, he claimed, was based 'almost entirely' on contemporary sources. There he found a sympathetic narrative of a just but wronged king, quite unlike the monster portrayed by later Tudor writers whose vindictiveness, glorified by Shakespeare, had misled generations. Kendall's biography was the historian's answer to *The Daughter of Time*, published four years earlier. Tey had successfully raised the notion of a historical conspiracy to darken Richard's reputation: Kendall offered the corroborative evidence, with 65 pages of footnotes.[22]

It blew Philippa away. 'At the time', she says, 'I was considering screen writing. My love is writing stories that challenge people's perceptions of established truths. It's really important that we question.'

And here it was: a cracking story that needed to be told. 'It had everything,' she says, 'power, politics, romance, betrayal, courage. I just thought if it's grabbed *me* like this, then surely it's going to grab other people, up on screen in the cinemas.'

Suddenly, in the languid peace of a rippling pool, Philippa needed to find out everything she could about Richard III. She would write his story. This one wouldn't be a two-dimensional caricature, but a portrait of a fully rounded medieval man and king. A complex man for sure, and a conflicted man, but not a psychotic, murdering.... 'You know, Machiavellian', she trails off.

She read all the histories. But it wasn't working. None of them presented a believable man. 'I was going to walk away from it,' she tells me. And then a new book came out, and for the first time she could make sense of Richard's life. She could make a film with this. She got in touch with the author, Michael K. Jones.

(After talking to Philippa, I read Jones' book, *Bosworth 1485: Psychology of a Battle*. It is a fascinating, engagingly written narrative with many new insights and, for me, useful new academic references in its footnotes. Yet I also found its arguments at times tortuous, so that an imaginative, if reasonable, hypothesis in one part of the book can reappear as fact within another discussion.[23])

Act II, Scene 1

So the screenplay was in its first draft, pretty rough and ready, and Philippa wanted to go down and walk some of the places that Richard walked. She had a good visit to Bosworth, and ended her trip in Leicester. She'd contacted some local Ricardians, Richard III Society members, and they'd directed her to New Street car park. There's a bit of medieval wall there that might be part of the Greyfriars precinct where Richard was said to have been buried.

It was her last Leicester stop. 'It was a lovely warm sort of late spring day', she remembers, 'and the car park was very empty.' She walked in, had a look around, saw the wall – an unloved, small thing, half-hidden, when I see it, behind graffiti, a bag of garbage, vegetation and the parking attendant's wooden shed – and thought, right, that's done, time to get home and write the screenplay. She was finished in Leicester.

In the privately owned New Street car park, behind the attendant's shed, is a small stretch of stone wall said to be all that survives above ground of the medieval Greyfriars friary.

Act II, Scene 1

Then she saw another car park on the other side of the road. It had a private sign, and a barrier. But she had this overwhelming urge to go in.

'So I slithered round the barrier,' she says. 'It was quite empty. I was drawn to a red brick wall ahead of me, and as I walked towards it I had to stop, because I had the strangest sensation. It was a warm day, but I had goose bumps so badly I was actually freezing cold to my bones. I knew then. I absolutely knew I was standing on his grave.'

She pauses, then says, 'And I know that sounds bonkers.'

I ask if she was looking for Richard's grave. Not until then, she says. Her interest was in his life, not his death. But then, well, it all changed.

That was in 2004. A year later, she went back. Perhaps, you know, perhaps she had been a little daft. She stood on exactly the same spot, and had exactly the same experience. But something was different. A few feet to her left, on the ground, someone had painted a white letter R.

Scene 2

THE SAME

A friary

Philippa knew that Richard III had been buried in Leicester. But everyone told her his grave had been lost.

Archaeologists such as Richard Buckley, who quite frankly were not really bothered about what had happened to the king's remains – their interests lay in the people, and the ones they dug up were always anonymous – tended to believe in the old story: the tomb had been wrecked, and its bones cast into the river. Richard III had no physical presence in the city.

Some Ricardians preferred to think that their king had never suffered such indignity, and told Philippa that what was left of his battle-scarred body still lay in the ground. It was under the old Parr's Bank, an imposing white stone fortress raised in 1900, with great columns and carved allegorical friezes at the front and round, domed towers high above.

It was here, just round the corner beside a Grey Friars cast-iron street sign, that the Richard III Society had placed their plaque in 1990. It commemorates the king's burial in the friary church. It doesn't actually say the grave was there, but with the words *Requiescat in pace* (rest in peace) and a reproduction of an 18th-century engraving showing monks carrying a coffin in front of what was said to be the Greyfriars church, it's easy to read it that way. When the plaque was commissioned, the site

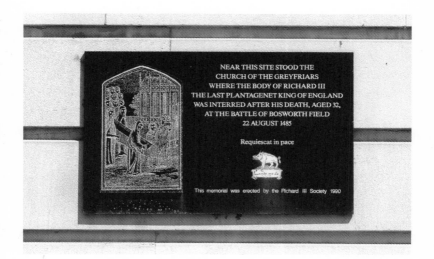

The Richard III Society erected this plaque in Grey Friars street in 1990, to mark the king's burial site; the unidentified funeral scene is taken from an 18th-century engraving.

was occupied by the National Westminster Bank. The NatWest had moved out in 2000, and five years later, when Philippa had returned to Leicester to sneak a second frisson in the private car park, the building was still vacant.

On the face of it, whether he was lost in the river or under offices – or more likely, scooped up and lost when the original bank was built – Richard III had gone. Indeed, this was the official line: up to the grand denouement in February 2013, the British monarchy's website concluded its summary of Richard III's reign by saying that he had been buried without a monument; and later, it said, his 'bones were scattered during the English Reformation'. Historians gave the matter little attention.[1]

Yet Philippa's car park experience told her the grave was still there, and she was not one to ignore instinct, however improbable. Cold shivers didn't solve anything, but they proved a potent catalyst. Thus began the second part of her saga with Richard III. With the clarity of a woman on a mission, she knew what she had to do. 'My problem', she told me, 'was I had three huge questions to answer before any search for Richard's grave could begin.'

First, if the weight of opinion was that Richard's bones had been thrown into the River Soar, she had to disprove that – or, as she put it to me, 'I needed to see research that showed that was not the case.'

Then she had to find the church. People seemed to have a rough idea where the friary precinct had been, but that was a large area. Where was the church within that precinct? 'Could it be', she recalled, 'where this car park was?'

And finally, if that worked out and they found a skeleton ('Even if by some happenchance we managed to dig the car park'), how could they show the remains were those of Richard III? It was a very Philippa Langley project. She would set out not so much to find Richard's grave, as to prove that it was where she intuited it to be. It was, you might say, a marketing person's approach to research.

'And it was then', she told me, as if so far all had been perfectly normal, 'that strange things started to happen.'

She went back to Edinburgh. Within months someone published some new research, in which they claimed to have traced a living relative carrying DNA that would look the same as Richard III's. If Dr John Ashdown-Hill was right, his discovery meant it would be possible to test the identity of an excavated skeleton. 'So straight away', said Philippa, 'I had one of the problems answered immediately.' They might have dug up Richard, but been unable to prove it was him. Not now. 'I now knew', she said, 'that we could identify Richard III if we found him.'

John Ashdown-Hill seems a gentle, almost delicate man, with a dapper moustache whose dark colour now offsets his close-styled silver hair. His carefully elocuted voice and light sense of humour, however, belong to a driven, determined researcher. He trained in French and history. At first he taught languages, but for a couple of decades he has been following his real passion as a freelance history writer. In a curious parallel to Richard Buckley, he traces his interest in old things to seeing

Victorian coins when shopping as a child. Early TV broadcasts introduced him to Shakespeare's history plays, and since 1996 he has been a regular contributor to both the Richard III Society's journal and to its less formal bulletin.[2]

He became involved in the search for a close living relative of Richard III when Belgian colleagues asked for help. They were hoping to identify remains that might have been those of one of Richard's sisters. Margaret had died in 1503 as the wife of Charles the Bold, Duke of Burgundy. Her body had been buried in the Franciscan friary in Mechelen. As with Greyfriars in Leicester, the buildings had been destroyed in the 16th century and the grave lost. And as in Leicester, the Richard III Society had made its mark with a plaque, erected in 2000.

Over the years, archaeologists had found three sets of human remains that could conceivably have been Margaret's. In 2003, five centuries after her death, it was decided to see if DNA could be used to settle the case. Ashdown-Hill set out to locate a modern sample.[3]

The following year he found what he was looking for in the person of Joy Ibsen. Mrs Ibsen, a retired journalist born in Shrewsbury, in England, had settled in Canada in the 1940s. According to Ashdown-Hill's research, her family – herself, her brothers and her children – were unique possessors of mitochondrial DNA (mtDNA) identical to Margaret's, copied down the female line through 16 generations from Margaret's oldest sister, Anne. When Ashdown-Hill relayed this startling news, he found she had no idea of the royal connection.

'Her face lit up after the conversation ended,' recalled her husband Norm, who had been sharing dinner with her when an unexpected phone call came through from England. She was happy to provide DNA samples, which were analysed first by Oxford Ancestors at Ashdown-Hill's expense, then by Jean-Jacques Cassiman at the Université catholique de Louvain.[4]

As far as the immediate task went, the result was a failure: none of the Mechelen samples matched those from Joy Ibsen. There was, however, a bonus, which might at some time prove useful. For Anne of

York's mtDNA, copied from her mother, would have been the same as all her siblings'. Among those, separated from Anne by two sisters and seven brothers, was Richard III.[5]

Philippa had barely begun her quest, to find the first of her big questions solved. Given the bones, she thought, she could now prove they were Richard's. All she had to do was find them. Remarkably, it was Ashdown-Hill who would again help her on her way.

He had been asked by the BBC to contribute a column to an online series called Local Legends. A large stone plaque by Bow Bridge in Leicester, noted the website, says Richard III's remains were nearby. But was that true?

The historian's answer was plain. There was no evidence to suggest the remains had been thrown into the river, nor that they had ever been dug up, nor that any stone coffin had anything to do with Richard. 'The more simple reality', he wrote, 'is that Richard III's body probably still lies where it was first buried, somewhere beneath Grey Friars Street or the adjacent buildings.'[6]

Or, as Philippa described it to me, 'Ashdown-Hill showed that the story the bones had been thrown into the River Soar was a nonsense. It really does not hold any water.'

That just left the church. Could Philippa show it had been in the car park? In this case, it was archaeologists who gave her the answer. Once again, it was the one she wanted.

Another year, another step forward. In 2007 there was an excavation at the old NatWest bank, where the Richard III Society had put its plaque. It was a small project, and the report was dry and technical. In fact, she told me, it had been 'dismissed locally as being of absolutely no importance'. But for her, it changed everything. They found no evidence whatsoever of Greyfriars church! Nothing! Richard's grave could not have been under the bank.[7]

'So I knew', she said, 'that the church must be further to the west. And in the west we had those three car parks.' Three open spaces – New

Street car park to the west, the Social Services car park across the road to the east and, beyond a high wall continuing east, a former school playground – with no buildings to cover or destroy the grave, just waiting to be investigated. Philippa had answered her own questions, and the answers were good. Which left her with a new one. Now what?

Back in 2005, enamoured with Ashdown-Hill's research, she had asked him to write to Time Team, Channel 4 television's long-running series in which a group of professional archaeologists attempted to solve a point of local history over three days. In October of that year he had duly rung the production company, and followed up with a letter. His proposal was strong on his genealogical research (he included a copy of an article he had written for the magazine, *Your Family Tree*). But though he also sent a photo of the actual car park in which Richard III's grave was later to be found, taken for him by a local Ricardian, his description of Greyfriars, if honest, was not encouraging: 'the layout', he wrote, 'is totally unknown'. Understandably, Time Team declined to take it further.[8]

Up to this point, Philippa had not met Ashdown-Hill. But in February 2009, in her capacity as Secretary (and founder) of the Scottish branch of the Richard III Society, she invited him up to Edinburgh to give a talk. He spoke about Richard's DNA and the Greyfriars church. As she listened, she realized that his work pointed to the same conclusion she had reached in her own research. Richard was buried in the Social Services car park.

They went for lunch at the Cramond Inn, a white-painted pub down by the estuary of the River Almond on the far west of the city. 'We put all of our research together', she remembered, 'and everything said, he's there. He's absolutely there.'

Suddenly it all seemed clear. If no one else was going to find Richard, she would. 'I'm going in search of him', she proclaimed, 'and I'm going to do it.'

A couple of people at the meeting knew someone at Time Team, and thought they'd try again, but Philippa guessed what the response would be even before they said no for the second time. So that was that.

She asked Ashdown-Hill to write to the local archaeologists: they'd understand. University of Leicester Archaeological Services would be the perfect team. He tried a few times, but they never got back.[9]

So Philippa went further afield, got on the phone and asked other archaeological contractors. She didn't come out and say she wanted them to dig up Richard III, but otherwise she was quite specific. She was looking for a grave under a car park in the Midlands, could they help? But archaeologists didn't seek out graves, and anyway, they didn't have the local knowledge. She should ask around in the Midlands.

So it was back to Leicester. This time Philippa went to the City Council, who, after all, owned the car park. But first, she approached television. In July 2010 she'd watched a programme on Channel 4 about the archaeological exhumation of soldiers' remains from an unmarked First World War grave in France, and their individual reburial in a new war cemetery. She was impressed, and noted that the film had been made by Darlow Smithson Productions, an independent London-based company. She contacted Julian Ware, DSP's then Co-Creative Director. Ware is a tall, charming man, an experienced broadcaster with an expansive vision. He responded positively.

Then she pitched the project to Leicester City Council. Look, she said, I know where Richard III is buried, and Channel 4 want to make a film about it, and it's all in your car park. And the council said yes. They had just one question. 'Which archaeologists are you going to hire?'

They heard the saga about Time Team, and the archaeologists who don't look for graves, and they sent her to the council's museum service. And the museum people said to Philippa, why don't you ask Richard Buckley? He'd be perfect for the job, he knows Leicester. Here are his contact details. He works at ULAS, University of Leicester Archaeological Services.

Her heart sank. ULAS had already said no. But Philippa Langley was not yet ready to give up. In January 2011 she gathered her thoughts, looked at the number, and picked up the phone.

People call ULAS from time to time with ideas for excavations. They imagine, said Richard, the archaeologists have the resources to drop everything, and do what they want. 'Which of course', he added, 'we haven't. All the work we do is for external contracts.'

Yet there was something about Philippa that encouraged him to keep listening. He'd already given quite a few talks for the Richard III Society, promoting the study of medieval history and archaeology, telling them about ULAS's work in Leicester, such as the big Highcross project. 'I never thought for a minute', he told me, 'that the search for Richard would be successful.' But if that was a non-starter, quite quickly he realized that the dig Philippa was proposing would be about the friary. And that appealed to him.

They would be able to research a part of the town that they had never been able to look in before, to check out one of Leicester's great medieval institutions. It wasn't that they hadn't been interested, but their work was determined by development. They'd excavate where planners thought important remains might be destroyed. That was what happened at the NatWest bank in 2007, where an investment business had hoped to build flats (though it never happened). There had been one modern research excavation in Leicester, at the Augustinian Abbey in the north of the city. After much searching, archaeologists finally located the site in the 1920s, and excavations were continued between 2000 and 2008 by ULAS, as a training project for archaeology students at the university. But, said Richard, 'Nobody had ever done a research excavation within the walls of Leicester.' Not until now.

'OK', he thought, 'here we go.' Ooh yes, it would be exciting to have some funding for research. He told Philippa it was all very interesting, but he needed to look into it. 'Only if my research comes back with anything,' he said, 'am I going to be prepared to take this further.' And Philippa thought, that's fair enough.

I asked Richard if he had found Philippa, well, a little eccentric? 'Oh yeah,' he replied. So what had he said after the call? He laughed. 'I'm not sure I should actually tell you, really,' he said. He paused. Then, smiling, he quoted himself: 'There's this bonkers person on the phone – but we'd get the chance to look for the friary.' That is, at least, how he told it to me.

But he was hooked. He slipped into project manager mode. How could Philippa's vision be turned into a productive excavation? The first thing was the king. He was aware that Richard III had been buried in Leicester's Greyfriars, and he knew where Greyfriars had been. But perhaps there was truth to the story that the body had been dug up and thrown in the river? So straight away there was only a 50 per cent chance of being right.

The second thing was that the site of the friary was now heavily built up. Medieval layers such as those where Richard's grave might have lain would have been destroyed by house foundations and cellars, and the open spaces would be riddled with service trenches.

Leicester was notoriously a town without any local stone. There was a premium on building materials, and people quarried abandoned structures. This meant that when archaeologists came across Roman or medieval foundations, what they usually saw was just the trench: someone else had been there before them to take away the bricks and imported stone. They might find the friary, but if all its masonry and floors had been ripped out – and perhaps Richard's grave, even if the robbers had no idea whose it was – it could be difficult to make much sense of it.

The council would never give permission: where would their staff park their cars? And where would all the money come from? Richard knew how expensive urban archaeology could be. 'I always think of all the problems first,' he told me, laughing. 'Would we be allowed to make a huge mess in the car park on the off chance that Richard may not have been dug up and thrown in the river?'

Philippa and Richard arranged to meet in the Holiday Inn, a 1960s vision of towering modernity stranded in a roundabout of traffic lanes where St Augustine Road enters the city. John Ashdown-Hill was there

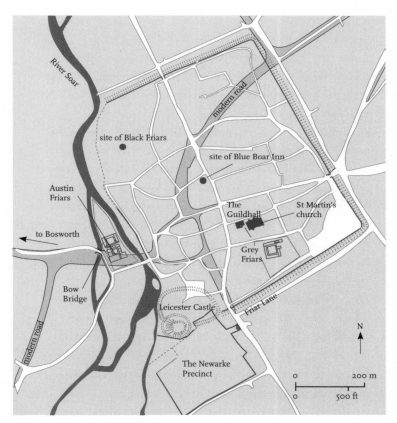

Medieval Leicester sits largely within the rectangular plan of the old Roman walls, with a new precinct to the south known as the Newarke (redrawn after Buckley and others).

too. By then he'd written a book in which he'd rounded up all the evidence he could find about the friary, Richard III's tomb and the fate of his grave – each of these topics was treated to an entire chapter. Another chapter summarized his genealogical and genetic research. Published over a year after he and Philippa met in Edinburgh, it was a manifesto for Philippa's project.

'If we had access to Richard's body,' he concluded, 'we'd know his height, what his face looked like, whether he really was deformed, and how he died.' He found it 'almost incredible' that the Greyfriars site had not been examined. He reproduced Diana Courtney's photo of the Social Services car park that he'd previously sent to Time Team, captioned 'Richard III's remains probably still lie somewhere beneath this tarmac'. And finally, he signed off with a teasing challenge: 'Perhaps one day the search for Richard III will begin!'[10]

Richard advised them to commission a desk study. 'We'd always known where the Greyfriars was,' he told me – he'd drawn a map in 1987 that became the standard for medieval Leicester, with Greyfriars written on it in the right place. What they didn't know was the arrangement of buildings within it. And neither did they know whether it was likely that anything of those buildings still survived underground – still less a feature such as a grave. Before embarking on a costly dig, they should find out what they could that might help them decide exactly where to place their trenches to best effect. Or whether it was worth doing at all.

'What always strikes me', he said, 'is that people who are not archaeologists won't see the problems. I can see them all. I perhaps came over as the killjoy to start with,' he admits. 'But I was on board pretty quickly.'

A unique partnership was launched, between two people driven by an interest in the past, brought together by different goals that could be achieved in only one way. Importantly, Philippa and Richard both had clear ideas of what they wanted out of it. To find a king and to understand a friary were not the same thing, but they weren't going to argue about that. They respected each other. As the project moved from one extraordinary event to the next, that regard would be tested.

Other meetings followed with the City Council. Quite often Philippa would ring up Richard, and within a month or two the Richard III Society provided the £1,140 fee and she commissioned the desk project.[11] 'Good,' he thought, 'you've got to do your homework.' He put Leon Hunt on to it, a Nottingham University graduate and experienced fieldworker who had come to work with ULAS in 2003. Hunt had written 150 such studies – they called them desk-based assessments, or DBAs. But never one like this.

Once he started looking into it, Hunt found there was actually quite a lot of useful information to guide an investigation on the ground. While Ricardians had been relentlessly attacking the many-headed hydra of myth and prejudice about Richard III, and archaeologists had by and large been ignoring the whole thing, some precious records had been gently gathering dust in the city's archives, biding their time. Well, it had come now.

There was no question about the fate of Richard III's body after he was slain in battle. Henry VII had it brought back into Leicester for full public gaze, slung naked over the back of a horse. Everyone would see that the king was dead.

Richard III's namesake, Richard II, who died in 1400, had been the subject of a famous conspiracy against his successor Henry IV. Rumours spread down from the north that Richard was still alive and would return to seize the throne that was rightfully his. Henry sought to quash the protest and make an example, and he found the opportunity at Leicester Greyfriars. Five of the friars were convicted of conspiring against their king, and executed in London.[12] Conscious of the parallel or not, the new Henry VII was not going to allow any such nonsense. Richard III's bloodied and bruised corpse, swelling and stiffening in the August heat, was displayed for two days in a college church in the Newarke, a specifically Lancastrian religious development – the 'new work' – in the southwest part of the town beyond the castle. There, as Henry reported in proclamations issued to his kingdom, Richard 'was laide oppenly that every man might se and luke upon him'.[13]

From there the body was carried through the streets and buried in the church of the Greyfriars, 'without any pompe or solemne funeral'. The specific site was in the church's choir, appropriate for such a prestigious figure but also one that was not accessible to the general public.[14] It may be that Henry ordered the burial. He would know where the grave was, and tucked away in the choir the tomb was beyond public reach – and veneration. Killing Richard in battle was only part of his victory.

All of that we know from sources written close to the events they describe – Polydore Vergil recording the funeral 'in thabbay of monks Franciscanes at Leycester', and John Rous specifically mentioning the choir – and there is no reason to doubt their veracity. We can also be certain that ten years later Henry VII had the grave memorialized with a tomb in alabaster, a creamy, soft stone that looks like marble and was immensely popular in the later Middle Ages for funerary monuments. We don't know what the tomb looked like, except that it bore Richard's image, whether in full sculpture or in shallow relief. When the friary was dissolved by Henry VIII in 1538 it was probably quite rapidly taken apart and the stone reused. In any event, from this moment on we have no contemporary records of what happened to Richard III's monument or his grave.[15]

Which is significant. In particular, there is no description of the grave being rifled or of bones being carried off. The first we hear of this is in 1611, three generations after the friary had been dissolved and precisely 50 years after the last note of any material being removed from the site for use elsewhere.[16]

*

We met the propagator of this story in the previous chapter. He was John Speed (1552–1629), a pioneering mapmaker and historian – some argue the first true English historian – whose maps we now value more than his histories. Richard's tomb, he wrote, was 'pulled downe' after the Dissolution of the Monasteries, 'and utterly defaced; since when his grave overgrown with nettles and weedes, is very obscure and not to be found. Only the stone chest wherein his corpse lay is now made a drinking trough for horses at a common Inne.... His body also (as tradition hath delivered), was borne out of the City, and contemptuously bestowed under the end of Bow-Bridge.'[17]

Other antiquarians and historians copied or elaborated on Speed's description, until it was fixed in stone in the engraved slab that can still be read beside the River Soar. But where did Speed get it from? We have no idea. What we do know, however, is that in the only point for which it is possible to check his facts, he got it wrong. The putative grave site he visited, 'overgrown with nettles and weedes', was apparently not at the Greyfriars at all, but at the Black Friars, another by then demolished friary, in the northwest of the city. As John Throsby, one of Leicester's great antiquarians, wrote in 1791, 'Mr. Speed, in his plan of Leicefter ... places this houfe [Black Friars] in the fituation of Grey Friars, and Grey Friars where this fhould be'.[18] The Black (or Dominican) Friary was close to the river, a little downstream from the Austin Friars. Perhaps Speed could see the ivy-covered Bow Bridge as he rummaged cautiously among the nettles, and recalled how Richard's body was carried naked into Leicester over that same bridge.

Yet even as Speed toured the city picking up what historical information he could, he missed a key monument. It was small, but bore an informative inscription: 'Here lies the Body of Richard III. some Time King of England.' We don't know precisely where it stood, but it was somewhere within the Greyfriars precinct, where Richard had been buried. Significantly, we know about it thanks to someone who was living and working in Leicestershire. This was Christopher Wren (later to become father of the famous architect), who just a year after Speed's book was published was shown the inscription on 'a handsome stone pillar, three foot high'. We might guess that the pillar was a decorative capital salvaged from the friary, but however it looked, it now stood as an ornamental feature in a garden. It was shown to Wren by the man who put it there, 'Mr. Robert Herrick (sometime Mayor of Leicester)'.

The Herricks were a powerful group of Leicestershire families. Wren was tutor to a young Herrick at Beaumanor Hall, about 16 km (10 miles) north of the city. Robert Herrick, whose memorial slab or ledger stone (as I write) now lies in the floor of Leicester Cathedral a few paces from that of Richard III – surrounded by testimonies to Herrick ancestors and descendants – had bought the eastern part of the Greyfriars plot and built himself a fine townhouse. It is debatable if he had any evidence to back up the claim that the king's body actually lay under his paths and flowerbeds, or whether he was just acknowledging historical fact that Richard had been buried in the friary from whose grounds he had created his city retreat. But if anyone could be expected to have known that the body had been removed, it would have been a Herrick and a former mayor of Leicester – and one who had developed the old friary site, to boot.[19]

The clear conclusion, and one that neither Richard Buckley nor Leon Hunt had expected to reach so simply, was that other things being equal, Richard's body should still be in the ground at the Greyfriars site. They were not the first to realize this. As they knew at the outset, Ashdown-Hill had made the same case, on the BBC website and in his book published the year before; it was partly this that had encouraged Philippa to press ahead with her project. Yet Ashdown-Hill was far from the first.

In 1920, Leicester historian Charles Billson wrote that Richard's remains, 'if undisturbed', must lie beneath Grey Friars Street or the facing buildings. In 1962 Audrey Strange (who would later publish an article concluding that the king's bones lay under one of the car parks south of the cathedral) wrote to Leicester Museum, suggesting they dig up the friary. 'I am afraid there is no likelihood of the Grey Friars being excavated at the moment,' replied David Clarke, the Keeper of Antiquities. 'It is a private car park.' He must have liked the idea, for in 1965 the *Leicester Mercury* noted his belief that the grave was still there, safe below the tarmac.

David Baldwin reviewed the evidence in detail in 1986, when he was a history lecturer at Leicester University. 'It is possible (though perhaps now unlikely)', he wrote, 'that at some time in the twenty-first century an excavator may yet reveal the slight remains of this famous monarch.' Rarely can such a portentous archaeological prediction have been proved right.[20]

As Leon Hunt continued with the desk assessment, that proof was yet to come. The important remaining caveat was Billson's 'if undisturbed'.

Was the grave still there? Or had it been unknowingly destroyed at some time as the open space of the friary precinct had been steadily built over and dug into in the 470-odd years since the Dissolution? That question was tied up with another: where exactly had the friary church stood?

*

If you walk five minutes from St Augustine Road, crossing the river over Bow Bridge, dodging the traffic below the Holiday Inn and continuing along Peacock Lane, you find yourself in front of the cathedral and looking down the eponymous St Martins. Continue along St Martins (which with Peacock Lane used to be called St Francis Lane), and turn right at the corner. Walk down Grey Friars (noticing a bronze plaque on the wall of the old bank), turn right at the next corner and walk down Friar Lane, past the narrow alley of New Street off to the right and along a pleasant early 18th-century red-brick terrace until you get to the far corner of number 35. In those few minutes, walking St Francis Lane, Grey Friars and Friar Lane, you have traversed three of four sides of the old Greyfriars boundary as it appears in the earliest map. Continue past number 41 (like 35, now occupied by a firm of commercial solicitors), and you can peer up a small gap back towards Peacock Lane.[21]

Seeing it like that, you could be forgiven for imagining the entire plot has been built over. The premises are mostly three-storey 18th- or 19th-century businesses and public buildings, all interesting and some of them lovely. They date from Leicester's industrial heyday, when the city was one of the country's wealthiest – in just 40 years up to 1901, its population trebled. The original friary precincts probably extended further at either end, so that Grey Friars as well as New Street cut through it, slicing it into three; beyond Grey Friars to the east – on your right as you stand on Friar Lane facing north – the block is solid with buildings. But behind the grand façades of Grey Friars and Friar Lane in front of you is a surprising amount of open space.

Peacock Lane and St Martins bisect this view, with Leicester Cathedral to the right and the car parks opposite that now fill much of the medieval Greyfriars precinct (see map page 105).

The way to work out what happened in that space over preceding centuries is to look at maps – Hunt called his study 'map regression analysis'. We are particularly lucky that the first large-scale, reliable map to survive, detailing Leicester's streets and what went on behind them, was surveyed immediately before the friary land was subdivided. It was published by Thomas Roberts in 1741. Overall, it is striking how rural the city looks: the great bulk of the land seems to be orchards. Immediately south of the cathedral is a large, wedge-shaped plot marked Gray Fryers – the one we walked around, cutting through down the modern street named Grey Friars. Half of it is orchard, distinguished by 20 independently drawn little trees. There are buildings only along part of the south street frontage, with an unusually large complex (though frustratingly indecipherably drawn) in the southeast corner. This is almost certainly Robert Herrick's mansion. The rest of the land is his garden, including walkways that separate quadrants and meet at a circle.

By 1740 the site had become the property of one Roger Ruding, who had inherited it and sought to realize his windfall. He arranged for a street to go through the middle – rather unimaginatively called New Street – and sold it off in parts; Herrick's house and gardens, known as The Grey Friars, were bought by a wealthy tradesman. Division continued down the years. The street of Grey Friars itself was laid out in 1872. The details of all this need not concern us,[22] but what is of special interest is what happened when New Street was built, and houses were raised along it and St Martins. The houses had cellars. Digging them out, workmen found bones.

We owe our knowledge of this to the ever-alert John Throsby, whose interest in antiquities encouraged him to pay anyone who brought him finds. The New Street development occurred before he was an adult (he was born in 1740), but in later life he recorded what happened.

Much of the Greyfriars land, he wrote in 1789, 'was purchafed, in my time, to build thereon; it was fold to different people, and was the occafion of that ill-contrived and unpleafant paffage, called New-ftreet. When the workmen were digging to fink the cellars, I remember, though very young, that the quantity and the perfectnefs of the human fkeletons found there, very much attracted the attention of the people of Leicefter.'[23]

A couple of years later he recalled the memory again, with a different twist. 'When the workmen were digging for the cellars', he said, 'to the range of houfes which face St Martin's church, they caft up, I remember, many human bones; one fkeleton lay entire: the Friary church probably ftood there.'[24]

Perfect human skeletons, one of them complete: this was precisely what ULAS's small dig east of Grey Friars street in 2007 had failed to find, encouraging the belief that the friary church was probably not at that far east end of the plot. But over two centuries before, Throsby had used the same logic to argue the opposite. Perfect skeletons meant a church. And he could point to where that church had been: on the south side of St Martins, near the north end of New Street, facing St Martin's church (what is now the cathedral) – in modern terms, under the houses on

Peacock Lane and St Martins either side of New Street, or the car parks immediately behind them, New Street to the west and the Social Services to the east.

On the face of it, then, Throsby's evidence was critical, key indication of where in the plot the church might have been. This evidence was consistent with a couple of medieval texts. One describes a brutal street murder in 1300, in 'the lane which leads to St. Martin's church and towards the church of the Friars Minor' (i.e. Greyfriars). The other, written in 1543 only five years after the Dissolution, says Greyfriars was 'at the end of the hospital of Mr Wigston', which was immediately west of the cathedral. Both passages imply the friary was across the road from St Martin's, in the case of the second, in New Street car park – as the Ordnance Survey marked the friary site on its maps, and where a small part of supposed medieval wall still survives.[25]

But how reliable was Throsby's memory? Could it even be possible that one of those skeletons was Richard III's? After all those stories and debates, had his bones been turned over like potatoes and covered in brickwork when no one was looking?

The good news was that in the most detailed early map of this area, by Thomas Roberts, none of the land had been built on; and a surprising amount of it was open now, notably in two car parks and an old school playground. The question was, what had happened in those spaces in the intervening centuries? Had buildings that might have destroyed archaeological remains been cleared away, or had there never been any? It was time to compare Roberts's map with later surveys, to chart the friary precinct's history of occupation.

We first see New Street on a map in 1804, with buildings facing out all round the block. More significant, however, is John Fowler's map, published in 1828, which identifies individual properties and shows considerable additional detail. At that time, apart from the development either side of New Street and along the lanes enclosing the precinct, the friary grounds remained entirely under gardens.

Total mapping appears with the arrival of the Ordnance Survey, the national organization established in the 18th century by governments facing the prospect of war. The survey spread rapidly beyond Jacobite Scotland and the English coast threatened by Napoleon, with pioneering and ambitious precision and accuracy. It printed its first map of Leicester in 1888, updating it in 1904, and again in 1915, in 1930, in 1955, and on into the present. As you turn from one map to the next, as if watching a movie through time from the perspective of a crow, the spaces fill in. But remarkably, already by 1904 the layout looks recognizably modern. There is the school playground. There is the New Street car park, and there, with its distinctive crenellated L-shaped plan, is the Social Services car park. Only at the north end towards St Martins – precisely where Throsby ventured the friary church might have stood – are parts of the latter built over. Those structures are gone now. So what exactly were they?

The answer to that lies in hand-coloured maps drawn up with extraordinary detail by a business that really needed to be clear about what was happening on the ground. They were produced by Charles E. Goad's civil engineers for insurance companies, and are known today as Goad plans. The Leicester maps are held by the county Record Office. To see them, I drive south for ten or fifteen minutes into a spacious leafy suburb, where, for no charge – and there is even free parking! – inside a light and high-ceilinged reading room in a decorative old school built in 1881, I can lay out the maps and take 18th-century histories off the shelves.[26]

I can't find what I'm looking for in a card index. I ask the librarian for help. She leads me to rows of what look like hundreds of red plastic folders, and pulls one out. 'Let's try this one,' she says, leafing through the pages. And then, 'There it is.'

'It helps', she adds with a smile, 'to remember numbers in this place.' She returns to the desk, where a lady wants to know what a consanguine terrier is, and a man comes up to tell her he's found something. I open the folder. There are 27, well-thumbed typed pages listing Goad plans compiled between 1888 and 1958. I find the one I want, fill in the details on a printed card and hand it in. While I wait for the map to be brought out of store, I settle down with Throsby's *Antiquities of Leicester*.

The map is a beautiful thing, made in 1938. Peacock Lane runs across the top and Newarke Street the bottom, with the friary precinct occupying a substantial chunk. Hundreds of small paper clippings have been glued on to a stiff white card, the buildings coloured pink and their every detail described in neat script. There are still gardens west of New Street, but Leicester is now a city learning to accommodate cars, and the 'motor parks' have arrived; the Social Services car park is over 75 years old. Beyond the block are symbols of Leicester's lost industry – hosiery factories, a leather warehouse, sawmills, a cardboard factory, a litho printer and typesetting factory, and many more in this vein. At the far west of the friary precinct is the Birmingham & Midland Motor Omnibus Company's Leicester Garage – pulled down only in 2009 – where presently is another, expansive car park.

But the area I'm interested in was never transformed by factories, remaining instead a collection of genteel offices for workers who now arrived in their motor cars. The southwest part is newly occupied by the County Council.[27] Buildings encroach into the northern space. There are garages and a library, with 'concrete floors', and some small unnamed outbuildings. These do not look like multi-storey structures with basements. If Richard III's grave was still there undisturbed in 1804, it was probably still there in March 2011.

This time it was Richard Buckley's turn to call Philippa Langley.

Scene 3

THE SAME

A university

'Blimey!'

Richard Buckley was remembering Philippa Langley's early submissions. She sent him stuff after their first phone conversation, when he had agreed to consider her idea that it would be worth looking for Richard III. He hadn't taken it seriously, but he soon realized they could only find the king if they could identify the friary where his grave was said to be, and he was keen to have a go at that.

Any thoughts he might have had that Philippa would share his excitement about the quest for the medieval church, however, were soon dispelled: for her the search was already over. She wanted Richard to know what would happen next.

They were going to make a television programme! It would be presented by Richard Armitage, a tall, dark-haired actor, star of TV drama series Spooks/MI5 and Robin Hood and (at that moment undergoing early shooting in New Zealand) the movie *The Hobbit*, in which he plays Thorin Oakenshield. Philippa had found her king. Now she would net a 'burnished and indecently handsome love god'.[1]

Nearer the reality of a busy university office, with one foot in academia and the other in a muddy trench, were Philippa's plans for reinterment. They hadn't even found Richard III, let alone dug him up, but here she was, plotting the reburial of his remains. The previous September

– months before she'd made first contact with the archaeologists – she'd commissioned a tomb design.[2]

Richard Buckley was amused. 'You'd plan a project in terms of something that was going to be a complete long shot,' he said, 'but you'd spend a lot of time designing a tomb and a coffin. She's very optimistic,' he added. 'I find that funny.' He was always quite open about his belief that they would never find Richard III. 'Every phone call I had with her,' he said, 'I told her, "You realize we are very unlikely to be successful?"' When she said that she was planning to order a coffin, he suggested she get some legs made for it so she could use it as a novelty sideboard.

Designing the tomb was like commissioning cover artwork for your first blockbuster novel before you'd written a word (paying special attention, perhaps, to the lettering of the author's name). However, this was far from a sign that Philippa was not to be taken seriously. In fact, it was the reverse. She was going to find Richard III. Of that there was no doubt. All that remained was the exhumation.

But while for Philippa the searching was over, for Richard Buckley it hadn't yet begun. These were different positions they were coming to appreciate, and to find compatible with their respective places in the mission. It worked well. They talked and they listened ('Richard Buckley will always give you the time of day,' said Philippa with admiration), and they had no cause to interfere with each other's priorities. Significantly, they each had their own, separate schemes: the Richard III Society called theirs Looking for Richard, and the University of Leicester ran the Grey Friars Project. As it grew beyond anything either of them had yet conceived, however, the differences contained the potential for misunderstandings and even conflict.

If the archaeologists imagined that Philippa was simply looking for a grave, the reality was more complex. At an understandably triumphant conference held by the Richard III Society within weeks of the formal announcement of their project's success in 2013, Philippa gave a joint presentation with Annette Carson. Now a retired copywriter, Carson had authored books on aerobatics, rock guitarist Jeff Beck and, in 2009, Richard III.[3] Philippa had asked her to join the team as historical adviser.

'Let's make no mistake,' Carson told a packed auditorium at the University of Leicester. 'This project was about Richard III, it wasn't about digging something up.'

A curious remark, perhaps, to make of an archaeological dig. Carson, it seems, had been a little unnerved by the sight of archaeologists handling Richard's remains: her preferred image of the king was James Butler's noble statue, not 'a series of bones which have been subjected to a lot of poking and prodding'.

But it emphasizes how for the Richard III Society the excavation was only a step in a long struggle to change the public attitude towards a 'maligned king', to quote Carson's book title. They wanted to persuade people that he was a good man and a good ruler, and to show how, again in Carson's words, 'bigotry, toadyism, propaganda and gossip' during his lifetime, and 'calculated propaganda' after his death, had created a distorted view of his achievements that was further warped by Shakespeare.

Philippa agreed, if she wasn't quite so dismissive of the dig. The Looking for Richard project, she told the captivated audience, was a search for a grave and the king's remains. But it was also a quest for a man, the *real* Richard III, the human being – she spoke as a screen writer, she said, not as a scientist or a historian – behind the myth.[4]

If we are to understand how Richard III's remains came to be found, we need to fathom the power that this image of an unjustly wronged monarch has over Ricardians – it might have been the archaeologists who excavated a skeleton and proved its identity, but they would never have looked unless pushed. It is the power that inspired Paul Murray Kendall, who wrote the book that Philippa took with her on holiday in 1998. It is the power that motivated other authors too, from George Buck as long ago as 1619, to Horace Walpole (1768), whose logic convinced John Wesley and Jane Austen, to vicar's wife Caroline Halsted (1844), who 'fell in love with' Richard, to the geographer and traveller Sir Clements Markham (1906).[5]

There have always been other writers keen to take the opposing view of Richard as borderline psychopath – or journalists hammering out the odd throwaway line about a hunchback – to ensure regular new recruits to the case for the defence. We saw in Act II Scene 1 how Josephine Tey's novel enlivened the Richard III Society in the 1950s. Shakespeare's indestructibly potent play showcases a living monster – the worse for his intriguing streaks of humanity – from one theatrical season to the next, born anew in the hands of talented directors and actors, challenging Richard's supporters to take up their swords.

The comparison doesn't entirely explain it, but we can gain a perspective on this if we consider J. F. Kennedy. Both the king and the president died young – aged 32 and 46 respectively – and violently, and while in office after short terms: Richard III's lasted two years and 58 days, Kennedy's two years and 307 days. They were both members of powerful and wealthy political families that knew much personal tragedy; it is said that Kennedy is unlikely to have been president if his brother Joseph had not been killed in the Second World War. Oddly, they both suffered serious back trouble: Richard III, we now know, had deforming scoliosis, while Kennedy endured recurrent and severe back pain for which he had unsuccessful surgery.[6] And I suspect that long after the moment, many people remembered what they were doing in 1485 when they heard the news of Richard's death.

All of that is curious enough. The key point, however, is that it is easy to imagine these two men as having been cut down just as they were ready to make their glorious marks: they were stolen from history, so that their times in power were associated with death, cruelty and fear (Richard) or a failed military invasion and a brush with nuclear war (Kennedy), rather than the constructive peace that lay ahead of them.

For Ricardians, Richard III was killed by a usurper with no claim to the throne, whose followers and descendants needed to overturn Richard's

Richard III's DNA suggests he had blue eyes, confirming that this painting owned by the Society of Antiquaries, made after 1512–20, was probably copied from a life portrait.

Act II, Scene 3

benevolent character to justify his death. There was a conspiracy, which needs to be exposed. Philippa, said Annette Carson at the Leicester conference, wanted her to join the project 'to help ensure that the true facts about [Richard III] were always set out for the public to see, to counteract the villainous portraits the media always revel in'.

Kennedy's assassination launched conspiracies on a perhaps unmatched scale. In this case it wasn't that anyone needed to justify his manner of death to the public, but the opposite: his true killers, it was argued, whoever they might be, sought to conceal their identity and their reasons for murdering Kennedy by manipulating evidence. Their actions and motives needed to be exposed, to honour a politically wronged leader.

Why is JFK relentlessly popular, asked Robert Dallek in 2011, when he achieved so little? The people, he replied, want a heroic, inspiring leader. He was young and handsome, said one of many online comment posters. He was one of us, said another. We love him for what he might have achieved; we can judge him only by his intentions, not by his performance. He was for peace, and paid for it with his life. He had everything, and he lost everything. His death came at a moment of cultural change.[7]

These are strong feelings. You can imagine them reflected in the face of a bronze statue in Leicester, of a man holding up a crown with an expression that says he knows he will never be able to do the things he wanted to do. Kennedy inspires powerful emotions. There is something similar in what drives Ricardians, but with added zeal: they believe that most people do not understand the target of their attentions. The unbelievers need to be told the truth. It would take a lot to discourage Philippa, a story teller who had caught the Richard III bug, from tracking down the real Richard III. The grave was but a marker on the journey.[8]

Yet imagine the appeal of finding that grave. Late medieval history is not distinguished by regular and spectacular new discoveries. In the Yale edition of Charles Ross's biography of Richard III, there is a 16-page foreword by the Welsh historian Ralph Griffiths. He considered how ideas about Richard had changed in the 18 years since the original text had been published. Several writers, said Griffiths, had 'sought to digest, rearrange and reinterpret the body of sources which Ross used', rehearsing plausibilities, shifting emphases and adjusting verdicts. He credited the *Ricardian*, the Richard III Society's journal, for its contributions. Historic texts had been edited and published, portraits of Richard had been scrutinized and his library reviewed.[9]

All of that was important, the stuff of historical process (and its low-key nature testament to the quality of Ross's text). But it is not a story to fire news editors and cause headline writers to reach for puns. Over a similar period, understanding of Stonehenge – to take a single prehistoric site – would have been transformed, with both new thinking and substantial new finds, aided by fast-moving developments in forensic-style sciences. Thinking about it, in the past 18 years that has actually happened at Stonehenge. Twice.

The promise of uncovering Richard III's grave hinted at unparalleled new information, of a material kind central to Ricardian concerns. Had Richard not been given a respectable burial, and had his bones never been disturbed? Had his coffin not been recycled as a horse trough? Had his arm not been withered, his back not deformed, his shoulders not uneven? How, precisely, had he died? Here, if the quest proved successful, would be the chance to share intimately in his pain, and to offer the respect he had been denied with a new memorial tomb, the ultimate station in the trail of modern plaques and testaments. Perhaps, even, through a form of sympathy like the medieval healing ritual of royal 'touching', it would prove possible to cure the world of the myth of Richard the Bad.[10]

*

In spring 2011, the next step on Philippa's journey was to visit Richard Buckley. He had called to say he had something to show her, and she was intrigued. She pitched up at his offices, and found he had all these maps laid out on one of their finds tables. He explained how they'd started with the oldest, and followed through right up to the modern ones, and they'd found this map made by Thomas Roberts in 1741.

'I'd never seen it,' Philippa told me. 'I'd never seen it, and believe me I had trawled every single piece of Ricardian research, and I'd never, never seen it. It was incredible, it was just dynamite.'

The map was amazing. It showed the Greyfriars area, and it had what looked – Richard was talking about it as her eyes tried to take it in – it had what looked like a gatehouse on the south side, which could be the remnants of Herrick's mansion house. Then she saw the garden, and the paths that met at a circle. She could hardly contain herself.

'There's a formal garden,' she said to Richard, 'and it's got four pathways and a central area. If you've got the grave of a king and a three-foot stone pillar that says, "Here lies the body of Richard III, sometime king of England", wouldn't you put it in the centre of your garden and have all pathways lead to it?'

Richard had to admit it was an interesting theory. He hadn't been aware of the pillar until Leon Hunt told him about Wren's memoir. And this was right in the area of the car parks behind the Social Services and the old school. 'It was right in the place', Philippa told me, 'we wanted it to be.' And at that point, she looked up at Richard with a smile and widened eyes. Well?

Richard told her he was ready to come on board. Obviously, his search would be for the church, Philippa knew that. He wasn't going to look for a grave, because that's not what archaeologists do. 'But', Philippa told me, 'the two were mutually beneficial, because if he found the church, I could look for the grave. And if I found the grave, he'd found the church. So we kind of did it on that basis.' Putting it like that, if she found the grave, whether or not they found the church seemed not really to matter.

It had been a long haul for Philippa – discovering Richard III's story in Waterstone's in 1998, deciding at the pub in 2009 to look for the burial, and commissioning the desk-based assessment from the archaeologists early in 2011 – but now things were moving fast. She had the DBA at the end of March. The archaeologists needed to produce another study, and then they could start digging. Philippa's job was to raise the money.

Richard prepared the new report. He called this one a written scheme of investigation (WSI).[11] It would detail what they were going to do on the ground and why, as far as it was possible to know at this stage. This would help them to decide what kit they needed and how many staff, and how long it would take, allowing them to cost it and programme it into their other work. Central to all those decisions were the questions of precisely where they would put their trenches, how many there would be, and what size and shape they would make them. Designing the trenches would use all of Richard's experience as an archaeologist working in Leicester for 30 years, drawing on the information that Leon Hunt's assessment had collated.

By comparison with their other work, this was a small project, and technically what they call an evaluation, not an excavation. They would test the ground to sample what might be there of interest, and see what survived. In a more typical job, they would then report to the city planners. In such an instance a developer would have paid for the evaluation. The archaeologists might tell the planners there was historic stuff underground of public interest that new building work would destroy. If the planners decided anyway to allow construction to go ahead, they would probably ask the developer to pay the archaeologists to do a proper excavation. A good WSI would ensure that the archaeologists got all they wanted out of the site, efficiently and fast, minimizing costs for the developer and finishing without getting in the way of often very tight construction schedules.

In this case, however, there was no developer: the only people who might destroy things would be the archaeologists themselves. In the jargon, they would seek out the medieval archaeology and characterize it. They wanted to find the friary church. If they succeeded, they didn't need to excavate it, just work out from the layout of the walls where the choir should be, and then look for a grave. If that too was successful, well, then they would excavate.

One evening in July, Richard attended a book launch in the Guildhall, a magnificent timber-framed structure built around 1390 as a meeting place for the town's more powerful businessmen. It's remained in some form of corporate use ever since – from a very early public library in the 17th century, through a court, mayor's offices, school and police HQ, until finally opening as a museum in 1926. No more than a footpath separates it from the west end of the cathedral, which, when the Guildhall was built, was a church frequented by merchants (Leicester has been home to a bishop since 1927, when the relatively modest St Martin's church became Leicester Cathedral).

The University of Leicester Archaeological Services had produced an illustrated history of the city on the back of the huge Highcross shopping centre excavations. Mike Codd had crafted 22 detailed historical paintings

Leicester's Guildhall, built around 1390 opposite the west end of what is now the cathedral (at far left in photo) and was then St Martin's church, in use as a town hall in Richard III's time.

showing Leicester through the ages, and Richard and his colleague
Mathew Morris had written the text.[12] Sir Peter Soulsby, who had become
the city's first elected mayor in May with an overwhelming majority,
commended the book to university, city and council luminaries, and
Codd's original paintings stood around the edge. It was the sort of event
with which the Guildhall must have felt very comfortable.

One of Codd's paintings was a cloud's view of the medieval town,
looking southwest as if coming down over the A46 from Newark. The old
walls around the Roman city are still prominent, though the 14th-century
settlement barely fills half of the enclosed space. You can see the River
Soar meandering its braided way through the woods and fields beyond
Bow Bridge, with the Austin friary on its island, and Black Friars inside the
walls in the northwest corner, to the right. Towards the left, in an area of
dense housing, is the prominent spire of St Martin's church, and beyond
that, squeezed into the space between St Martin's and the crumbling south
wall of the Roman city, the buildings of Leicester Greyfriars.

Their church, envisaged as a low-key almost barn-like structure,
is close to the town wall, south of the friary cloisters and other buildings.
Richard told Mathew they were going to look for that church. He
introduced him to Philippa Langley, who was also there, and they talked
about Richard III. Philippa wasn't impressed with the painting, as she
and Ashdown-Hill had decided the church was north of the cloisters,
close to St Martin's where the Social Services car park is.

Ashdown-Hill had argued that churches were always north of the
cloisters. By and large this is true, but it is not an invariant rule. The
excavation on which Richard had worked as a schoolboy had shown
the Austin friars across town had put their church south of the cloisters,
where it could be near the public road; unlike the rest of the complex,
the western part of the church was open to everyone. At the Greyfriars,
Philippa had found a medieval map in the Record Office that showed
two churches close together, either side of St Martins lane, leaving space
for the cloisters only to the south, and placing the friary church firmly

under the car park. Richard had tried to discourage her from putting too much weight on the map: it purported to show medieval Leicester, but it was purely schematic. She never really gave the map up, though, and later, when she watched the first television film of the dig which at that point they were far from sure was going to happen, she was disappointed to see that her mantra, 'church, road, church', failed to make it past the editing process.

Meanwhile, Philippa had been thinking about ground-penetrating radar, or GPR. GPR had helped archaeologists map out a large, First World War grave in France, before any excavation occurred, in the project that had impressed Philippa in Darlow Smithson Productions' film for Channel 4. GPR had come up when she talked to the City Council, hoping to persuade them to let her dig in Leicester. Now she needed to commission the survey.

She'd asked Richard about it: 'Do you think this is going to be worthwhile?' And he said, 'Look, I've done three ground-penetrating radar surveys in Leicester, and they've all been hopeless, they showed us nothing. But', he added, 'this is archaeologically virgin ground, so it's worth a shot.'

Actually, Richard was completely against it. 'When it works, it's brilliant', he told me. But in Leicester it hadn't. 'People thought we'd get a plan of the friary, find the church, then dig the hole. It doesn't work like that. Here walls are almost always entirely robbed out, floor levels often don't survive, and the complexity of different periods of archaeology confuses things.' In essence, there's rarely anything of interest underground in Leicester that GPR is good at finding.

That was Richard's opinion, but GPR was the only geophysical process that might find anything in the conditions, what with the tarmac and everything. 'We were all really hopeful', said Philippa, 'that this amazing scanner would give us a lot of information to take forward.' She rang Dr Phil Stone.

Phil Stone, a radiologist, is chairman of the Richard III Society, a gently spoken man with glasses, a fine head of silver-white hair and a Father Christmas beard. He had helped Philippa earlier with society research funds for the desk-based assessment. 'What is it now, dear?' he asked, in a kindly tone that Philippa recognized.[13]

The GPR survey was conducted by Stratascan, a geophysical contractor based in Worcestershire near the border between England and Wales. It cost Philippa, or the Richard III Society, £5,043. For that she got what its manufacturer, a Swedish company called Malå, describes as 'the most technically advanced GPR system on the market' – the Mira – and a man to drive it. With a large, low box hiding the technical kit attached to the front of a mini tractor, it looks a little like a hi-tech estate lawnmower. The same machine had produced spectacular results on some Roman towns investigated by Time Team, where buried wall foundations were revealed in 3D – only GPR can do that. What might it find in Leicester?

Philippa had arranged for the three car parks to be empty on the day of the survey in August. They made quite an event of it. Philippa and John Ashdown-Hill were there, and Phil Stone, and meeting with Philippa for the first time, Annette Carson. Richard Buckley had been invited along too, and a city councillor. DSP, hoping to get a Channel 4 commission, filmed a short promo. The shiny yellow tractor trundled around, automatically collecting its data. Initial results visible on the laptop mounted by the driver's seat were difficult to make sense of, but they would wait for the full report after it had all been processed back in Worcestershire.

It was a disaster. A variety of underground responses showed on a map in lines and blobs of different colours. The technical language made it sound important, but what it came down to was that for about a metre (just over three feet) below the tarmac was rubble – made ground or demolition debris – and under that pipes and cables. There was nothing at all that looked like a wall, still less the plan of a church. Philippa had paid £5,000 to find a few drains and some manhole covers.[14]

Ironically, in due course excavation would prove the GPR survey correct in what it had shown, not least in its accurate mapping of what the archaeologists decided was probably the site of the school bike sheds, and a medieval stone coffin. With no walls or other graves that might have indicated a cemetery, however, in 2011 the coffin remained unidentified. Which was just as well. When excavated, it would turn out not to be Richard's grave, and could have resulted in a wild goose chase.

'It was a really difficult moment,' said Philippa. 'We'd found nothing. We couldn't even see the outbuildings.' But that was only the start of the problem.

Richard Buckley had costed it all, including reinstating the car park after they were done, for which the city's Highway Maintenance team would charge them over £15,000, nearly half the archaeology budget. All the parking spaces needed to be relocated – Philippa had helped negotiate that. 'Logistically it was quite difficult,' said Richard, 'but that's what I like about urban projects. I like the complexity.' Altogether, they needed about £35,000, and naturally, Richard's first thought was, where's it going to come from?

Philippa had brought in a major sponsor, Leicester Shire Promotions, a company marketing tourism in the city and the county. However, seeing that the hi-tech GPR survey had failed to show any sign of the friary, they pulled out. Those manhole covers had cost Philippa a lot more than five grand.[15]

Now what was she to do? The dig had been planned for April 2012. The months were flying by, she'd lost her sponsor and she'd spent a pile of the Richard III Society's money for nothing. By Christmas 2011, the project, Richard told me, 'was dead in the water'.

Philippa got on the phone.

Sarah Levitt, Head of Arts and Museums at Leicester City Council, had supported Philippa from the start. 'Her belief in the project', said Philippa, 'opened doors. She had real vision.' Since her arrival in Leicester in 1997, Levitt had, in her words, turned 'a traditional, under-funded and inward-looking institution' – Leicester's museums, the first of which opened in 1849 – 'into a modern city service'. She was keen to make the museums relevant to Leicester's unusually diverse population.

Unfortunately, in 2011 she had the task of telling these citizens that three of their museums were going to close. 'They are not part of the core business of the council', she said, in language to which people across a recessionary Britain had by then become all too accustomed. But the help she gave to Philippa would prove to be one of the best investments the council could have made.[16]

Hold it off until the August bank holiday weekend, said Levitt. Give yourself more time, and the council will be able to sort out the staff parking. And that is what they did. Only later did Philippa realize the significance of that weekend. The dig would start on 25 August, three days after the Battle of Bosworth: the day of Richard III's burial.

As they entered 2012 and Philippa and Annette Carson continued with the fundraising, the debate about exactly where the friary church might have been became increasingly academic. If there was anything of the friary buildings left in the ground, the archaeologists were going to find them. Of course, they had no idea that, all this time, Richard III's remains were quietly lying there, just below the rubble concealed under the smooth tarmac of the Social Services car park. Neither could they possibly know that, but for a combination of luck and Mathew's archaeological skills and experience, when it came to it the bones might have been crushed into pulp before anyone saw them.

*

Mathew Morris, though originally from Cambridgeshire, had studied archaeology at Leicester ('It was a really good university,' he told me, 'the nicest one, with the best archaeology course and good students'). Afterwards he returned to Cambridge, to excavate and work in a museum, but was drawn back to Leicester by the offer of a job on the Highcross project in 2004. He stayed with ULAS, where in 2011 he was an archaeological assistant, his name the last in a list of 21 staff. He'd wanted to be an archaeologist since a primary school trip to see an excavation at an Anglo-Saxon cemetery, with skeletons lying in the graves. He enjoys digging, and has the confident air of a man happy in his job. However, it is unlikely that he ever imagined, as a nine-year-old boy fascinated by those skeletons, that one day he would himself find the skeleton of a king. For Richard was to put him in charge of the Greyfriars dig.

Soon after the book launch, Mathew was in the office rather than out in the field. So as Richard prepared the WSI, every so often he would come over and ask for Mathew's opinion on his plans for the trenches, on how they might make some sort of use of those geophysics plots, on the best way to do things. Philippa kept coming back with details she wanted to add. Chris Wardle, the City Archaeologist in the planning department, suggested revisions. At first, Leon Hunt, who'd written the DBA, knew much more about it than Mathew. 'But', Mathew told me,

Mathew Morris, director of the excavations that found Greyfriars friary and Richard III's remains, poses for the press at the grave, lower right of centre (he wears a hard-hat for work).

Act II, Scene 3

'he has no real urban experience, so he didn't want to run the excavation. So I ended up running it.' 'Mathew', Richard told me, 'is a very good archaeologist.'

In most jobs, you would expect to find the information you needed in the WSI, making it an essential document ('Can you do this tomorrow?'). By the time the Greyfriars report was finally handed over to Mathew, however, it was all a little irrelevant. It had been rewritten five times, and they had discussed the strategy as it went along. Mathew already knew what he had to do.

Like Richard, he saw the project as a good chance to explore an area of Leicester they didn't usually get to see. It would be intriguing, and exciting: they might discover anything. It seemed so improbable that they would find Richard III, he didn't consider that aspect seriously. It's difficult to imagine now, after all that has happened, but at the time the 'Richard III bit' was secondary. This was, after all, the Grey Friars Project, not a quest.

But first, Mathew had bigger things to think about. In the spring he was back out by Highcross Street, directing an evaluation of a large parcel of land where there had been a Victorian brewery that had succumbed to vandalism and as yet unfulfilled ambitions for new development. They dug seven 30-m-long (98 ft) trenches, and found copious amounts of Roman archaeology, including parts of a street surface and a mosaic floor, but little substantial of more recent date. They were in that part of the town that Mike Codd's medieval painting showed mostly as gardens and meadows. He seemed to have got it right there.

Over at the Richard III Society, in June Philippa announced her project, with the planned late August date for the dig, in their printed newsletter. The chance to investigate Greyfriars had finally come, and with it the opportunity to 'potentially recover the remains of our king so that they can be reinterred with true honour and dignity'. There would be a memorial service in the cathedral on the second of October, which should give everyone enough time to tidy up.[17]

It understandably got Ricardians talking and excited about what might happen. Which was good, because almost at once, in July, Philippa's key sponsor, who though facing its own challenges had come back with £15,000, wobbled again and pulled ten grand. What made it worse was that Sarah Levitt had set the first of August as a deadline: if they were unable to raise the funds by then, they would have to postpone the project to the following year.

That was it, thought Philippa, game over. She rang Annette Carson. We need to raise £10,000, and we've got two weeks in which to do it. And Philippa (former marketing student and sponsorship manager for the *Scotsman*) and Annette (award-winning PR and advertising copywriter), aided by the ever understanding Phil Stone, launched an international appeal of a kind that perhaps only the Richard III Society could manage. With its branches across Britain, Canada, the United States, New Zealand and Australia they begged 'Ricardians and their friends to band together and make it possible for this once-in-a-lifetime excavation to take place'. Others took up the cause, not least the King Richard Armitage website, an online petition to promote a 'historically accurate' movie, whose two heroes are neatly encapsulated in its title.

Within minutes, the money poured in, absolutely flooded in. 'I think there was one day', Philippa told me, 'I actually sat at my computer from seven in the morning till three in the morning, dealing with emails that were, literally, coming ping, ping, ping, it was that fast.' The money arrived from everywhere the society had branches, and also from Holland, Belgium, Germany and Austria, and even Turkey and Brazil. They raised the £10,000, and the dig was saved. By the time they closed the appeal, they had nearly £13,000.[18]

With a month to go, all the money was in place. Just over half of the total of £33,000 came from the Richard III Society. After struggling to maintain its commitment, Leicester Shire Promotions held to £5,000, and Leicester Adult Schools (backed by a former mayor) brought in a further £500. The City Council, which had helped Philippa so much in the planning, felt it would be politically inappropriate at a time of severe financial stringency to put up cash, but they had agreed to offer £5,000 in reserve. The university, however, had given £10,000. The dig was a reality.

Richard Taylor, then the university's Director of Corporate Affairs and a man to be underestimated at your peril, was grappling with one of the most severe challenges to hit English higher education in recent times. With continuing cuts in central government subsidies, annual student fees were rising, and from 2012 the universities were allowed to charge an unprecedented £9,000 for a year's tuition. In the event, many sought the maximum, and student applications fell.

Taylor argued that universities needed to be clear about how they positioned themselves in the market, and that their reputations were critical assets. This was not language to warm the hearts of all academics, though at Leicester's Department of Archaeology, where ULAS had been operating successfully as a commercial outfit for over a decade, it was rhetoric they understood. Taylor's line was that Leicester was a top university, and among its peers by far the most socially inclusive – 'elite without being elitist'.[19]

He saw the dig as an interesting project that people would engage with, and, along the way, would raise the university's profile – and there was little doubt that he himself was excited about it. And what if it succeeded? The idea that Leicester's archaeologists might solve a centuries-old mystery with TV-style forensics from university scientists; do this while helping to restore the reputation of a wronged monarch, at the same time as putting paid to a slur on the city's ordinary Tudor citizens; and all because they'd found a king whose remains had lain at the feet of those unfortunates needing the help of Leicester's social services – well, it might have been designed by the university's marketing office.

Initially, Taylor's grant made Richard Buckley a little uncomfortable: if the university was going to give away £10,000 for a dig in Leicester, is this how he would have spent it? There were so many more things in the city he wanted to know about, starting with the castle. 'What always worried me all the way down the line', he told me, 'was that, yes, it would generate some interest, but there was no chance of it being successful!' He laughed. What would he say to the sponsors when they failed to find anything?

Richard learned that the dig was finally going to go ahead just before he went on holiday. He would return on 23 August, the day before launch. He stayed for a fortnight with friends in the south of France, joking about a curious project that was sure to be a failure. Perhaps it was more from fear than conviction, but he was downbeat about it, and no one could have guessed how much was at stake.

With Richard away for two weeks, returning just before the press launch, Mathew was starting to worry that he didn't know what he was doing. They had had no last-minute talks. Would the diggers turn up? They'd never had a press launch before. Press launch?! They'd hardly ever had any journalists before. He'd done a short interview, once, for local BBC Radio Leicester. Perhaps that would help.

And there was to be a camera crew there, filming for Channel 4. He'd watched a lot of Time Team programmes, and they seemed to get on fine despite all the cameras. In fact, only a couple of years before, ULAS had actually helped out with a Time Team dig, a few miles from Leicester in the grounds of Groby Old Hall, a crumbling, 15th-century red-brick manor house. One of its inhabitants had been Elizabeth Woodville, Edward IV's wife and mother of the princes who disappeared in the tower. Philippa Gregory, whose best-selling series of novels focusing on some of the women at the centre of the Wars of the Roses had then just begun with *The White Queen*, took part to help out with the history. The archaeologists dug away in the background, and no one bothered them. It would all be fine. If Richard came back from France.

One week to go. Over at Bosworth, a few days before the anniversary of the confrontation, the Battlefield Centre held a weekend of events and celebrations, with a re-enactment of Richard III's death. This was an impressive sight, with armoured knights on horseback, archers, pikemen, gunners, cannon, hawks and flags, and an amplified commentary to enliven the damp, smoky air.

The church of St James, Sutton Cheney, where myth says Richard III heard his last mass before the Battle of Bosworth, and the Richard III Society holds an annual commemorative service.

'Richard for England and St George! Come on, then, give our king a really good cheer!'

A weak cheer drifted from the crowd.

'I still can't hear you!'

Enter, field left, an army of rather downhearted-looking footsoldiers.

'If you wish to cheer, or boo, the Tudors or the Lancastrians, here's your chance!'

There was a scatter of half-hearted booing.

'Can I hear that a little bit louder, please?'

If only he'd been there in 1485, history might have been entirely different. As a crown-wielding Henry VII was booed and the late king's body was carried away, slung authentically over a horse (if tastefully clothed), the announcer had some news for the spectators. 'I am reliably informed', he said, 'very soon there's going to be a dig in Leicester to see if they can find 'im.'

Act II, Scene 3

97

The Richard III Society had a stall at the re-enactment, signing up new members and selling books. Late in the morning they had held their usual service at the medieval church in Sutton Cheney, a small, shrunken village east of Bosworth Field. Richard, say some, attended his last mass here early on the morning of the battle – 'This church has strong links with King Richard III' is the diplomatic wording on St James's notice board. Every year loyal Society members gather here to commemorate the battle and honour the dead. On that day in 2012, as usual, the Prayer of King Richard was read from his Book of Hours. Celebrants lowered themselves on needlepoint kneelers made by Society members, and admired the wreaths and banners hung around the Society's brass plaque, fixed there in 1967.[20]

One week to go. It had been a day when, it seemed, dreams might come true.

Sometimes they do.

Act III

EXCAVATION IN
2012

Scene 1

GREYFRIARS

A car park

'It's a good start on the roads around Leicestershire and Rutland, with no major incidents to report. There's a rather cold and windy day of weather in front of us, but we can hope for a few sunny spells here and there.

'Good morning, I'm Jonathan Lampon and you're listening to BBC Radio Leicester. History's being made in Leicester today as the search begins for the remains of a king of England. It's five minutes past six and we start with Barry White...'

It was grey in the east, the sky barely growing light as the sun began to rise across the horizon. In the west some lights flickered from the Holiday Inn, a useful vantage point from which to survey the entire field. Dawn brought relief from a night troubled by uneasy dreams. He looked pale and death-like, as he consumed his modest breakfast. There was something, he said at last, that he must tell them.

That last paragraph is a fantasy. The words – with the obvious exceptions – are those of historians who like to release their inner novelists when describing the Battle of Bosworth.[1] This is the half-real half-fictional world we inhabited, early on the morning of Friday 24 August 2012, in Leicester to attend a press event whose main features were historical re-enactments, rather than the reality they appeared to be, and the celebration of something that had not happened, and possibly never would.

It was a curious and rarely entered world, of an archaeological dig that was designed to retrieve something very famous yet not known to be there. The matter of the quest meant it could not be ignored, not least for fear that with no control, the information that did get out – and surely, it would – could be false, misleading or likely to make fools of everyone. The best way to lead was to keep ahead of the gossip with real news. The problem for the university was that, as yet, there *was* no news. In addition to which, all it had to show people was a car park: a small, empty parking lot round the back of some council offices.

Ather Mirza, Director of the University Press Office, remembered leaving his first meeting of the three partners: the university, the City Council and the Richard III Society. Everyone had agreed that the dig should be launched with a bit of a splash. But how on earth would he get the media to come and film a piece of tarmac? He decided, he told me, to stage-manage it. Which is exactly what he did, with a council car park as mise-en-scène.

He had a good start: the dig was to begin on the anniversary of Richard III's funeral. The whole event had a surreal touch, especially for those journalists only half awake before seven in the morning. The cast list included men in convincing medieval armour wielding convincing pikes, others in luminous yellow jackets spraying yellow lines on the tarmac, a historian, a scriptwriter, a forensic psychologist (research interest: psychology of love and destruction), a geneticist, an archaeologist, a cabinetmaker and a woman slowly pushing up and down a bicycle-like contraption wired up to a life-support system, as if there was no one else there. There was even, standing in his white hut despite the exclusion of all but a few cars, a parking attendant. As Mirza said to me, he had brought in 'all the academics who the media might possibly want to talk to'.

Philippa Langley was there, to explain the mission. Richard Buckley described the archaeological strategy. He was expecting that maybe Radio Leicester and the *Leicester Mercury* would come to see what they were doing, and was looking forward to it, but loads of people came: he was blown away, and not happy. 'There was so much interest,' he told me, 'we were being set up to fail and look very silly when we didn't find the grave.'

John Ashdown-Hill talked about genealogy, clutching a copy of his recently reprinted book and a polyester Richard III flag (you can buy them on eBay for £5.99). Stratascan had sent Claire Graham to demonstrate ground-penetrating radar, though this wasn't quite what it looked. Graham is a GPR specialist and had worked with Robbie Austrums on the survey, but is also their Sales Manager. She had brought a simpler piece of machinery than the one they had used almost exactly a year ago to do the actual survey, when fortunately it appeared not to have found a grave or the drama might have been wiped out at a stroke. Turi King, a geneticist at the university and the first person invited by Richard Buckley to join the team, stood under a luxuriant fig tree – a reminder that the car park had once been gardens – with Michael Ibsen, a Canadian-born woodworker who carried copies of genes from Richard III's family. King took a DNA swab.[2]

A former journalist who had started out on the *Leicester Mercury*, Mirza had presented what he would have wanted on that first day. It worked. All the national media came. There was a sense of promise, of what might be found, and the press were enthusiastic. 'Wow,' thought Mirza, 'this story's got legs, it's going to run.' They'd set the stage. Now, as the dig progressed, they would create the narrative.

Mathew Morris had thought it would be simple.

His jobs at the launch were to erect the gazebo, a pop-up white barbecue tent for the journalists' buffet in case it rained, and then to get the trenches laid out. Richard Buckley was tied up with all the interviews, allowing Mathew to focus on preparing for the excavation. They wanted to cut the tarmac on the Friday, so they could save time on the Saturday and bring in a mechanical digger straightaway.

He tucked the gazebo round the corner by the council staff bike shed, and secured it by tying sandbags round the legs. It stayed there for the rest of the dig, a lunch hut and a shelter for sudden rain. Then he and

Leon Hunt, who wrote the desk-based assessment and was site supervisor for the dig, marks out Trench 1 on 24 August 2012, watched by Claire Graham, knights and world media.

Leon Hunt could prepare for the road cutter, which was due to arrive after lunch. The council had wanted the trench sides to be clean and straight to facilitate resurfacing, so they started marking out guide lines with a can of yellow aerosol paint.

But there were media everywhere, wandering all over the place, with their unmovable satellite trucks parked where they were trying to put the trenches. 'They wanted to film us spraying out lines,' said Mathew, 'the press wanted footage. We got through two cans of spray paint, when one would have been more than enough.'

He worried about the cutting. This circus had to be out of the way by two o'clock, when the man with the powered circular saw would arrive. They didn't know how hard the asphalt would be. It might take half an hour or half a day – and then he'd have to come back the next day. In the event, the vans went, they checked for live electricity cables with a hand-held CAT scanner, and it was all done in an hour. 'The tarmac turned out to be really crap,' said Mathew, 'he went through it like butter.'

How did they decide where to put the trenches? 'It was a little arbitrary,' said Mathew. They had the strategy, one here, one here, within half a metre. But then you'd get on site, and find an overhanging tree, or an unmapped fence post, things like that, and they'd jiggle them about; there was always a little bit of flexibility. The guiding principle on that day was the orientation of Christian churches.

A typical church plan is a crucifix. The vertical stem forms the nave, the place where the congregation gathers (and in medieval friaries, where the wider public were welcomed); the top the choir (where the clergy sit) and beyond this the presbytery or chancel (holding the high altar); the horizontal bar is the transept, separating the nave and choir/presbytery at the crossing, and often containing chapels in its protruding wings.

At a friary there would be other buildings around the church, such as an infirmary, kitchens and a library; the all-important chapter house, where the friars would meet daily, sitting on a bench that ran round the edge; and a square garden or courtyard (garth), enclosed by a walk (cloisters), typically south of the church where it could catch the sun. The church, however, was the key structure, and with its spire or tower rising from the crossing, the one that dominated the streets around. All other church buildings followed its alignment, which was approximately east–west, so the transepts ran north and south. A Franciscan friary such as Greyfriars would be expected not to have had protruding transepts, but just the crossing separating nave and choir, known as a walking-place.

The church faced east, in the sense that you worshipped facing the church's east end. So most attention to the architecture and decoration at the west end was devoted to the outside, which you would see as you entered through the largest doors. Inside, you would look east towards the altar, beyond which the church's east end was designed to impress mostly from the inside. Hence this was where, often, you would see the grandest stained-glass windows, through which the rising sun might shine.

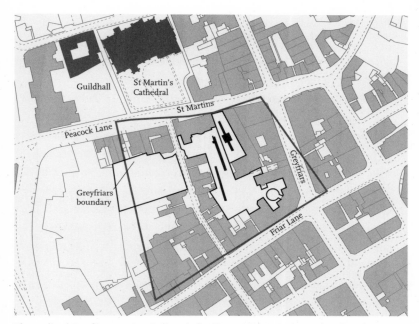

The medieval Greyfriars precinct, indicated after Thomas Roberts's 1741 map, and modern streets; the three car parks and Trenches 1–3 are outlined in black (see plan page 117).

When Leicester Greyfriars was built in the 1220s, the astonishing achievements of European Gothic architecture were approaching their peak. One of humanity's great triumphs of design, engineering, craftsmanship and sheer genius of artistry was well expressed in England in Salisbury Cathedral, whose Lady Chapel was going up at the same time as Greyfriars, soon to be followed by the entire breathtaking building. As well as finding indications of the friary's plan, the archaeologists hoped they might retrieve fragments of masonry and glass, and gain some insight into the quality of its architecture. Salisbury would have commanded master builders and materials beyond the resources of Leicester's friars, but what did their home look like?

Because the church would have been long and narrow and aligned roughly east–west, the best hope of picking up any of the friary walls in small trenches was to make these long and narrow and aligned north–south. They would need to find more than one bit of wall or they wouldn't know what it was, but if they were in the right place, north–south trenches should cut through several. The plan was to dig two trenches and then, as Richard described it to me, think, 'Where on earth are we in the friary?' They would then decide where to put their third and last trench.

The private owner of the New Street car park, the largest of the three, had preferred not to interrupt its service. By good fortune, the two parks left for them to excavate were aligned largely north–south. So aided by the GPR survey – which finally proved very useful in suggesting where not to dig, avoiding service pipes and what might be disturbed ground – Richard had proposed two partly overlapping 30-m-long (98 ft) trenches in the longer space, the Social Services car park. Together they would give a 50-m (164 ft) slice through Leicester's history.

They had to leave a foot passage through the site in case of emergency. They couldn't undermine the buildings on the sides, or cut off any fire escapes, and they had to avoid the underground services and leave enough room for their excavation spoil. There was not a lot of jiggle space for those two trenches. Looking around, Mathew could see an array of painted white lines, the parking grid that packed cars in against the walls running down either side of the lot. There in front of him were two long straight lines. For Trench 1, to the east, Mathew and Leon set out the edges a metre either side of the white line. To the west and mostly further south, they used the white line there for the eastern edge of Trench 2. Somehow it all fitted.

The written scheme of investigation (WSI) gave Mathew four objectives, which added up to finding the church; there was no mention of a grave. However, when the archaeologists lectured about it later, they elaborated five goals to illustrate their approach on the ground. The first was to find remains of the friary. Mathew would then try to identify the orientation and position of buildings, from which he hoped to work out where the church had been. Then he would seek to locate the choir, east of the church crossing where John Rous had recorded that Richard III had been buried. Finally he would search for human remains that could be identified as those of the king.

They judged the likelihood of each goal. Objective one was 'a reasonable expectation'. Two was 'a probability'. Three was 'a possibility', and four was 'an outside chance'. Five, the only one that really mattered to the Richard III Society who had initiated the project and put up half the money to get started, was 'not seriously considered possible' – or, as another version had it, 'not realistically considered'. All along, the archaeologists had said that looking for a king was not the sort of thing they did. Which was just as well. If they'd approached sponsors with their research strategy, the project would never have happened.

Philippa's approach was a little different. A year before almost to the day, she and her fellow Ricardians had arranged a photograph in the council car park. On the ground, they propped up a little framed reproduction of one of the many surviving portraits painted of Richard III after his death. In front of this they spread out Ashdown-Hill's bright new flag, the late medieval royal standard, split into quadrants of which two contained three gold lions passant on a red field, and the other two, three fleurs-de-lys on a blue field. They arranged the portrait and the flag so that, in the space between them, could clearly be seen, though faded and scuffed, a white-painted capital letter R. For Philippa and her supporters, there was only one objective.

*

'It's bone.'

They'd barely started, up at the north end of the first trench, the cathedral end, and Mathew had stopped the shiny red digger and climbed in. He shovelled away the loose rubble and dirt, then reached with his left hand into his back trouser pocket, took out his trowel, and crouched down into the shade, so that his white hard-hat was two feet below the level of the tarmac above him.

'I think it may be human bone.'

They'd arrived on site at eight o'clock in the morning. The confusion and distractions of the previous day, as they'd tried to mark out their trenches around – and under – TV satellite vans and a zoo of wandering journalists, academics and medieval knights, had moved on. Sometimes the details might be haggled over, but they were all now broadly agreed about strategy towards the media and the general public: they stayed outside the car park.

Philippa and Darlow Smithson Productions needed some exclusivity for their film, so that it had some original content – though it had still not been formally commissioned. Like all broadcasters, Channel 4 knew well how far they could string along an independent production company without committing money, and still get the story if they wanted it (and at no point would they contribute funds to the excavation).

The archaeologists were expecting to disturb human remains; not Richard III's, but there would have been graves both inside and outside the church, and they would have been surprised if they found none at all. The Ministry of Justice, who issue licences for the excavation of human remains, require their removal to be screened from the public. There was a further need for concealment at the far south end of the excavation, where the council retained a small parking area. Taxis would stop there to drop off and collect vulnerable children and their carers, clearly not something to be splashed around the world. Which left, with just the two small trenches, very little that could safely be opened to uncontrolled viewing.

Finally, the University Press Office wanted to create a meaningful narrative from what was likely to be a random set of discoveries. If allowed to go public as they occurred, poorly understood finds and half-digested ideas could have caused confusion, and dissipated the story's power. That would have been in the interests of neither academic reputations nor publicity for the university.

The downside for the archaeologists was that this meant they couldn't open the site to the public during the dig, which was always a shame. 'It

would have been nice', Mathew said, 'to have had more public interaction.'
Still, perhaps they would find something interesting, and in the end
people would be able to see it.

Yes, it looked human. The bone was lying horizontally. The digger's
bucket, with a clean, sharp edge selected to scrape a flat surface as it
worked along the trench, had neatly sliced the top off the brown, stained
bone, revealing pale lines against the dark brown soil. The driver wasn't
able to see it because the bucket was in the way, which was why Mathew
had been standing in front, watching, in control, holding up his hand,
and shouting. Hang on a minute.

It was almost certainly part of a leg. But was it just a single bone?
Perhaps it had been disturbed by an earlier excavation, scatter from a grave
dug through by an unknowing Victorian navvy. Or was it connected to
another bone, still articulated as would be the case if it was in a burial?
It was close to the edge of the trench. As Mathew removed the loose earth
with his trowel, he could see the knee end was out of reach, under the
tarmac, and at the foot end there seemed to be nothing there. He wasn't
going to be able to find a joint.

The digger was a red, six-ton Kubota KX161 with rubber caterpillar
tracks and a bucket at the end of a hydraulic arm at the front, with a
small white cabin for the operator. They'd hired it from an independent
company based in Leicester called JoinPoint, which had worked
with them on the Highcross site. Mathew didn't know the driver,
Steve Stell, but though he hadn't done any archaeology before, he was
really good; he could do exactly what was asked. He was a bit nonplussed
by all the media attention. Later, after the weekend was over, he'd come
in on the Monday holding up his newspaper. 'Look at this,' he'd say,
'I'm in the bloody *Sun!*'

Mathew had arranged for the digger to start at the top end of Trench 1
because of the needs of access. In normal times the narrow car park had a
one-way through route. Drivers would come in off Grey Friars, take a
cobbled passage through a red-brick arch around the side of the council

offices, and in due course leave at the far end of the car park out into New Street. With the fence and screen across the south end of the excavation, however, what was left of the parking area could only be reached by driving back and forth through the arch. This was too narrow for the digger and the trailer needed to convey it. There had to be enough space for them to come and go at any time, which meant working from the top, piling the spoil between the trench and the wall to the side as it went down, then coming up Trench 2 from the bottom to end back up near the entrance from New Street. In the end, this proved not to be an issue, as it stayed there all through the dig. But JoinPoint could've come and picked up their machine at any time if they'd needed it elsewhere.

The digger began with a narrow-toothed bucket, to break up the surface. In no time he was at the bottom of the car park, having left in his wake a path of piled, broken tarmac with two very straight edges, as if the artist Richard Long had made an unusually rapid appearance. Back he came, switching to a wider, flat-bladed ditching bucket, and pulling the debris out to one side. Then back again to start digging.

The Goad maps showed outhouses at the top, and sure enough, the first thing they found, right at the end and close to the surface, was a solid, modern brick foundation. That needed the toothed bucket. As Philippa and John Ashdown-Hill watched it hammer through the fresh red brickwork, the dust of white mortar clouding in the breeze, they thought, this isn't the sort of wall we were expecting. Neither had they said anything to the archaeologists as, at the start, the shiny little red digger had parked its rubber tracks right over the R. Within minutes, the bucket had smashed through the symbolic letter and lost it in the pile of fragmented tarmac accumulating like breaking pack ice. They were meant to find a king there, not the foundations of a Victorian toilet.

But mostly there was gravel. Mathew was expecting to find medieval archaeology no more than three feet down, 70 cm to a metre, but there was a further half metre of red-stained gravel. They were going quite deep. There wasn't much Victorian garden soil, so perhaps it had been taken

The Social Services car park, looking north towards the old school (right) and cathedral spire (left). Taken during excavations in 2013, this photo shows Trench 2 infilled with new tarmac.

out and built back up again. Their journey through time had begun with a peek into the lost world of gravelled motor parks.

They continued going down and down and not really finding anything, just lots of dark soil with very thin bands of mortar in it. Only with hindsight did they realize these were probably wispy remnants of church floor surfaces; at that stage there was no way they could tell. Mathew was starting to worry that the trench would be too deep before they hit medieval archaeology, that too much of it had gone. The night before, his great fear had been that both trenches would be done by lunchtime: there would be nothing in either of them, after all the hype of the press launch. What if they didn't find anything? It wasn't looking good. Then he had spotted the bone.

There were a couple of concrete slabs that were just too big for the bucket to rip out, so at first the digger had to go over them. Now he worked one loose. As the beam rose like a lid opening, Mathew could see a bone sticking out of the section, the side of the trench: the concrete slabs had protected it at the first machine pass. That looks a bit human, he thought, watching from high up. Which, he soon confirmed, it was. He covered it with a plastic finds bag, and protected it with soil and bricks. They would return when the finer excavation began.

They would have just carried on, working along the trench with the digger, taking out a bit more gravel and getting down into the earth where they hoped to find medieval remains. But while the muddle of the previous day's press event had gone, with journalists tripping over each other's cables and knights in armour sipping coffee at the gazebo, they were still not quite alone. Now they had a film crew with a director from Darlow Smithson Productions. And DSP, in on the project even before the archaeologists knew about it, were not about to miss anything.

The archaeologists had had no idea how much filming they were going to have to do, and how long it would take. This was not Time Team. From this first day, Mathew and Leon Hunt were doing pieces straight to camera. In the end it worked out fine. Mathew, Leon and Richard were the three main archaeologists, and they shared the work, one supervising the digger while another spoke to camera about a new find, and so on. Straight off, DSP had wanted to film bits during the morning about finding brick walls. They hadn't programmed that in. It was like the yellow lines, when they'd mark out the trench and get ready for the next job, but then have to go out and buy another tin of paint and spray it all again.

So rather than have the digger driver sit there doing nothing while Mathew handled a brick with an air of studied curiosity for the thirteenth time, he let him take the rest of the gravel out on his own. They knew how deep it was then, there was just Victorian rubble underneath, and the digger could stop safely as soon as he hit brickwork. He could do stuff without supervision while they were mucking around with the filming.

But that created a problem. The trench was cut 2 m wide, with a little give for the 1.6-m-wide bucket: they didn't want to bash the edges with it. The digger's rubber tracks, however, were about the width of the trench, and when Mathew brought Steve Stell back down to machine the top of the earth out, he had to drive inside the trench he had just excavated. It was a little bit too tight: a track caught on the side and popped off.

They lost a couple of hours' work over lunchtime, while they waited for the digger driver to collect some chains. They were hanging around for him to get the track back on, and Mathew began to wonder. Was that bone really human? Was it just loose, or could it be a burial? He had a spare moment, so he popped in for another look.

He did exactly what he'd always do in such a situation. Working with gentle speed that belied his skill, like a production-line craft potter, he dug a slot across the bone, just 5 cm across, looking for another bone. The only difference was that this time he wore rubber gloves. If it did turn out to be significant, they would need to DNA test it. He couldn't risk exposing loads of bone and contaminating it with his own DNA. It was a policy in the written scheme of investigation.

And sure enough, as he scraped out his narrow cut in the soil, he found another bone, from a right leg, where it should be, parallel to the first. This was a burial, of an adult lying on his or her back. He labelled it Skeleton 1.

Mathew wasn't surprised, but it was a good start to the dig. He knew human remains had been found when the cellars were dug next door nearly three centuries before. Another burial confirmed they were in the right area. It wasn't going to be Roman, it was at a medieval level. There was no sign of a church at this stage (though the location up near the cathedral was quite badly damaged by the Victorian outhouses, so they hadn't proved its absence there), and the ground looked like garden soil. They were probably somewhere outside the church. Richard Buckley was pleased, too. When he heard the news of the bone, he thought, good, we're on the right track. We could be in the graveyard and missing the building, what we'd expect.

Mathew made the mistake of saying to Philippa, yes, it's a grave. So they spent the next 40 minutes or so filming the whole thing. Then quite suddenly, the sky darkened. The cathedral spire glowed briefly as the sun shone on to thunderous clouds. The temperature dropped. Lightning flashed. It rained.

'They all legged it', said Mathew, grabbing coats and heading to the gazebo or corners in old buildings around the car park. He climbed out of the trench to fetch something to cover the bones. When he got back, he found Philippa in his waterproof jacket; she left him there and ran for shelter. Turi King, the project geneticist, had just turned up to see what was going on. She'd brought cookies, so they sheltered from the storm nibbling comfort food. The DSP crew ducked under cover as well, from where they could film Mathew getting soaked, while Leon Hunt, holding an umbrella, supervised the digger at the other end of the trench.

Mathew was concerned that the water would wash out the burial. He stayed there to cover it up, laying down clean plastic finds bags, padding them with soil and holding them down with bricks, nursing the bones while the storm rumbled and flashed over Leicester.

The idea that the grave might be Richard III's hadn't entered his head.

*

'Once you say you've found human remains,' Ather Mirza told me, 'you distort the whole story.' At the University Press Office, they made it very clear that the focus of the narrative should be on the archaeology – finding the friary, the next bit of pottery, the next tile. 'I used to tell the archaeologists,' said Mirza, 'if you don't want the world to know, don't tell me.' He learned that they had found a burial over a week later, on the day the Ministry of Justice gave the archaeologists permission to dig it up.

Fortunately, there was plenty to tell in the meantime. They'd always said that the fifth and final objective was, in Richard Buckley's words, a long shot. However, there were four others to meet before they searched for 'the mortal remains of Richard III'. They achieved the first of these on the first day. This was no ordinary excavation.

As they dug down from ground level, they learned what they had to get through before they reached any possible remains surviving from medieval times. At the northern end of Trench 1, and as they were soon to find, occasionally also elsewhere in both trenches, there were 19th- or 20th-century brick foundations or demolition rubble. There was a deep deposit of gravel that had built up across the whole area since it had been in use as an early car park; there seemed to be little Victorian garden soil beneath the gravel, so most of it had probably been carted away. Below all of that, as they entered what they called 'the archaeology', they started to encounter thick layers of building debris. These were not further accumulations of red brick, but random chunks of pale coloured stone, several obviously shaped with the smooth curves of fluting and beading indicative of door or window frames, or perhaps stone ceilings.

Before the sensation became dissipated somewhat by interviews for Darlow Smithson Productions and poses for the university cameraman, Richard Buckley had started the day with a spring in his step. With a year and a half of discussion and planning behind them, now they could at last get on with some new archaeology, and find out what was really there beneath the car park. By the end of the day, when Richard returned to catch up with progress, his early optimism was more than renewed.

About two thirds of the way down from the top end of Trench 1 they had found an east–west wall, exactly as the project design said they might. To be more precise, they had found an excavation that had once held a wall foundation, what they called a robbed wall, with part of a low stone wall still surviving alongside and large quantities of rubble. It looked as if there had been an important, high-status medieval building in the vicinity.

Act III, Scene 1

They didn't yet know where they were, but they'd found the friary. Within hours, they had met objective one.

Because of the delays caused by the filming, the thunderstorm and the digger throwing a track, they were unable to complete Trench 1 on the Saturday. On Sunday morning, however, they knew what to expect as they dug down, and they got the rest done in half an hour. They found another robbed wall, parallel to the first and near the southern trench end, though a live cable prevented further investigation there with the digger.

Machining out Trench 2 also went really easily, finishing on schedule by mid afternoon. They spent the rest of the day cleaning up, removing loose rubble and overburden to expose the medieval layers. At the top end of Trench 2, where it overlapped with the bottom end of Trench 1, they could see the same east–west robbed wall they'd found on Saturday. Intriguingly, there was another robbed wall attached to it at right angles, disappearing under the tarmac as it ran south on a slightly different alignment from the trench edge. Meanwhile, on the other side of the trench and further down was a second north–south wall, parallel to the first. If these two walls had been standing at the same time and continued opposite each other, they would have been separated by quite a narrow space, 2 m (6 ft) across. Whether that indicated two buildings side by side, or an indoor passage, might be resolved by what lay between them, presently covered by stone rubble.

Monday was the August public holiday, and Mathew, Leon Hunt and Pauline Carroll, a former administrator of the university's School of Archaeology and an experienced excavator, continued digging and cleaning alone. The others arrived on Tuesday, and they were set up for the rest of the project, with a small but extremely skilled team of men from ULAS: Mathew, Leon Hunt, Tony Gnanaratnam (who had directed the

Opposite, top Looking for Richard III: three excavation trenches in 2012 to locate the friary (T1–T3), and a larger area in 2013 to establish details of the choir and presbytery.

Opposite, bottom Hypothetical Greyfriars plan based on evidence from the excavations and typical friary layouts; identifying the chapter house was a key moment in unveiling the story.

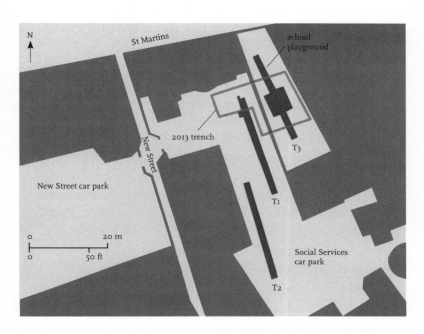

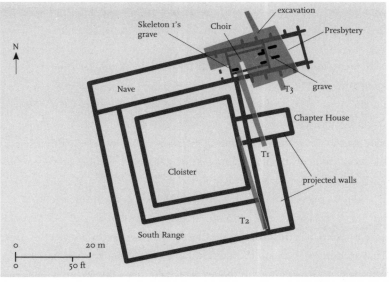

Act III, Scene 1

dig across the road at the NatWest bank, delighting Philippa by finding no evidence there for Greyfriars church) and Jon Coward. Three other ULAS staff, Tom Hoyle, Steve Baker and Neil Jefferson, would put in a few days. They would also be joined by seven volunteers, who between them worked for 22 days. Among these were Martyn Henson, a school teacher who had once worked for ULAS and still wanted to be a professional archaeologist but couldn't afford the pay; Kim Sidwell, another experienced ULAS excavator, now working for the university's Student Support Services; and Ken Wallace, a retired teacher who found fame after he discovered vast quantities of prehistoric coins on a hill in Leicestershire in 2000. Karen Ladniuk, a Brazilian lawyer and member of the Richard III Society who had heard about the dig, flown to England and presented herself on site, was the only volunteer without previous excavation experience. Pauline Houghton and Andrew Mcleish completed the list.

ULAS usually worked Monday to Friday, but they didn't stop for Greyfriars. They already had a tight three-week window, with the prospects looking tighter still thanks to the intensity of the filming. 'When you've got a project you're interested in,' said Mathew, 'it's very hard not to be there when it's still going.' Over the whole three weeks he took only one day off.

Mathew set up Jon Coward and Tony Gnanaratnam in Trench 1, Leon Hunt and Martyn Henson in Trench 2, and prepared himself to keep the film crew off their backs. They spent a couple of days cleaning up, working out what they had and removing rubble. As the week went on, they started emptying out medieval pits and robber trenches, lifting all the loose stone off the floors, and getting a handle on where they were – which bits of the friary they had found.

On Wednesday it rained. They tried to keep going until lunchtime, but spent most of the day sitting in the gazebo, and by two o'clock they gave up. This was the only day they lost to weather, a curious piece of luck. That summer was one of the wettest the UK has ever experienced, beating various records back to 1776 (before which comparisons become harder).

Archaeological trenches across Britain were filled with water, and with August sunshine 95 per cent below normal, there were few of the usual bronzed diggers.

Once they'd removed the debris between the wall lines running down either side of Trench 2, it was clear they had found a corridor. There had been a floor there, now marked by mortar bedding with impressions of tiles which had been prized out for reuse. Surprisingly, as the eastern wall disappeared out of the far southern end of the trench, a small part of actual wall survived intact above floor level, a very rare find in stone-poor Leicester; a stub of stone moulding, with wall plaster still attached, was a jamb from a doorway giving access from the east.

In Trench 1 they cleaned up the two parallel east–west walls, which appeared to have belonged to a 7.5-m-wide (25 ft) building. Here too there was some low upstanding masonry. At first they thought this had survived from the building, but as they emptied the tops of the robber trenches and removed rubble from the interior, they realized they were dwarf walls raised against its inside; perhaps, thought Mathew, some kind of refacing or repair work, although they looked a little like benches.

That took them all of the first week, and by Friday afternoon they were ready to begin Trench 3. Where they'd dug in the north end of the Social Services car park, the remains had been badly damaged by outhouses. So rather than put the new trench up there beside Trench 1, they looked over the high wall to the east. This might be the last opportunity to excavate in the Alderman Newton's playground. The derelict late Victorian building had been on the market since 2007, its lower windows boarded up. The estate agents had allowed them to excavate there, but once it had sold they might never get permission again.[3]

So they laid out Trench 3 in the playground, another strip 30 m by 2 m (98 ft by 6.5 ft), and cut the tarmac. On Saturday morning they machined it out. There was no accumulation of parking gravels here, and they hit the archaeology sooner, no more than 75 cm (2.5 ft) down, as they had expected it to be in the earlier trenches, where they had had to go down twice that depth before they hit medieval layers.

Straight away they found a nice medieval tiled pavement: it just popped up. But as they cleaned it, they could see a real mix of tiles, all of them very badly worn, and it didn't look right. Then they found an east–west robber trench, and another, showing where two large walls had been, with really good floor surfaces in between. How did these fit with what was in the car park, which was invisible from where they stood? It was time for a proper survey. So on Sunday they cleaned up the new trench, and surveyed everything they had done in the past week with an electronic distance measuring device (EDM).

'I legged it up to the university,' said Mathew, pointing at the computer in front of him in the ULAS office where we were talking, 'and downloaded it all on here. I dropped the EDM plan on to an Ordnance Survey map, and coloured in the bits where we knew the walls were.' He paused, and gazed at the black screen before turning back to me.

'I was sitting there looking at the computer, and it dawned on me that we knew where we were in the friary – and we'd found the church. So I rushed back down in the minibus to show Richard, thinking he wouldn't still be there.'

But he was, talking to people, catching up on the day's events, and they carried the plan around the site, fitting it all together. The corridor in Trench 2 was the western cloister walk, with two walls of the rectangular chapter house showing in Trench 1. 'Then the benches,' said Mathew, 'the little bits of dwarf wall, fell into place. They were the benches around the edge of the chapter house.'

Impressions in the floor showed that tiles there had been laid in a diamond pattern; building material among the debris suggested the walls had been of local grey sandstone, and the roof of local slates, with glazed pottery tiles on the ridge. This was critical evidence. Knowing where the chapter house had been was an important part of planning the friary.

Then at the top, continuing beneath the high brick wall that separated the car park and the playground, was the church. The southern of the two large robbed walls indicated in Trench 3 lined up with a deep pit in Trench 1, confirming their suspicion that that might too have been a large robbed-out wall. The church was a little over 10 m (33 ft) across, and there was evidence for the base of at least one substantial buttress.

They had identified a cloister walk, the chapter house, and the church: objectives two and three achieved. As a bonus, they seemed to have found one of Robert Herrick's garden paths, made from medieval tiles he'd collected, perhaps, from the undergrowth, where they'd been abandoned by scavengers looking for better things.

Now they had found the church, they needed to narrow their search, to learn more about its layout and see if they could define the presbytery, the choir and the crossing. There were likely to be graves inside that part of the building, one of which could contain the remains of Richard III. Indeed, they had already found a grave. They could now see that Skeleton 1 was inside the church's eastern half. It could be in the choir.

On the first day, Richard Buckley had watched Mathew supervise the digger, and seen them hit Victorian foundations as anticipated. 'I'll leave them to it,' he said to himself. 'I don't want to interfere, they're running the site. I trust them, they're all very good archaeologists.' They'd cut their teeth on some huge excavations in Leicester, up to ten years before. They'd dug up 1,300 burials. They were good at machining, good at recognizing things.

Nonetheless, he was surprised to see evidence in the first week for what looked like the cloister walk, and then the chapter house, and then, blimey, they'd found the church. A few days' digging had unsettled a year and a half of complete conviction that they could never, ever find Richard III.

Next week they would start looking. They would excavate Skeleton 1.

Scene 2

THE SAME

A grave

'It looks to be two legs parallel with each other,' explained Mathew, as he and Philippa stood up to their shoulders in the bottom of Trench 1. 'That to me suggests it's an articulated human burial rather than just loose bones knocking around in the soil. So now that we know it's articulated, we can't touch it until we get the licence to deal with the human remains.'

However, what they could do, he continued, is clear around the bones, remove all the free rubble and dirt, and see if there were any more burials or other features to indicate a graveyard. It had been a good first day.

In the event, as we have seen, they found no other burials or human remains in Trench 1 or Trench 2. The discovery of that first grave, however, was the sign they needed that they were in the right place, and the moment for Richard Buckley to apply for an exhumation licence under the Burial Act of 1857. He considered the budget. Allowing for each grave a day to excavate, a day to wash anything recovered and a day to analyse it, they could manage six. He filled out a simple, three-page form, in which Section 3 asked what he expected to find. Against 'Estimated age of remains', he wrote 'Medieval 13th–16th century'; and against 'Estimated number of set[s] of remains', '6'.

You might think that archaeologists like to find graves: ancient burials can be extremely informative about the worlds and lives of people from the past, and occasionally they offer fine artifacts that make popular museum exhibits. Yet excavating and analysing burials can be time-consuming and costly. Human remains found unexpectedly on excavations – as many are, especially when they are older than historically documented cemeteries – are not always welcomed. Their discovery can add significantly to budgets and cause delay, especially in the type of commercial projects ULAS normally takes on, where schedules are tight. Archaeologists do not excavate graves lightly.

Archaeologists are also of course aware that long-forgotten graves were dug by mourners and celebrants who knew the buried individual; that what might be incomplete, damaged and delicate remains are the real physical traces of someone who was once alive. Many archaeologists think a great deal about death. When you excavate ancient graves, and handle remains that tell personal and intimate stories of individuals who have no voice but yours, you cannot avoid it. The complex ethics of how ancient human remains are studied, published, conserved and, perhaps, displayed, are major topics of debate around the world.

Yet how archaeologists as ordinary people deal with the experience of revealing the remains of another person is not something they often discuss. There is no training in emotional issues at an archaeological dig. We might see analogies between excavating an ancient grave and working in a morgue or at a recent crime scene (indeed some archaeologists specialize in the latter, and can make important contributions to human rights abuse investigations). Rarely does an excavating archaeologist have to handle remains as complete as those in typical modern situations. Their behaviour, however, can be telling, often characterized by long periods of silence as they pick at the delicate exercise of forensic exhumation, punctuated by clinical descriptions of their progress and occasional expressions of gallows humour.[1]

Practically speaking, to dig people up, you need permission from the authorities. In recent years there has been a bit of a tizz about this among archaeologists in England, as the responsibility for issuing licences passed from one national government department to another. The new section (the Ministry of Justice) treated archaeological remains as if they were modern, so that questions of supposed cross-infection became an issue, excavation needed to be screened from the public, and, at first, all excavated remains had to be reburied within a given time limit, typically a few months. Archaeologists were not impressed. The new rules created much new paperwork for an outcome that could see the remains they wished to study being taken away before they had even begun.[2]

Around the time that Richard Buckley handed Philippa the desk-based assessment for the Grey Friars Project, the Ministry of Justice, lobbied publicly by archaeologists, conceded that reburial should be an option, not a requirement. For Philippa there was never any doubt that once found and excavated, Richard III's remains would be reburied – and that this would happen in Leicester (as Richard Buckley said to me, 'If Philippa had gone to see the City Council and said, "I want to rebury Richard at St George's Windsor", they wouldn't have supported her').[3] For the archaeologists, however, any other remains they might excavate in the search for Richard III – which, as they envisaged it, would be *all* the remains – would be important evidence for Leicester's early population. These should be kept for future studies.

Section 4 of the licence application form asked what it was intended would happen to any excavated remains. The options given were 'Reinterred', 'Cremated' (a very odd thing for an archaeologist to contemplate for historic material), 'Left in situ', and 'Wish to retain'. Richard ticked the last box, noting that any remains would be deposited at Leicester's Jewry Wall Museum around July 2014. This is the city archaeology museum, with some of the country's largest standing Roman walls, not far from Bow Bridge but the other side of the Holiday Inn, where it offers a rival attraction to the narrative of Richard III in street furniture and memorials. Then he added a qualification.

'Please note,' it read. 'In the unlikely event that the remains of Richard III are located, the intention is for these to be reinterred at

St Martin's Cathedral, Leicester within 4 weeks of exhumation.' To emphasize how very unlikely this was, a further comment pointed out that though Richard III was buried in the area in 1485, his remains 'may subsequently have been exhumed and thrown into the nearby River Soar after the Dissolution in 1538'. Richard was taking nothing for granted.

The licence came through on 3 September, the second Monday of the dig. By then, apart from the burial, they had largely finished in the first two trenches, and had opened the third in the school playground. They had found enough wall foundation trenches to show where parts of the friary's cloister, chapter house and church were, but not enough yet to establish which part of the church they were in.

Philippa and Darlow Smithson Productions were keen to film at least one skeleton, even if it turned out not to be Richard III. The archaeologists didn't know whether or not Skeleton 1 was in the choir, where they

September 2012 press photo, looking south down Trench 1, with spoil against school wall; the small extension bottom right was made to allow full excavation of Skeleton 1.

believed Richard had been buried, but it did seem to be inside the church, a good place. So they decided to make this the first set of human remains to exhume. Both Turi King, project geneticist, and Jo Appleby, project osteologist, were free to be at the dig on Tuesday. Mathew had been there continuously for two weeks. He took Monday off, and prepared to return the next day to supervise the excavation of Skeleton 1.

The body's lower legs were inside Trench 1, but the rest of it was still under the tarmac. So the first task was to extend the trench, by opening up a square on the west side. DSP wanted to shoot them cutting the tarmac, machining it off along with the upper layers of gravel, and then excavating the skeleton, so they could edit the sequence to make it appear it had all happened in one simple process. Mathew knew from experience this would take too long. So they got the man in early with his diesel-fuelled circular saw, pre-cut the tarmac and covered it up so no one would notice they'd done it.

The film crew arrived, with the presenter Simon Farnaby, a tall, curly-haired comedy actor at that moment best known for his regular appearances in the popular children's television series Horrible Histories ('That's the man', exclaimed my young daughter as we watched him at the dig on Channel 4, 'who got pooh in his face!'). His *Spotlight* CV notes that he is 'highly skilled' at golf, pool and snooker.[4]

Paul Finnigan, a skilled driver the archaeologists had worked with before, immediately set to, with the wide ditching bucket on his digger, and prised up the tarmac, which came away leaving remarkably straight edges. Mathew stood in the trench, keeping an eye on the carefully packed dirt and bricks that concealed a sheet of blue plastic protecting the body's two legs. Immediately below the tarmac, the ground was tough. Finnigan had to hammer through red bricks and concrete. At length he was able to scoop out the gravel and edge down to the level where Mathew knew they would have to start working by hand, about a foot above the grave.

Despite Mathew's precautions, however, the filming took so long that by lunchtime Jo and Turi, who had been hanging around all morning, were still in their coats and jeans. Eventually they were able to don protective white hooded overalls and start the excavation. From above the trench you could make out two anonymous white figures, crouched down in the hole, working with trowels, hand shovels and white plastic buckets. By two o'clock they were still digging. They hadn't even reached the level of the skeleton.

Outside the dig, no one knew they had discovered human remains. They'd hung thick sheets of blue tarpaulin over the wire fence around that end of the trench, which would otherwise be in plain view from the street over the car park wall and gates. But Mathew was adamant that they couldn't leave anything exposed overnight. 'It was just obvious', he said, 'they weren't going to get anything done that day. So I called a halt to it.'

Mathew still didn't know where in the church Skeleton 1 lay. He had taken advantage of having the digger driver on site to widen Trench 3 over the wall. The archaeology there was looking good, and he had every hope they might learn more about the church layout. And then human remains turned up in that trench as well.

So Mathew sent Jo and Turi over to see if this was another articulated skeleton. It turned out to be charnel, disturbed remains that had been reburied at a level higher than the church floor in a small pit. It was impossible to say exactly where these remains had come from, but one possibility was a raised tomb: all the tombs at floor level inside the church had been demolished. The important bits were all there, about half of the skeleton, the longbones, an intact skull, a few pieces of rib and the pelvis – enough for Jo and Turi to say that Skeleton 2 was female. Of their six potential sets of human remains, they had one young woman and one as yet uncharacterized individual. The odds on finding a king were shortening.

On Wednesday Turi had to fly to Innsbruck, in Austria, to attend a forensic conference. With most of the action in Trench 3, that would leave Mathew and Jo alone in the council car park to find and excavate Skeleton 1. This time, things should be simple.

Act III, Scene 2

*

If Skeleton 1's discovery was marked by a thunderstorm, its excavation was on the hottest day of the dig, effectively Leicester's brief summer in a long, wet season. Jo suffered the full get-up over her clothes: a disposable white suit and hood, face mask and white rubber gloves. Mathew hung around above, emptying her buckets of spoil, helping to record and bag finds, and offering moral support. When they came to lift the bones, he wore a mask and gloves, but he was pleased not to be in the trench. After Jo, he was the team member with the most experience of human remains, but the prospect of cooking in the sun in a white onesie – 'I'm a cold weather man' – had no appeal. Anyway, he said, there were no suits tall enough for him.

They would not finish until half past seven, a long, hot day. They were always in sight of the trench, though they had the odd break because of the heat. Then Jo would have to put on another suit. During the afternoon she didn't take many breaks because of having to take everything off and put things back on again. 'I did get overwarm at one point,' she told me, 'it really was genuinely very warm.'

Mathew put everybody else in Trench 3, and left Simon Farnaby and his crew to get on with it – they had three days of filming, this was their second day, and they had a lot of shots to get. In a week's time, what the archaeologists were to uncover would become the centre of a media firestorm. On that Wednesday, 5 September 2012, people would come and look, and talk, and film. For most of the time, however, around that small square extension to the trench there were just Mathew, Jo and some bones, concealed behind high walls and a blue tarpaulin screen, as oblivious to what was happening elsewhere as the world was ignorant of the scene at a grave in a small Leicester car park.

The week before, Jo had been away on holiday, sitting in Suffolk in the rain. She'd gone in to work on Monday morning to find Richard Buckley standing outside her office. 'Oh, Jo,' he said, 'by the way, we've found some human bones. You needn't worry, because they're not going to be Richard III, but if you could just pop down to the site and excavate them, that would be hugely useful.'

Jo Appleby had only joined the University of Leicester School of Archaeology that January, as Lecturer in Human Bioarchaeology. It was her first proper university job. She grew up in Essex, then studied for a degree at Cambridge, a second degree at Southampton, and a doctorate back at Cambridge. She then spent a year and a half working for the Cambridge Archaeological Unit, and four years as a research fellow back at the university again. Tall, with long dark hair tied at the back of her head and a crystal-elocuted diction – which she puts down to having to speak English to that part of her family descended from a Danish grandparent – she will make a strong mark on the busy lecture circuit to which all the team are to become accustomed.

Her work concerns mainly prehistoric human remains. When she arrived on site that September morning at eight o'clock, she was planning to spend the winter writing a big grant application; she hoped to get funding for an excavation in Russia, working on Bronze Age burial mounds out in southwest Siberia.

She looked down at the still half-buried leg bones that Mathew had exposed. Following their line up into the dark earth of the extension, she imagined the rest of the body. If people bury their unburnt dead (rather than one of the many other things people do with them, including storing them in boxes and bundles, feeding them to birds and animals, and publicly displaying them – the latter popular for Christian saints), they typically place the corpse on its side or back. Skeleton 1 was almost certainly an individual laid flat on its back, and Jo could see that its skull should be just within the trench. It could be male or female, and of any age other than very young. The previous day, however, Jo and Turi King had dubbed it the 90-year-old friar, an imaginary member of medieval Greyfriars who'd been laid to rest after a peaceful life.

The plan now was to remove the remaining earth with a mattock down to just above the level of the skeleton, and then for Jo to change to small hand tools. When she began they were still quite high up, and it would have taken too long to continue working from the top by hand. She went carefully, letting the weight of the mattock head feel its way through the earth. 'And then', said Mathew, 'there was that crunch when you know you've done something you didn't really want to do.'

Jo had found a skull.

A quick sweep of the loose dirt with her hands revealed the top of a head, curving down at the front to the dark hollows of the eye sockets before it disappeared into the ground. It was time to call DSP.

Simon Farnaby, wearing a long-sleeved checked cotton shirt and faded jeans, stood over the trench, looking down. Philippa stood beside him, and Mathew watched, his high-vis jacket open over a black T-shirt.

'I'm quite excited,' said Farnaby, 'because that appears to be a hole in the skull.'

Jo looked up.

'That's not an old hole, that's a hole that's been there for ten minutes. I was just basically taking it down with this mattock here, and unfortunately that's gone into the top of the skull.'

Farnaby: 'Rrrrrright.'[5]

At that moment, watched by Philippa and Mathew, Jo was being interrogated for a television programme, and filmed with two cameras. This was no ordinary dig.

'She'd just clipped the edge of a skull,' Mathew told me. 'We've all done it, and it's really annoying, but there was no way she could predict it was going to be there.' It was far too high to be linked to the legs. They assumed it was charnel, an extra skull, so they weren't particularly worried. But as she removed more earth, Jo found it still had the lower jaw in the right place, which seemed a bit wrong, and vertebrae coming off, the start of a neck. 'We were thinking,' said Mathew, 'this doesn't seem like charnel.'

He was getting worried again. The film crew kept interfering and asking Jo to do bits to camera, and by lunchtime she still hadn't made much progress. So he told the others to go over to Trench 3, saying they'd call them back when the skeleton was uncovered and there was actually something to film. He wanted to let Jo get on with it for a couple of hours. Anyway, Carl would be there to record anything that happened.

Carl Vivian is from the university's IT department, where he makes films and videos and does a bit of teaching. Tall and lanky with short, dark hair, he looks like one of those sports shop assistants who would rather be up a mountain than advising you about a backpack that might be useful on the train to work. Asked to record the dig from start to finish, he was the perfect foil to Darlow Smithson Productions. Partly out of diffidence, he just filmed and filmed, often with his camera on a tripod, standing on the sidelines, getting what he needed without interfering, asking no questions and waiting for something to happen. DSP were filming entertainment; Vivian was creating a record.

They were back on their own now, while Philippa watched from a distance, sitting in a chair at the end of the trench. Jo spotted some trauma, a small hole on the top of the skull. Because it was a little loose from the mattock blow, the face came away along a suture line that wasn't fully fused, and she could see an extra hole, a large one, in the back of the head as well. It was time for a rethink.

She put away the mattock and continued working by hand. She didn't want to scratch the bone, so she used sterilized wooden clay-modelling tools, rather than a metal trowel. As Mathew watched, he thought to himself, 'We don't do that in commercial, we just don't have the time to be that careful.'

They'd begun by trying to come down on to the skeleton in plan, so they could see it fully laid out and perhaps outline the grave pit. Instead, Jo now worked from the known to the unknown. First she cleared the legs, slowly peeling away the red-brown, stony soil with the tip of her modelling tool. She was able to follow the right leg into undisturbed clay, and find, as with the left, that there was no foot. She was not displeased to see that the feet had been removed before the dig had begun.

Excavation in 2013, showing Richard III's grave (ringed), Greyfriars church (shaded pale) with presbytery (outer lines to right/east) and choir (inner lines) as shown by floors and foundations, and sites of infilled Trench 1 (wider vertical lines) and removed wall between council car park and school playground (narrower vertical lines).

'Bone is a composite material,' she explained. 'It has an organic part and a mineral part. After you die, the organic part gradually deteriorates, and that changes how the bone behaves. When you're alive or you have recently died, if you have a fracture it has a very smooth edge. When you've been dead for a long time and your bone is degraded, then a fracture is raggedy, it's very distinctive.'

The lower leg bones of Skeleton 1 had that raggedy break.

'My money would be on the Victorian builders,' said Jo. 'They may not have realized. Even if they had, they would not necessarily have owned up. Builders don't in our experience.'

Next she cleared the arms, and then the pelvis and the hands. It was now obvious that the skull and the legs were parts of the same individual.

The body must have been laid with the head propped up in an unusual way.

When she had held the skull and looked at the gaping hole on the base where there shouldn't have been one, she had wondered if Richard Buckley might have been wrong when he told her that Skeleton 1 wasn't Richard III. Now it all seemed quite normal, with arms and legs in the right place, and she began to relax. Maybe they hadn't found Richard III. Maybe he was somewhere else. Maybe at the bottom of the River Soar.

Mathew was yet even to entertain the notion that they might have found a known individual. The trauma to the head, however, gave the skeleton a special interest. 'This is going to be a really interesting analysis and write-up,' he thought.

Philippa came over for a look. All this time she had been in a parallel world to the one inhabited by the archaeologists. Though she hadn't yet taken in the significance of the head wounds, she was just as convinced that Skeleton 1 was Richard III, the body under the R (or at least, it had to be said, near the R), as the archaeologists were convinced it was not.

Now, as she looked down at the bones in the freshly dug trench, she saw something that challenged her belief. 'It was really odd,' she said later. 'He looked to have no battle wounds and he seemed to be quite tall. I'm 5 ft 9 in., and you could see his leg bone was pretty much the same length as mine. I thought, "Maybe this isn't him."'

From the start of the excavation, Philippa had always referred to Skeleton 1 as 'him'. DSP filmed a sequence with Simon Farnaby and Philippa watching Jo and Turi remove soil on the Tuesday, when only the leg bones had been exposed. Earlier, Philippa had told Farnaby that Skeleton 1 was Richard III. 'I just thought she was insane,' he said. 'This is ridiculous, it's the first thing that was found. What's the chance of the trench being cut in the right place? I mean it was bizarre.'

'Are you nervous about this?' he asked her. 'Strangely, I am,' she said. 'I feel sick.'

'I suppose it's a weird thing digging up dead bodies,' said Farnaby.

'Yeah,' said Philippa. 'It is. The whole point of this journey, this project, was to try and honour this man.' She paused, and looked from Farnaby down into the trench. 'I mean it might not even be him.' And her voice broke.[6]

Now, with the whole skeleton exposed but for the torso, that momentary doubt seemed to have been confirmed. Jo read her thoughts. 'This just looks like a well-nourished friar,' she said. 'It's not him.'[7]

Philippa was devastated. It seemed that everything she'd worked for since the day she stood and shivered in that same car park nine years before; her dreams and the hopes of the people she'd inspired to come along with her: all these might have been for nothing. She left the site and went for a walk. She was away for a good two hours.

So when, finally, Jo started on the ribs and torso, she was completely alone in the car park, with Mathew, Carl Vivian the silent cameraman, and Skeleton 1. 'When I'm excavating skeletons,' she said, 'I always try to do the ribcage and vertebrae last. Otherwise the ribs tend to get dislodged by other bits of the excavation.'

Meanwhile, in Trench 3, Leon Hunt had opened a larger area between the two robbed walls of the church, and the archaeologists were cleaning it up, finding chunks of carved stone. When he returned to the university at night, Richard Buckley would often go to see Deirdre O'Sullivan, to chat about some of the things they'd found. Another illustration of the remarkable way in which the university seemed to be able to offer almost all the expertise they might need at the dig, O'Sullivan is a lecturer in the School of Archaeology with considerable excavation experience, specializing in early Christian archaeology. Her current research focuses on the Dissolution and friaries.

In Trench 3 they'd found inner walls parallel with the main ones. Deirdre O'Sullivan wondered if these might be the bases of choir stalls. They thought it would be a good idea to get another opinion, and had invited Glyn Coppack down from the University of Nottingham. Coppack is researching early medieval religious houses, including the analysis of old excavations at Fountains Abbey in Yorkshire, one of the greatest

Cistercian foundations in Europe. He knew all about friaries and monasteries, and they were expecting him to visit the site that afternoon. Then he, Richard and O'Sullivan could come to some conclusion about where the different parts of the church had been.

The human spine is a tough, flexible tube that both protects the spinal cord, a central nervous system that connects the rest of the body to the brain, and provides a key part of the skeletal structure. It is composed of 33 interlocking vertebrae. The upper seven form the neck (cervical); the next 12 connect with the ribs (thoracic), followed by five in the lower back (lumbar); at the end are five sacral bones, fused into one in older adults, and the coccyx, four more-or-less-fused bones that in many other mammals would be the beginning of a tail.

As Mathew watched Jo at work on Skeleton 1, he could see a few vertebrae going down from the skull, and a few vertebrae going up from the pelvis. You could draw a straight line between the two. Jo was following the spine up from the bottom, delicately cleaning away with the tip of her wooden knife.

And then something very strange happened. The spine disappeared. Jo was digging around, slowly widening a hollow in the earth, and there seemed to be no more vertebrae. Had they dissolved? That seemed very unlikely, as the rest of the bones were well preserved. Neither was there any sign that someone had dug them away at an earlier date, in the fashion of the feet. Then she found the twelfth thoracic vertebra. It very clearly was not where it should have been.

She cleaned the bone, and followed the line up to the eleventh vertebra. There it was, firmly against the twelfth, but continuing in an arc that veered away from the centre of the body. It wasn't supposed to do this. The spine was severely curved.

*

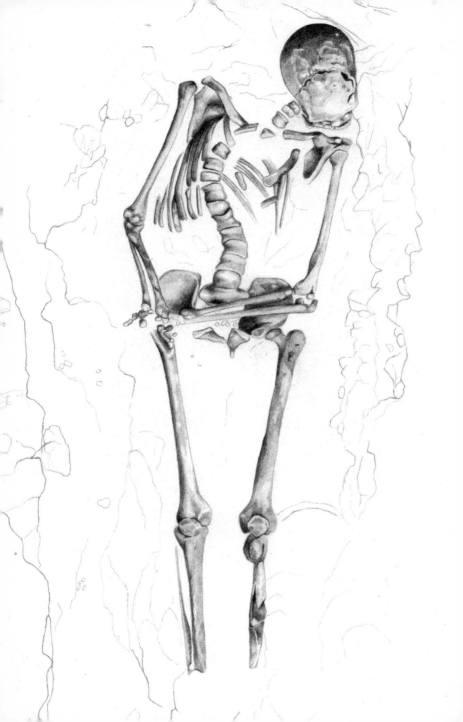

Jo had a huge adrenalin rush. She didn't speak, but said to herself, 'I think this is Richard III.' She sat back. 'This is not how it happens. Archaeologists don't go looking for things and find them!' Her hands were shaking. 'I can't go and tell them', she thought in shock, 'until I've uncovered all the spine, right up to the neck.'

Mathew had been watching as Jo tried to find the back bones. They weren't there. And then they were. 'Hang on a minute,' he thought. It was so blatantly curved. It wasn't something caused by the way the body had slumped in the ground, it was so blatantly... They sat together in silence, Mathew looking down at it from above, Jo looking at it from inside the trench.

'Good grief,' thought Mathew. In the church. Curved spine. Battle trauma. Male skeleton, in his thirties – Jo seemed to be happy that it was a youngish male. Good grief, thought Mathew, it's ticked every single box you'd ever want if you came up with a checklist before you started the excavation. This is Richard III.

In a detached sort of a way, he suddenly realized that Skeleton 1 was going to be really important. They had to dot every i and cross every t, do everything so carefully, make sure that every last detail was properly documented, that all was correct. 'I didn't have time on the emotional level', he later told me, 'to think about what we'd found.' Neither of them could afford to let their feelings interfere with their work. Jo leaned forward and carried on digging, gently prising the earth away from the bones, uncovering the ribs and following the spine up to the shoulders, so that it lay there exposed from the earth, looking like some curious fossil serpent entombed in rock.

The situation, as Richard Buckley put it, was slightly bizarre. They were only allowing certain people to see the burial. The Ministry of Justice insisted the remains be screened from the public gaze. There was also always the possibility that they couldn't complete the excavation in the

Skeleton 1 as it lay in the ground after Jo Appleby had removed soil from above; feet are missing, hands are together over the right hip, and the spine curves away from the centre.

available time, and they'd have to temporarily fill it in. So they had to be very careful to make sure that it wasn't public knowledge that they'd excavated a burial.

Ather Mirza's team had been issuing press releases almost daily. They all seemed to end with Richard Buckley saying that finding Richard III was 'still a long shot', but they left little doubt that everyone was very excited about progress. In the previous week they'd found medieval remains (Tuesday), it had rained (Wednesday), and they'd found more medieval remains (Thursday). On Friday they'd held a press briefing in the old Guildhall opposite the cathedral, fronted by Philippa, Richard Buckley and Richard Taylor, and Leicester City Councillor Piara Singh Clair. 'First week of search for Richard III exceeds expectations,' said the release. They'd found the friary.

The notices were picked up by the national UK media, and the dig was being closely followed by local press and radio. That morning Mirza had fired out the strongest message yet. In a 'huge step forward', the team had found the friary church – the burial place of Richard III. The dig would be opened to the public on Saturday, but it was the best day of summer, and there was little traffic in the semi-pedestrianized streets, so why wait? There was a crowd outside, along St Martins and New Street, trying to get a peek at what was going on.

Mathew had been popping backwards and forwards all day, to keep an eye on what they were doing in Trench 3. The only way to do this was to walk round the streets, out through the car park gates into New Street, round the corner and down St Martins, and through the gates into the Alderman Newton's playground. There were hordes of people watching activity at Trench 3: because no human remains were being excavated, unlike Trench 1, it was not screened.[8]

The rest of the team needed to know what they'd found, but they were all on the other side of the wall. The main spoil from Trench 1 was piled up against this wall, and they'd got in the habit of climbing up it for a quick look at Trench 3, and to pass tools across. But Mathew couldn't just stand on the spoilheap and yell out that they'd found human remains: it would be around the world in minutes. So he had to walk calmly out through the crowds, nonchalantly enter the other car park and sidle up to Richard Buckley to deliver a quiet but potent message.

Richard wasn't interested.

He'd spent much of the afternoon at Trench 3 with Glyn Coppack and Deirdre O'Sullivan, talking about friaries. Unknown to either Mathew or Jo, they'd come to a momentous conclusion. Coppack had approved their theory that they had uncovered remains of the church's choir and presbytery, and agreed with O'Sullivan that they could see the actual footings of the choir stalls. They had formally achieved their fourth objective: to find the church choir. Skeleton 1 was exactly where it should be if it had any chance of being Richard III.

Unaware of all this, Mathew was trying to tell Richard that there was something in Trench 1 he ought to come and see. Richard, Coppack and O'Sullivan were standing in Trench 3, looking at the mortar bedding for the floor tiles, the choir walls and the architectural fragments. 'Yes,' Coppack was saying, 'I think it's Early Perpendicular masonry. Yes, I'm happy with that idea.'

Mathew tapped Richard on the shoulder. 'You really need to come and look at the skeleton.'

'Look,' Richard said to Mathew, 'I really am a bit busy, I've got guests. I'm having a discussion with Glyn Coppack, he's come all this way from Nottingham, I can't talk now.'

Mathew waited a bit, then he persisted. 'You really need to go and look at it now.' In the end he realized he had no option but to tell him there and then. 'The burial's got curvature of the spine,' he said, 'and trauma to the head.'

Richard had not expected that. He swore. He stamped his feet. He swore again. He just could not believe it. He swore, again.

On his way in, Mathew had passed the DSP crew, and said quietly, 'You're going to want to film the skeleton now – but don't all rush back at once and make it look like something important's been happening. Just trickle back.' While he was talking to them, Jo had jumped out of the trench, run up the spoilheap, and stuck her head over the wall. There was a DSP man close by, and she told him, 'I think we've found Richard III.' Which, as Jo said, 'Got a bit of reaction.'

As I listened to people telling me about their memories of that day, it was usually at this point that things started to become confused. While Mathew was trying to get the attention of Richard Buckley over in Trench 3, Carl Vivian was filming the body in the ground. He shot the slow pan up the skeleton, the legs, over the hips and up the curved spine to the skull (sequence 16) fifteen times. He knew that that was what every television programme in the world would use (as indeed they did). His hands were shaking. Once everybody came back, it would be a circus again, he just wanted to take his final shots, in the quiet, him and Skeleton 1. 'Then', he said, 'it all becomes a bit of a blur. Things were moving very quickly.'

Philippa had returned from her solitary walk, her pink and blue shirt changed for a blue and green check and her long blond hair tied back, to find the atmosphere at the dig had transformed. The skeleton had a curved back.

DSP set Simon Farnaby up beside the grave, then brought Philippa in to film her reaction; they had co-opted Vivian as their third camera. This moment when Jo described the complete skeleton to Philippa, broadcast around the world, is easy to mock, when the originator of a scientific project succumbed to emotional shock. Yet remarkable as the discovery of Richard III is, it is also extremely rare, possibly unprecedented, for any major research breakthrough to be recorded in such detail as it actually took place.

Early in 2012, when Philippa and DSP were trying to persuade Channel 4 to commission a film, the broadcaster said they'd love to do it – provided they could guarantee that they would find Richard III. Of course, research never works like that, which is why all the great stories are told after the event, are recreated from records and memories, often mixed with a good part of 'this is how it must have felt'.[9]

The closest comparable moment I can think of to the archaeological discovery of Richard III's remains is the uncovering of Tutankhamun's tomb, almost exactly 90 years before. It came at the end of years of fieldwork in which Howard Carter, supported by Lord Carnarvon, was determined to find the boy king's grave, a quest that seemed futile to almost everyone else. As it became apparent that they had succeeded, world media interest was huge. This was by far the greatest archaeology story ever told in modern times, and there is almost no limit to the imagery and verbiage recording it all. But what really happened, when Carter first entered the tomb?

The archaeologists left us a wonderfully atmospheric description, recording how they slowly cleared sand and rubble, following steps down, until they met a sealed doorway. 'With trembling hands', says Carter, 'I made a tiny breach in the upper left hand corner.' They tested for 'foul gases', and finding it safe, Carter 'inserted the candle and peered in, Lord Carnarvon, Lady Evelyn and Callender standing anxiously beside me to hear the verdict'. It goes on. The candle flickered as air rushed out of the chamber. It took time for Carter's eyes to adjust to the feeble light. Then, finally, the famous exchange.

'Can you see anything?' asks Carnarvon.

'Yes', replies Carter, 'wonderful things.'[10]

This passage is based on a carefully composed journal entry for 26 November 1922, in which Carter records, 'Lord Carnarvon said to me "Can you see anything". I replied to him Yes, it is wonderful.' Carnarvon apparently remembered the answer as, 'There are some marvellous objects here.'[11] The dig diary for that day notes, in total, 'Open second doorway about 2pm. Advised Engelbach.' Truthfully, it is impossible to be sure what actually was said.[12]

Yet when Richard Buckley, Mathew, Jo and Philippa gathered round the remains they knew as Skeleton 1, and together saw, for the first time, what it was, their every word was recorded. By three cameras.

'So what we're actually seeing here', says Jo, 'is that this skeleton in fact has a hunched back.'

Philippa's jaw drops. That is not a turn of phrase, her jaw actually drops. 'No,' she says, quietly. She straightens up. 'No,' again.

Then she looks round at Farnaby. 'Now I know why you wanted to ask me that question. You blighter!'

Farnaby laughs. 'Well, we don't know for sure,' he says, striving to return to script, 'there would have been plenty of hunchbacks.'

Jo, prompted by Farnaby, continues.

'There's a bit more. When you were questioning me earlier about the skull I was a bit evasive about it. There is actually a wound, it's not very visible on the surface of the skull, but *inside* the skull you can see that some of the bone is broken away and he's actually been hit in the head with something. And when you turn over the skull there's also some damage to the skull base.'

As Jo talks, Vivian has a tight facial close-up on Philippa. Her eyes raise. You can see profound shock.

The last time she saw the skeleton, she thought it couldn't be Richard III. Now she is being told it is, and it's not what she had wanted to find. The physical quest has become a triumph, but the personal one a disaster. Despite everything the Ricardians had said, despite years of believing that Tudor historians had created a fantasy of a deformed and evil king, Richard III *was* deformed. That knowledge is the legacy of her project. There in front of her is his distorted back; and there is his head, brutally attacked.

Philippa asks if the wounds occurred before or after death? Jo says she can't tell, but they certainly date from at or around that time.

'OK, don't get me wrong, here, right?' says Philippa, 'But that curvature is *major* curvature, I mean that's seriously something going on. So, how do you get armour on that? It goes against everything that the specialists have been telling me, the guys that fight, the guys that do combat, the

At a staged conference in February 2013, Jo Appleby tells the world's press about wounds on Skeleton 1's skull, the first occasion on which images of the remains were released.

guys that wear armour, the guys that do medieval horsemanship, they're saying there's no way if he had a hunchback and a withered arm he could do it.'

Jo is describing her immediate reaction to what she can see, which is substantially less than half the skeleton – some bones are still buried, and apart from the skull, only upper-facing surfaces are exposed – and none of the detail. Handling the remains later in the lab, when they are cleaned and under bright light and magnifying lenses, with comparative material, reference works and other specialist opinions to hand, she concludes the man in fact did not have a hunched back; he suffered from scoliosis, which gave him a badly curved spine, but left his profile reasonably straight and his head facing normally.

'I haven't spotted a withered arm,' says Jo. 'The arms are OK.'

'The arms are OK?' repeats Philippa. 'Ah, *some* good news then.' She pauses. 'You know what, I feel really weird, I feel I've got to sit down.'

She sits down.

'It's circumstantial evidence at the moment,' says Jo, smiling beneath her white face mask, 'but I think just to be on the safe side, we might do a DNA test on this one.'[13]

When the filming was over, and Mathew had sent all the archaeology staff home, it quietened down again. Turi had texted Jo from Innsbruck.

'Skellie up? 90 yr old friar? :)'

Now Jo could reply.

'Youngish man with head injuries and hunch back. I'm not kidding. Think we might take some samples for you!'

'No way!'

Later, Turi texted her husband. 'I think we've found him.'

'Found who?' he replied. No one had expected this outcome.[14]

Jo lifted the skeleton, transforming it into a collection of loose bones. Any relationships between these would need to be reconstructed from the dig photos and her knowledge of anatomy. It made sense to package them in body parts. As the sun fell and the light falling across the car park grew rich and warm, Jo, kneeling in her white overalls beside the grave, prised out the body bone by bone. Mathew sat above, in face mask and rubber gloves, completing an anatomy chart on a clipboard. Here comes the left leg in a clear polythene bag; here's the right leg, here are the hands – lying together, so difficult to separate, with all those muddy little bones; the lower arms, left and right, the right pelvis, the left pelvis, the upper arms. The head had already gone.

They left the back till last. Clearly this might become one of the most considered spines in the history of human archaeology. It needed to be treated with great care, the delicate vertebrae with all their undue wear and deformity raised from the grave without the slightest damage. We can only guess what sympathy and attention Richard might have received for his condition in life. In death, there was no lack.

The skeleton had one more surprise for them. As before, Jo worked from the base of the spine towards the neck. They had all but finished when she lifted two vertebrae, the second and third thoracic, to reveal a slug of corroded iron. The layers of corrosion concealed its true form, so it could have been almost anything, but its position, in the back of the neck, was undoubtedly suggestive of an arrow tip.

Before Richard Buckley had left the site, Philippa had asked him a favour. She wanted to carry out a little ceremony. John Ashdown-Hill listened from a respectable distance, hands in pockets, his head to one side.

'The remains that we've uncovered,' she said tentatively to Richard. 'I know we don't know a hundred per cent if they are Richard, but when we put the bones in the box, I'd quite like' – she glanced across at Ashdown-Hill – 'John has a Richard III standard, and I'd quite like to just put it over the box to get it into the van, if you're OK with that.'

'Absolutely fine,' cut in Richard, nodding with a smile. 'Particularly as there's good indication that they're the right ones.'

For Richard, who had been working with Philippa on this project since her phone call early in 2011, seeing the bones in the ground had a rare poignancy. These were not just anonymous remains, perhaps, but a real person, one whose name and face he knew, whose deeds he'd learned about at school.

'That's fine,' he said, 'absolutely fine.'

'Thank you,' said Philippa. 'We're never going to do this twice, are we? I'd just like to mark it. It just seems right, to put his colours over it.'

The confusion, shock and sheer astonishment that swirled around the precise, scientific rigour of the excavation, like a storm trying to penetrate a well-sealed house, was about to turn to farce.

In the melee, Richard left unaware that he hadn't told Mathew about Philippa's request. Most of the bones were now in a standard brown cardboard box with removable lid – known to archaeologists as a longbone box because of its size and shape. Philippa wanted Jo to load it into the university's white van draped in a bright blue, red and gold flag, the one that Ashdown-Hill had photographed beside the R on the tarmac long before the dig had begun. And DSP wanted to film it.

Act III, Scene 2

Mathew and Jo were by the van, hot, dirty and emotionally drained and getting ready to leave, when Philippa shouted across the car park.

'Jo, do you want to come and do this?'

Jo did not.

They had all had a moment of adrenalin-fuelled excitement when they saw the complete skeleton in the ground, and realized they were probably looking at the remains of King Richard III. In scientific and popular discourse, however, 'probably' has quite different meanings. For the Richard III Society, by and large it meant their king had been found. As Annette Carson put it at the Society's conference in February 2013, soon after the key scientific conclusion was announced: early in September 2012, before the intensive research had begun, 'We knew it was Richard III'.[15]

For the archaeologists, it meant they now had a testable hypothesis, a quite different position, and one we will follow in the next two chapters: were these bones those of Richard III? It signified the beginning of a completely new research project, and one that would consume vastly more funds and time than the excavation – which is to say, much more than anyone had imagined would be needed.

So having experienced the shock and thrill of discovery, the archaeologists rapidly focused back on to the scientific goals. This was not Richard III. It was not a 90-year-old friar (or as Simon Farnaby had put it, 'One unlucky monk'). It was Skeleton 1.

If you watch the Channel 4 films of the dig, you might notice, as the bones are bagged and boxed, that the containers are labelled R III, SK 1. This was not because the archaeologists were then calling the body Richard III. It was their name for the dig. But neither was that, as you might imagine, because they were expecting or even hoping to find the king – this was the Grey Friars Project, and their key goal was to learn about the friary. However, for the first two weeks of the excavation, the woman at Leicester Museum and Galleries who gives out site codes was on holiday. It would later become A11/2012, but Mathew needed a temporary code for the finds bags, which would be going up to the university to be washed. The choice was simple, a bit of a joke. Now they had the near-complete skeletal remains of a real person, but it was still Skeleton 1.

Mathew was a little uncomfortable about the flag idea. 'We didn't know it was Richard,' he told me. Jo was adamantly against it, as we see in the film, when a quick cameraman caught her reaction to Philippa's shout. 'I'm not sure I'm very happy about doing that, given that we don't know for sure it is him yet. I mean if we get the DNA and it turns out not to be, it just feels a bit of an inappropriate thing to have done.' Her body language was less measured.

Mathew felt he had to support Jo, and he found a compromise. 'It doesn't seem right Jo should do it,' he told them, 'but I've got no objection to you doing it.' Philippa can do it!

But Philippa doesn't want to do it.

'I don't think it's right for me to do it, somehow,' she says, clutching the folded flag, watching Mathew and Jo from a distance.

'Do you want to do it, John?'

Ashdown-Hill stands beside her, his arms in a curious echo of Richard III's in the grave, wrists crossing at his waist, one hand hanging limp.

'Do what?'

'Would you like to carry the box to the van?'

'I don't mind,' he says gently.

'Where's the box?' asks Philippa.

'Over there,' says Ashdown-Hill, pointing.

She hands him the bright bundle of cloth, and walks off behind the blue screen. Then, clutching the flag at two corners, Ashdown-Hill gives the camera a grin that blends nerves, perplexity and triumph, and unravels it with a flourish.

And so, late on a Wednesday afternoon in September, the remains of a then anonymous and undated man were carried across a car park in

Leicester in a recycled cardboard box, draped with the flag of late medieval English royalty, and laid on the floor through the side door of a small white Citroen van.

Some of the remains, that is.

The day before, Turi King had brought a big roll of tinfoil to the site. They'd forgotten what it was for, so when she'd rung around lunchtime to check on progress, Mathew had asked her. It was to wrap bones selected for potential DNA analysis, to protect them while minimizing the risk of condensation – ancient DNA being susceptible to damage from moisture. As Mathew drove from the dig to begin the short journey up to the university, Jo, sitting beside him, had the skull and the leg bones safe on her lap, wrapped in foil like culinary parcels.

As the van sweeps out of the car park in the Channel 4 film, past the high, fading green-painted wooden gates and round the red-brick wall into New Street, it is possible, perhaps, to discern a faint smile on Jo Appleby's face. About to enter its third phase, the project was now firmly in scientific hands.

Act IV

AN AUTOPSY

Jo put Richard III in the fridge.

They had left the site unguarded. Though the grave wasn't fully excavated, the trench was just dirt, and you couldn't see it from anywhere. The weather was going to be fine overnight, so Mathew had decided there was no need to cover it over. Jo's job had been to recover Skeleton 1, and she had other work to get back to. The team would excavate and record the grave the next day.

Up at the university with all the digging gear, the records and Skeleton 1, Jo and Mathew carried the foil-wrapped bones upstairs to where the samples that might be analysed for DNA could be put immediately into cold storage. Then they hid the rest of the remains behind a mass of other things in Mathew's ground floor office, made sure everything was well locked up, and went home.

For Mathew this was a 20-minute drive to his girlfriend, and for Jo an hour's train journey east to Peterborough, where she lived with her boyfriend, also an archaeologist. For both, it was their first chance to reflect in private. They'd excavated and studied many human remains, and despite the odd drama, exhuming Skeleton 1 had been mostly a routine exercise. Yet as they travelled out of Leicester and the tension drained from their bodies, it began to sink in that the work was no longer routine. 'Hang on,' thought Mathew, 'we've actually probably done this. Against all the odds. We've just found a king of England.'

It began in Edinburgh, if not in Waterstone's in 1998, then at the Cramond Inn in 2009, when Philippa announced that she was going to find the body of a king. Her quest became the Looking for Richard project, a relatively simple, emotive affair, which relied on historians and archaeologists to make her vision real. The excavation run by the University of Leicester had been the Grey Friars Project, a more complex, open-ended inquiry that hoped to locate a friary and learn about medieval Leicester, with five objectives. As much as was possible at this stage, all these goals had been achieved.

Now there were new projects. For the Richard III Society, there was the prospect of a reburial, with issues of design, ceremony, ritual and more to think about. For the archaeologists the future lay in the opposite direction, towards pure science. The dig had brought together the Richard III Society and the university in a unique partnership of innocence and experience, of high emotion and practised caution, and of historians and archaeologists – each with their often quite different ways of seeing things. Objectively establishing the identity of Skeleton 1 was a project on its own, in which the Society would not be involved. Like the Looking for Richard project, this one had a simple goal; but it would become one of the most intensive and wide-ranging exercises in modern archaeological science, beyond anything anyone could yet conceive.

On Thursday 6 September very few people knew that they had excavated a skeleton. Even most of Mathew's team, and visitors such as Glyn Coppack, had left the site the day before without seeing the remains laid out in the ground, and were unaware of the find's potential significance. Later Leon Hunt, site supervisor, told how he remembered Thursday. Mathew arrived in the van, screeched to a halt, got out leaving the door hanging open, and, looking as if he had not been to sleep that night, said, 'Did you actually understand what I was telling you yesterday?'

He described the remains and the exhumation. Then Richard Buckley arrived. 'I think we've found him,' he said. 'It was an astonishing thing,' said Hunt. 'Shock and bewilderment, knock me down with a feather.' And they got on with the dig.

Mathew brought Tony Gnanaratnam back over from Trench 3 to excavate and fully record the rest of the grave. He emptied out the soil and traced the edges of the grave pit. They'd already taken samples, but partly for environmental analysis and partly, as Mathew put it to me, 'out of not having other people nicking it', they bagged up the entire grave fill and took it back to the university.

In Trench 3 they confirmed that what looked like more graves were indeed more graves (or, in one case, a machine-excavated trench with

modern bricks in it), but with such a strong candidate for Richard III
in the first grave, there was no need to investigate another one. They had
a lot of recording to do. With approval from the City Council to continue
on site for a third week, they finished the excavation on the following
Monday, returning on the Friday to begin the process of backfilling over a
geo-permeable membrane, and final resurfacing. The grave for Skeleton 1
would remain open, though well protected.

Meanwhile, on the previous Saturday, three days after Skeleton 1 had
been removed, they had a planned public open day. Nearly 2,000 people
queued in the sunshine along St Martins and Grey Friars to see the dig.
The archaeologists printed display diagrams and stuck explanatory labels
in the trenches. They anticipated that they would be asked about human
remains – the stated goal of the project was, after all, to find Richard III –
so they prepared carefully worded answers that would give away nothing
without actually being dishonest. To their surprise, however, no one asked;
the dig itself was of sufficient interest.

At a press conference on the following Wednesday, however, everyone
asked. The Grey Friars Project, said a university statement, had excavated
the remains of an adult male, with significant perimortem trauma to
the skull 'consistent with an injury received in battle', an arrowhead in
the upper back, and severe scoliosis, a form of spinal curvature. Within
minutes the news went round the world. Quite suddenly, the car park dig
was international public property.

For the University of Leicester this was the ultimate public relations
opportunity. The astonishing story brought together traditional research
and – as was now clear it would – cutting-edge forensic science from
across many of the university's departments, involving large numbers
of academics. As if this weren't enough, it combined the research with
one of fiction's great characters, Shakespeare's ambitious, devious, cruel
and deformed king, based on a historical figure now apparently brought
to life in the most unexpected way. The press event happened to be less
than three weeks before the start of the new university year, when families

across the UK were already focused on higher education; Leicester was particularly keen to attract overseas students.

The discovery was undeniably good for publicity. But if things went wrong, it could prove a public relations disaster, and undo years of effort by Richard Taylor and his team, striving, with some success, to convince people to respect the university for the quality of its research and teaching. There were genuine and some might say intractable dilemmas.

Firstly, from the start the university had insisted that it would not support the project unless it could be seen to be good research. 'With things like this', Richard Taylor told me, 'one's always seeking to mitigate risk. We couldn't do this for a publicity stunt, or people would quite rightly have said, you're not a proper university, you're doing this for PR spin reasons. So it was really important that the university had valid research questions that needed to be answered.' Those questions – to seek the friary and find out more about early Leicester – were provided by Richard Buckley. They were also questions that, before the dig began, could not justify an investment of over £10,000.

No one, however, aware of how the world works, could doubt the university's need to ensure that people knew it had done the excavation, and was about to fund a new research programme. The dilemma here was simple: could the public – and the press – be trusted to engage with a sensational news story, while understanding that the ubiquitous presence of Leicester's brand did not in itself indicate that anything had been hyped?[1]

The second dilemma was more interesting and, at least in the field of archaeology, unprecedented. The sense among everyone involved that they had probably found the remains of Richard III was impossible to miss. Yet the project to establish whether or not those remains really were the king's had not yet begun. Concealing that human remains had been found would have been impossible – any attempt to do so would have been exposed and held to ridicule. They had to explain why they were suddenly pouring resources into their study, where typically a few days' work would have sufficed. Yet, by definition, they could not say that the skeleton they had found, in the course of looking for Richard III, was Richard III's. All this led to some distinctive press statements.

'I need to be very frank,' said Richard Taylor to a packed and pin-silent Guildhall. 'We are not saying today that we have found King Richard III. What we are saying is that the search for Richard III has entered a new phase. Our focus is shifting from the archaeological excavation to laboratory analysis. This skeleton certainly has characteristics that warrant extensive further detailed examination.'

Nonetheless, he added, 'We have all been witness to a powerful and historic story unfolding before our eyes. This is potentially a historic moment for the University and City of Leicester.'

Leicester's City Mayor, Peter Soulsby, echoed the mood. 'This is truly remarkable news,' he said. Further investigation was needed, but this was 'a potentially staggering find. If the experts finally conclude these are indeed the bones of King Richard III, this will have enormous implications for our city.'

Everyone was excited, and hopeful. 'I would like to say to anybody watching this or listening to this,' said Philippa, 'if you have a dream, fight for it. But more than that, instil in others your belief and your passion, and by doing that you'll create a team.'

As they spoke, from a panel that also included Jo Appleby, Richard Buckley, Lin Foxhall (head of the university's School of Archaeology and Ancient History) and Turi King, a large reproduction of a portrait of Richard III rose up behind them. Experienced journalists asked questions that challenged the distinction between remains that could be Richard III's, and remains that were. In their answers, it was apparent that Philippa and Richard Buckley were pretty confident the king had been found. Yet as Foxhall emphasized, the research had not yet begun. The bones had not been cleaned (no photos were shown), the DNA analyses would take 'up to 12 weeks', and there was a small artifact in the grave they had not yet had the chance to look at. There was work to do.[2]

After all, they might have said, perhaps Skeleton 1 was a knight called Mutton.

After the Dissolution of the Monasteries, John Leland, an antiquary and poet favoured by Henry VIII, travelled around England and Wales, staying in Leicester around 1540. He noted that, at Greyfriars, 'there was byried King Richard 3. and a knight caullid Mutton, sumtyme Mayre of Leyrcester'. This is likely to have been Sir William de Moton of Peckleton, who died around 1360, and about whom we know little else.[3]

Suppose that Mutton suffered from scoliosis, and died in battle, either of which is possible. How do we say which of Mutton or Richard III was Skeleton 1 – if either of them? Not least because reburial in the near future seemed a high probability, it was also necessary to learn as much from the remains as possible, as this would be the only opportunity to do so.

Learning about Skeleton 1 was one of the key topics at the first post-excavation team meeting, held at the University of Leicester on 25 September, just 11 days after the dig had ended. As they sat in a circle in a small, clinically functional room decorated only with banners proclaiming their institution's world-class teaching and research, the archaeologists already knew there was unheard-of interest in what they were doing.

Heavy press coverage of the Guildhall conference had been accompanied immediately by a request for a debate in Parliament ('That this House ... praises the work of the archaeologists and historians ... [and] calls on the Government to arrange a full state funeral for the deceased monarch'). A petition had been launched on Her Majesty's Government's website asking that the king be buried at a Catholic church. *The Times* had soon reported that the Queen did not wish for a royal burial – she thought Leicester Cathedral would be a nice place. York had responded with another Government petition, seeking the reburial 'with due dignity and respect in York Minster'.[4]

In Leicester, local journalist Peter Warzynski found Year Two children had their own views on the topic – mixed with some city tradition.

Petra (age six): 'He fell off a bridge and hit his head and then died. I think he floated down the river.'

Ihsan (seven): 'When he was killed, they built a car park over him and forgot where he was.'

Petra: 'We should keep the bones here because King Richard III school is here.'

Senior archaeologists had written to *The Times* – more excavation was needed before the scientific analyses could begin – and the *Guardian*: 'The identification of bones found in Leicester as those of Richard III may be supported by the telling absence of any trace of a horse.'[5]

It was exactly a month after the dig had started, and it seemed that already the world knew more about Skeleton 1 than the archaeologists who had dug it up.[6]

The meeting was chaired by Lin Foxhall, sharing a table with the manager of the School of Archaeology, Sharon North, taking minutes. Foxhall, tall and thin with shoulder-length white hair, retains her Pennsylvanian accent long after she left university there to study at Liverpool. She taught at Oxford and University College London before arriving in Leicester, where she is Professor of Greek Archaeology and History. Her research has sought to move understanding of classical antiquity beyond a masculine perspective, and she is involved in fieldwork projects in southern Italy and the wider Mediterranean; to put Richard III into perspective, in 2008 her trading networks project was awarded a £1.73 million grant ($2.75 m).

Around her sat Mathew Morris, Richard Buckley, Jo Appleby and Turi King. Also from ULAS were Anita Radini (their archaeobotanist, who would be dealing with environmental analyses), Nick Cooper (Post-Excavation Project Manager – with his dog, Max) and Debbie Sawday, a consultant on medieval pottery. Further academic staff included Ian Whitbread, who would be helping with artifacts, and Deirdre O'Sullivan, who would advise on friary archaeology. Kevin Schürer, an experienced local history and population statistics researcher and now

Pro-Vice-Chancellor (Research and Enterprise) at Leicester, would be conducting the essential genealogical work to back up Turi's genetics.

They brought an extraordinary amount of sense and skill to discuss a small archaeological evaluation – and in the coming months specialists from other institutions would be drawn into the project as well. Neither was it typical for such a meeting to be filmed, or witnessed by the university Press Office, but Carl Vivian and Ather Mirza were not to be left out. Yet the discussion was calm and focused, a sign of something that would become almost as important as the quality of the research itself. This was a high-profile project, but they were going to work together to solve the questions the dig had thrown up. No amount of the often publicity-seeking arguments that would rage around them would distract them from their purpose.

Because of the project's small scale, the work on the excavation itself resolved mostly into just two themes. They needed to establish the site narrative, how and when the grave and the friary buildings had been laid out, and how the different parts related to each other – Mathew would be doing that over the next few weeks, explained Richard. And they would see what light the tiles and architectural fragments could throw on those structures. They also discussed what other work they might do (further investigation of the friary site was now clearly a priority) and how and when it would all be published – already they were proposing articles for prestigious peer-reviewed journals *Antiquity*, *Genetics* and *Nature*. Which left the burial itself, with the DNA and genealogical research. The bones had not been touched since they left the site. Which was a good thing, for, as Jo explained, she wanted the first studies to take place with the dirt still on. Skeleton 1's last journey had begun.

*

The adult human body has 206 bones and 32 teeth. Counter-intuitively, perhaps, a child has more: the skeleton alters while we age. As we grow up, separate bones fuse together and harden, some change shape in different ways depending on whether we are male or female, and, of course, overall they get bigger; fewer teeth are visible in a young child's mouth, but growing permanent teeth already lurk within the jaws. It's easier to age a younger individual from their bones than an older, as most regular changes occur in the first two decades of life, but it needn't stop there. If we live long enough, our bones may show signs of degeneration. Injury and infection can leave their marks. Persistent rigorous activity can change bones as they accommodate more developed muscles – some of the men whose remains were retrieved with the wreck of the Mary Rose (which sank 60 years after Richard III died) had atypically large left shoulders and right forearms, possible signs that they were practised longbowmen.[7] Teeth, too, change, and may wear and decay.[8]

Such things help to make well-preserved remains particularly informative. Complete skeletons are rarely recovered: we have three bones inside each ear, for example, which are too small to survive most conditions. By losing both feet, however, Skeleton 1 had got off to a bad start – farewell to 52 bones. The discovery on the first day of the dig came about when the mechanical excavator took a soft slice from the left tibia, one of the two longbones in each leg; the left fibula, the slighter bone, had already gone, and likewise the three surviving leg bones lost their lower ends to the Victorian navvy's spade. Most of the small bones from the tips of the fingers and thumbs (the distal phalanges) had dissolved. The left wrist was all there, but a few of the small carpal bones were missing from the right. The rest of the skeleton, apart from a few absent teeth, was complete, if occasionally damaged: most of the softened, fragile ribs were broken, and there were two small areas of loss where Jo's mattock found the skull – fortunately not where there was anything of great interest.

Overall, though reduced to around 135 bones and 29 teeth, Skeleton 1 was in a good state and able to tell us a great deal about the person to whom it once belonged. Much of this information would come from examining and measuring the bones themselves. In addition, 13 samples would be taken for scientific studies, including six teeth, five small parts of rib and two parts of femur (thigh bone). That this could be done was fortunate. In many other soil conditions common across Britain, little would have been left. I have worked on excavations where bones were mechanically as well preserved, but where ancient DNA would be unlikely to have survived. I have worked on others where no bones were found at all.

One of Europe's great treasures was excavated just before the Second World War at Sutton Hoo in southeast England. A king had been buried in a ship with gold and jewels of fabulous artistry and wealth. We can guess he might have been Raedwald, who died around AD 625: but his remains had vanished, and we know nothing about his appearance, his health, his battle wounds or any of the other details we would long to know. Under the car park in Leicester, with nothing so much as a finger ring and only a shallow, irregular pit with one end dug away, if Skeleton 1 had entirely dissolved it's unlikely we would have known there was a grave there at all. You certainly wouldn't be reading this book.

If Robert Herrick hadn't acquired Greyfriars for his garden four centuries ago, perhaps there would have been no Skeleton 1. If New Street had been laid out 25 m (80 ft) to the east in 1740, there would be no Skeleton 1. There would be no Skeleton 1 if a large building had been erected in the wrong place. If in the few months before Philippa returned to the car park for her second visit in 2005, a workman had not painted a white R on the tarmac, perhaps no one would have searched for Skeleton 1.[9] If Mathew Morris had decided to lay out his first trench with the white parking line on the left instead of down its centre, he would not have found Skeleton 1. When the archaeologists returned to the site in 2013 to learn more about the friary church, they wondered if there might also have been no Skeleton 1 if a small building had not been raised right over the grave – the king could have been saved by a privy, and all who sat in it.[10]

Yet after everything, if Leicester's geology had been different – the same
geology that led to the city's builders digging up old stone wherever
they could find it, and removing almost all trace of the medieval friary
– Skeleton 1 would not have been found. Unconcerned, perhaps, about
Richard's fate at Bosworth, and later accused of defiling his grave, the
truth is that, deep down and out of sight, Leicester held on to its king.

Some of the earth still clung to the jaw as Jo and Turi, wearing white
suits, face masks and double gloves in a sterile room in the university's
Space Research Centre, gently pulled out teeth. This was the first task,
to get the essential DNA samples before the bones became contaminated.
The next was to scan the entire skeleton, laid out as it had been found,
to record it ahead of any possible damage. Then Heidi Addison, ULAS's
finds and archive specialist, cleaned the bones under a sink tap with a
toothbrush, before they went back to the Radiology Department at
Leicester Royal Infirmary for another full CT scan; this time the bones
were positioned on a bespoke polystyrene template to facilitate building
a virtual 3D model.

You don't often see crime drama autopsies conducted in an ordinary
room with furniture round the edges. Yet post-mortem imaging, which
dispenses with scalpels, spectacular eviscerations and the essential clunk
of something heavy dropped into a steel bowl, is becoming so popular
as an alternative to the traditional autopsy, there is talk that one day it may
become the norm. Computed tomography (CT) scanning is quicker and
cheaper than surgery, and can give detailed, accurate information without
destroying the evidence (the corpse); sometimes it can even see things
that surgery might miss.

CT scanning is attractive to museum curators hoping to learn more
about human remains in their collections – and a diversion for hospital
staff when equipment is otherwise idle. Ramesses III, we have thereby
learned, had his throat slit; Tutankhamun did not die from a blow to

the head, though he did have a broken leg; and Ötzi, the 5,000-year-old remains of a man found frozen in the Alps, had broken ribs, a flint arrowhead in his back, a punctured artery and bad tooth decay.

Scanning Skeleton 1 would greatly speed up its study while minimizing the risk of any damage, reason enough to do it. Yet there was a further, compelling case. If the remains proved to be Richard III's, they would be reburied. While everyone celebrated, the bones might effectively be destroyed. CT scans could not match the real thing, but at least there would be an accessible record for future researchers.

As it happens, the University Hospitals Leicester NHS Trust, serving a large Muslim population who typically find open post-mortems distasteful and want the body released as quickly as possible, has a longstanding research interest in post-mortem CT scanning.[11] It works closely with the East Midlands Forensic Pathology Unit (EMFPU), a university department based at the Royal Infirmary. Skeleton 1 was scanned by Claire Robinson, Advanced Practitioner Forensics in the Radiology Department, and Guy Rutty and Bruno Morgan, Chief Forensic Pathologist and Lead Consultant Radiologist respectively at the EMFPU; both men are qualified doctors and university professors. 'It was the best bone CT we have ever done,' Rutty later said of the results.

Yet Sarah Hainsworth, Professor of Materials Engineering at the university's Department of Engineering and another member of the EMFPU, took the scanning to another level, with the first known archaeological application of micro-CT (micro-computed X-ray tomography). This created exceptionally high-resolution images of the injuries and scoliosis-affected bones – at a cost. Recording each bone took six to eight hours, slightly less than was needed to do the entire skeleton with conventional scanning; for more typical engineering uses, the scanner could be left largely to get on with it, said Hainsworth, but this case involved 'skeleton sitting'. And the resultant digital files were enormous.

The scanned skull, a series of flat digital slices that software could combine to make a 3D image, went straight to the University of Dundee,

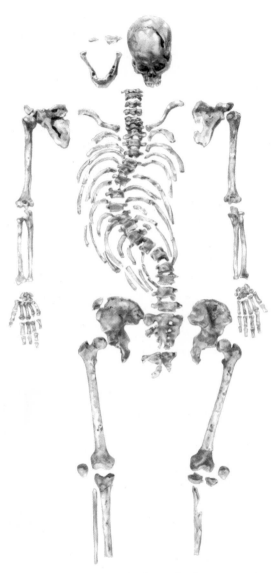

Skeleton 1 laid out in Leicester University; a variety of analyses were conducted on individual elements, and 3D scans will allow visual study of the skeleton now that it is reburied.

where Caroline Wilkinson would start on building a facial likeness. In Leicester, Kevin Schürer addressed genealogy, hoping to prove that Ashdown-Hill's identification of Joy Ibsen's children as possessors of mitochondrial DNA that should match Richard III's was correct – and also perhaps to find other living carriers of comparable DNA. And Turi King began what was likely to be the longest process of the project, seeking and if possible characterizing Richard's own DNA. Which left Jo to look at the bones.[12]

The archaeologists were clear from the start, from watching the remains emerge from the ground and later from their study of the grave and the records they made, that this had been no ordinary body. For one thing, the grave was a mess. During the subsequent 2013 excavation, when they worked throughout July and investigated an area about twice that

Graves of Greyfriars's own important people at the church's east end were excavated in 2013; all had originally been dug with more care than Skeleton 1's.

of all three previous trenches put together, Mathew's team exhumed three burials they had identified the year before but left in the ground. One of these was exceptional: a substantial stone coffin with a stone lid (quite unlike the old troughs claimed in the past to have held Richard), which when opened revealed a lead coffin and the remains of an older woman. The other two were typical of medieval graves in Leicester, even in the poorer quarters: the pits were neat, straight-sided and big enough to hold wooden coffins (indicated in the ground by stains in the earth and corroded iron nails) in which the bodies had been laid out comfortably on their backs.

Far from being deep, squared and regular, Skeleton 1's grave was relatively shallow with rough curved sides and base. The foot end is missing, but with the body's torso twisted to one side and the head crammed up against the other end, we can surmise that very little has been lost. The grave was too short, and the only surplus space would have been just enough on one side for a man to stand as he helped another above to lower the body into place.

Skeleton 1 had been laid on its back with its legs straight out, feet reaching east towards the altar in the conventional Christian way.[13] Unusually, however, the left arm, instead of matching the right which hung down the side, was bent and crossed the torso so that the two hands were together over the right hip, right hand apparently over left. No organic remains survived to confirm the hypothesis, but it seems reasonable, as the archaeologists suggested, to imagine that the wrists had been tied, which would explain why the right arm had not fallen down off the hip. Otherwise the body appears to have been handled casually. There was no coffin. Neither was there a shroud: though fabric almost never survives, Leicester's archaeologists have come to recognize shrouded burials by the way skeletons lie in a compact, tight tube, with arms tight and legs close together. With relaxed shoulders, flexed arms and parted legs, Skeleton 1 was not like that.

This is not to say that the body had been singled out for punitive treatment. There is a rare but consistent practice, found around the world and in many different eras, of burying certain people – hated, feared, marked in some way as deeply abnormal – face down, or prone. Skeleton 1 had apparently been buried with haste and disinterest, but not dramatized disrespect.

Though no coffin, there was one nail. A piece of old Roman iron, along with a handful of weathered Roman and early medieval pot sherds, had been disturbed by the grave diggers and thrown back in with the fill. This provided the first new evidence of date, meaning the grave had to have been dug between around 1300 and the Dissolution in 1538 (so Mutton and Richard are still in the running). This was the nail that had been identified as a possible arrowhead, but X-ray images cut through the corrosion to reveal its true form.

When Jo was excavating the skeleton, her first thought on finding the skull was that it didn't belong to the body whose legs stuck out at a lower level. It soon became clear that they were in fact linked, but I wondered, given the angle at which the skull lay, if the head might have become disconnected from the body before – or possibly even during – burial? In my own research, I had encountered a case where a body had been crammed into a short grave and the head lay at a higher level; only on forensic examination did we realize the poor man had been decapitated with a sword. Not so, Jo assured me, with Skeleton 1. The neck bones were all articulated, and the occipital condyles on the skull fitted exactly the superior facets of the atlas vertebra – head and neck were fully attached.

With the DNA samples taken and the remains scanned, cleaned and scanned again, Jo was able to begin her study in earnest. She laid the bones out on a work table in a room in the Archaeology Department, spacing them out so they would not knock against each other, a 3D exploded diagram of human anatomy. What stories did they tell?

Unlike bears, walruses and chimpanzees – to name a few – humans do not have a bone in their sex organs, a *baculum* (male) or an *os clitoridis* (female); fortunately for Skeleton 1's dignity, there are some parts of long-dead men we can never measure. Unfortunately for archaeologists, this means the human skeleton does not carry a label saying male or female – much research time would be saved if it did. Instead, more or less subtle differences are sought, reflecting the basic fact that, on average, men are bigger and stronger than women.

This is not a hit and miss affair. A huge amount of work has gone into compiling statistical formulae using skeletons of known sex (archaeologists use 'gender' for the cultural distinction, and 'sex' for the biological one, as they are not always the same) and, for comparable studies, known age. A group of remains that can be used in this way was recorded in London in the 1980s, when a thousand 18th- and 19th-century burials were removed from a crypt in Spitalfields during the church's restoration – the unusual scale of the archaeological project is revealed by its cost, said to be over five times that of building the church! Nearly four hundred of the individuals could be identified from coffin plates, so we know from these and other records when they were born and when they died, and something about their life histories – and even, in some cases, their appearance – all of which can be compared with the evidence of their bones.

The key elements for distinguishing men and women are the skull and, especially, hips. Interestingly, Skeleton 1 is a case where most of the evidence points in one direction, but is qualified by suggestions of the opposite. During excavation Jo had suggested it was male. Yet on more detailed analysis, she could see feminine signs – at one point she even emailed Richard Buckley to say the skeleton might be female (a moment that Richard remembers as one where he contemplated leaving the country).

The greater sciatic notches, the inner curves in the hip bones that partly determine the size and shape of the space through which a baby is born, are naturally wider in women. So, too, the notches are wider in Skeleton 1 than for a typical male. The third molars (wisdom teeth) are tiny. The limb bones are unusually slender for a typical adult man ('almost feminine', as Jo put it), and overall the skeleton does not show the strong muscle attachments associated with men. On several occasions, Jo discussed Skeleton 1 with Piers Mitchell, a Lecturer in Biological Anthropology in the Department of Archaeology and Anthropology at Cambridge whom she had got to know and respect during her time at the university there; he is also a hospital consultant in the National Health Service. He agreed with her diagnosis, that the skeleton was in some respects feminine, but he also supported her original judgment: it was male. Here was a gracile man, with quite a delicate frame and features – 'less chunky', as Mitchell put it, than the caricature macho leader. As I write, Richard Buckley is still living and working in Leicestershire.

You don't need to be an anatomist to see that Skeleton 1 was adult, but could Jo be more precise about the man's age than that? In this, as elsewhere, she was helped by the scans – among other things, they allowed the Forensic Pathology Unit to say Skeleton 1 was white, answering a question that archaeologists rarely ask.

There are all sorts of ways of estimating adult age, reflecting the difficulties (ageing younger people, because of the fast, substantial changes that occur as they grow, is easier and more precise). They considered the condition of the teeth – a little worn, with a few cavities – and the presence of those third molars, the closure of sutures (fixed joints between plates in the skull), degeneration of moving joints, the state of the pubic symphysis (the place where the two hip bones meet at the front) and ossification of epiphyses (the extent to which cartilage at the ends of longbones and in the back has turned to bone), among other regions. Yet none of these offers a precise and uncontroversial age, even in a perfectly preserved skeleton. Usually an age range is suggested. In this case, standard anthropological techniques made that in the 20s or 30s. The more sophisticated post-mortem CT methods narrowed the range to 30–34.

Having concluded that Skeleton 1 was male, Jo could estimate the man's height – the formulae differ slightly for men and women. If a body was laid out completely flat and the skeleton is particularly well preserved, sometimes it can be possible literally to measure an individual's height.

Typically, however, this cannot be done, and Skeleton 1 – with missing lower legs, a slightly folded torso and sharply angled neck, and bones having moved by various small amounts in the ground – is typical. The key database for estimating height was compiled in the 1950s, from study of American fatalities in the Second World War and the Korean War. The most useful bones (as with ageing, there are several ways to estimate height) are in the arms and legs, the longbones; just one bone can give a good approximation, though legs are better than arms.

Jo measured a thigh bone, and estimated Skeleton 1's height at around 5 ft 8 in. (1.73 m), which matched the Pathology Unit's estimate – based on averaging a variety of calculations – of 5 ft 7 in. to 5 ft 9 in. (1.70–1.75 m). This was a decent size for a man who had died between 1300 and 1538 – an inch above average.[14] Yet in life, he would never have stood that high.

He had a funny back.

*

'The appearance of the skeleton', wrote Michael H. Young (consultant orthopaedic surgeon, retired) from Cardiff to the *The Times* newspaper, 'may be a consequence of throwing a body into a hole in the ground. The spinal curvature cannot be accepted as conclusive evidence that the deceased had such a deformity in life.'

In February 2013, the team would release much information, and more through subsequent interviews and public talks, about their often incomplete research. They would then have to face something that no scientist or historian would choose. The conclusions of their work would be picked over by a public desperate to know more. People would exhibit strange ideas about how archaeologists, and scientists in general, conduct research, often appearing to believe that no one in the University of Leicester's project had any scientific skills, or even common sense.[15]

Meanwhile, science journalists, and sometimes scientists and other archaeologists, would point out that Leicester was unprofessional in not publishing the research in peer-reviewed journals. The dilemma for Jo and her colleagues was that by late that year they would have submitted or nearly completed key journal articles, but they could not enter much of the public debate. Peer-review is a slow, thorough process, and journals work to their own schedules. And they demand exclusivity: breaking an embargo could result in a rejected paper.

Jo was very curious about Skeleton 1's spine – as were Piers Mitchell and Bruno Morgan. They examined the bones, they scrutinized the 3D scans, and they concluded that Skeleton 1 suffered from severe idiopathic adolescent-onset scoliosis: he really did have a bad back.

Most of that diagnosis is a technical way of saying the spine was curved strongly sideways – severe scoliosis – but no one can say why – idiopathic. It has a Cobb angle of around 70–90 degrees; in modern medicine, young scoliosis patients with an angle of over 45 degrees are typically considered for surgery. As well as the curve to the side, there was also a twist, causing the spine to spiral. This was revealed in a physical replica of the skeleton made at Loughborough University, which could be handled in ways the original can not. A 3D computer model, derived from the CT scans, was used to create the replica by laser sintering, in which a high power laser fused small particles into precise, extremely detailed copies of the bones.[16]

Adolescent-onset means the man was not born with the condition, but that it appeared during childhood. The evidence for this lies in the individual vertebrae. These are broadly normal, so early growth was not affected. However, the bones in the curve are slightly wedge-shaped, and the spinous processes – the wings that stick out behind the vertebrae – are twisted to one side. As the boy's teenage growth spurt began, the first signs of scoliosis caused some of the bones to develop abnormally. Above and below the curve, however, the vertebrae were unaffected, and his neck and hips grew as they should have done.

As he aged, some of his back ligaments turned to bone, stiffening the curve, and he developed severe osteoarthritis. His twisted ribcage would have squeezed his lungs, possibly causing shortness of breath and severe pain, though he may have been unusually fortunate and suffered little in that respect. Late in 2013, Richard Buckley told me that he had given over 40 public talks, at which several people had 'stood up at the back to say, "I have scoliosis"', without apparent discomfort. However, Skeleton 1's condition was probably worse. It was a particularly rare form, and with such an extreme curve, present only in one among several thousand individuals – and five times more common in females than males.

It would have reduced Skeleton 1's height. Otherwise a little above average at 5 ft 8 in. (1.73 m), he would have looked 2–3 inches shorter (5–10 cm). His right shoulder probably rose above his left: his right clavicle or shoulder blade is misshapen from having to work harder, the inner end where it articulated with the top of the chest being noticeably enlarged. When Skeleton 1 was fully dressed, the visible signs of his affliction would have been a squat torso and uneven shoulders.[17]

Most of the illnesses and injuries that Skeleton 1 suffered during his life were probably minor, and they left no traces on his bones. However, analysis revealed that, when approaching death, he was infected with roundworms. Jo had taken soil samples from three areas. When Mitchell analysed these (dysentery and ancient parasites being a special research interest), he found many roundworm eggs (*Ascaris lumbricoides*) in the area where the intestines would have been, but none from the skull and few outside the grave. He found no sign of other intestinal parasites: if Skeleton 1 ate any beef, pork or fish, said Mitchell, it had been well cooked, as there were no eggs from tapeworms associated with these foods.[18]

Other studies showed that Skeleton 1 had indeed had a high-protein diet, and ate plenty of seafood. This insight came from analysis of nitrogen and carbon in the bone. These two elements each have two stable forms, known as isotopes, both absorbed by the body from food – nitrogen-14 and nitrogen-15 (^{14}N, ^{15}N) and carbon-12 and carbon-13 (^{12}C, ^{13}C). The ratios between each of the two forms reveal the relative proportions of land and marine food consumed: fish and shellfish have significantly more ^{13}C, and on average more ^{15}N, than do plants and animals that live on land.[19]

Two different labs each analysed two rib samples, and both found the same thing: Skeleton 1 had a varied, protein-rich diet that included seafood. One of the labs hazarded that over a quarter of the diet was marine, and that the rest of the food was heavy on meat. This was clearly someone who ate well.

That information about culinary habits was a by-product of an especially important study, which set out to determine when Skeleton 1 died: radiocarbon dating. Two laboratories were selected because of the significance of the date, in case anything should go wrong, and to provide considerable security in an area of reliably high-precision work. The labs were at the University of Glasgow, at the Scottish Universities Environmental Research Centre (SUERC), and the University of Oxford Radiocarbon Accelerator Unit (ORAU).

Carbon dating uses a third carbon isotope, this time an unstable, radioactive form, radiocarbon or carbon-14 (^{14}C). Extremely small amounts of ^{14}C are present in the atmosphere (and thus in every living thing), produced by cosmic rays from space hitting nitrogen. Carbon-14 is not absorbed by dead matter, and it decays (reverting to a form of nitrogen) at a known rate. So careful measurement of the amount of ^{14}C relative to other carbon in something that was once alive – the less ^{14}C, the older it is – can establish when it died.

The technique has been around for over 60 years, during which time it has been immensely refined. We cannot yet date a sandwich (as a disgruntled inquirer at the British Museum once hoped, apparently trying to catch out his corner shop), but radiocarbon dates on properly collected samples are now consistently accurate and precise, often to within a few years. There were no reasons to question the results on Skeleton 1.

Up in Glasgow, Derek Hamilton's initial two dates were six years apart. When averaged and adjusted for long-term variations in atmospheric carbon-14 (one effect of which is to reduce a date's precision), the result was that Skeleton 1 died – with a 95 per cent certainty – between 1430 and 1460.

Down in Oxford, Christopher Bronk Ramsey came up with pretty much the same date. His initial two were only two years apart, and his final estimate 1415–1450. So Skeleton 1 could not have been Mutton the knight, who had died long before 1415. On the other hand, neither, apparently, could he have been Richard III, who died after 1460. What was going on?

The problem was all that bouillabaisse. Having realized that Skeleton 1 ate a lot of seafood, both labs duly corrected their dates to remove a distortion that this had caused: overall the sea contains relatively less ^{14}C than the atmosphere, so if you carbon date an old fish it looks older than it really is – an effect that would have been passed on to anything that might have eaten it. Using established correction data, which make the dates more accurate but unfortunately less precise, Hamilton and Bronk Ramsey – quite independently – came to definitive results that were almost identical. Hamilton then combined the four dates with sophisticated (Bayesian) statistics, threw in the knowledge that the burial had to have occurred before the Dissolution in 1538, and sat back.

With a high degree of probability, Skeleton 1 died between 1455 and 1540. Mutton was even further out of the picture. But Richard III was in.[20]

So who *was* Skeleton 1?

Act V

AN INQUEST

The improbably curved spine at once distinguishes Skeleton 1, but this isn't the only feature to mark it out. While the scoliosis might tell us something about how the man looked and felt, there are other conspicuous indicators that tell us something even rarer in the archaeology of human remains. We know how Skeleton 1 died.

The research team were able to identify at least 11 wounds in the bones. All of them are perimortem – they could not have been inflicted after the burial, and none shows any signs of healing, so the blows that caused them must have been delivered around the time of death. Nothing in the wounds themselves can say whether this means immediately before, after or at the actual moment, but as two would have caused almost instant death, and at least four others were potentially fatal, there can be no realistic doubt that this man was killed with razor-sharp steel blades. It is quite likely there were other blows that inflicted flesh wounds but did not contact bone, and any of these might also have been potentially fatal. Skeleton 1's end was brutal, quick and extremely bloody.

Almost certainly he died in battle. The radiocarbon dates say this very likely happened between 1455 and 1540, a range that entirely captures the Wars of the Roses, from the first Battle of St Albans (May 1455) to the Battle of Bosworth (August 1485), the Battle of Stoke (June 1487) and even beyond to the Battle of Blackheath (June 1497).[1] Realistically, of course, the proximity of Bosworth makes it more than likely that Skeleton 1 met his death there, 24 km (15 miles) to the west. On this basis, then, we can hypothesize that he died in 1485, on (or perhaps earlier, as there are suggestions some skirmishing occurred a day or two before) 22 August.

As is typical for the period, there are no precise figures for how many died at Bosworth, with contemporary estimates ranging from three hundred to ten thousand. Charles Ross thought a further 15th-century 'speculative estimate' of one thousand dead 'may not be too wide of the mark'. Some of these men were probably left on the battlefield, 'buried in a ditch like a dog', as some said of Richard III's body.[2] But many of them would have been given at least a perfunctory ceremony, mostly in

Tradition says that many of the Bosworth dead were buried in the churchyard at Dadlington; in 1886 it was reported that local farmers frequently ploughed up 'skeletons and rusty armour'.

mass graves nearby. Which begs the question, what was it about Skeleton 1 that caused his body to be carried to Leicester and treated to a burial, however hastily conducted, in a privileged area of a friary? Clearly this was no ordinary soldier. The potential candidates for Skeleton 1 must be significantly less than one thousand.

No mass graves have yet been found at Bosworth. Nor are there records of any, apart from a rather ambiguous reference to 'the bodies or bones of the men slain' on Bosworth field, in a document in which Henry VIII gave permission for the nearby church at Dadlington to raise alms, the better to 'pray for the souls of them that were slain'.[3] We do, however, have the remarkable evidence of a grave, part of which was meticulously excavated and studied by archaeologists, from another Wars of the Roses battle, at Towton, Yorkshire. How do the wounds described for Towton compare to those on Skeleton 1? Did he die like a common soldier? Or was his death, like his burial, something altogether different?[4]

There is no doubt that Towton was an exceptionally cruel battle; historians have accepted that 20,000 men or more may have died.[5]

Emotionally, one resists thinking of a mass grave as a statistical sample, faced with the evident pain and fear experienced by individual, often young, human beings. But it would be wrong to treat the remains of 38 men, from a pit that was dug for at least 50 bodies – the others had been exhumed by a construction company before archaeologists became involved, working under a Ministry of Justice Licence, and were soon reburied – as if they were representative of that slaughter. Other graves might look different. The battle began, for example, with an exchange of arrows, so we would expect a grave close to an army's position at that moment to contain people killed or wounded by projectiles; in the excavated grave, arrowheads accounted for only two wounds. At Bosworth, on the other hand, it seems gunpowder weapons were more common than at Towton, and we might expect to see shot wounds in some of the dead.[6] Yet the types of weapons indicated by both the Towton grave and Skeleton 1 are mostly sharp blades. A specific comparison between the two sets of remains does seem valid.

The contrasts are striking.[7]

Taken as a group, the Towton men look like professional soldiers, or at least men who had seen battle before. Of 28 skulls examined, nine bore well-healed trauma from earlier physical conflict. The most extreme of the 16 wounds was to a jaw, where a slice of bone and the root of a tooth had been cut away, and the chin fractured – all of this had successfully healed. There may have been further soft tissue wounds, leaving scarred flesh but no indications on bone.

The perimortem wounds, the unhealed impact of Towton, are not spread evenly over the bodies. Of a little over 150 injuries, over three quarters occur on the head and neck. Of the rest, most are on arms and hands, with a scatter down the legs. There is not a single wound in the chest, back or hips. Neither are the injuries found equally on all sides. There are more cuts on the left side of the head than the right, and on the right arm than the left. Crushing blows to the skull are mostly on the left of the face and head.

These wounds were studied by Shannon Novak, an American bioarchaeologist who specializes in skeletal injury patterns and is currently at Syracuse University, New York – but who happened to have taken up a post in England, at the University of Bradford, the year the Towton grave was excavated. The evidence suggested to her predominantly face-to-face combat by right-handed assailants – more or less well-armoured men slugging it out with staffs (a variety of viciously tipped poles), swords, daggers and clubs. Arm and hand injuries resulted when men tried to parry blows. Far from the romanticized image of heroism and honour in battle, concluded Novak, the grave revealed the truth of medieval warfare: scenes of 'frenzied killing that involved numerous blows to the head, often after [the victims] were incapacitated and unable to defend themselves'. These men had not died easily.

In two respects, Skeleton 1 exhibits the same pattern: most of the wounds are on the head, and the number falls within the range seen for individuals at Towton. Otherwise, however, we seem to be looking at different deaths. On this evidence, Skeleton 1 was no common soldier.[8]

He has no visible wounds on his arms, legs or hands, in his shoulders or in his neck. He has an injury to one rib and another to his pelvis. There are a couple of areas where damage to the delicate bones in his face was probably caused by soil pressure in the grave, but in three other cases facial injuries were inflicted by weapons. Most spectacular, however, is a group of six injuries to his head.

A blow to the top was focused enough to leave a small, ragged hole – breaking the bone and opening two little flaps like trap doors on the inside – but not so hard as to penetrate deep into the brain. Bob Woosnam-Savage, Curator of European Edged Weapons at the Royal Armouries Museum in Leeds, thinks this was made with a rondel dagger, a weapon with a thick spike designed for two-handed stabbing. A contemporary illustration shows a man wielding a dagger in exactly this way, standing over his prone victim and driving the blade into his skull. Skeleton 1 would have bled, and probably reeled from the blow, dazed and vulnerable, but still alive.

Lower down are three shallow scars, where a very sharp bladed weapon, probably a sword, shaved off slivers of bone. In the larger two you can see spongy inner bone in the circular dished depressions, and there are striations where the blade whistled through. These marks are like signatures. Do they match? Probably, concluded the scientists, which would mean the blows were delivered by a single sword; but 'we cannot be certain'.

These cuts look almost innocent on the skull, though ultimately they would have resulted in fatal blood loss if not quenched. Skeleton 1, however, was dead before that could have happened.

At the base of the skull are the two largest and most significant wounds. Either of these would have led to almost instant loss of consciousness, followed by rapid death. Which was delivered first cannot be determined, but what is clear is that this man died when he was attacked at the back of his head, just above his neck.

Jo Appleby had discovered the larger hole as the skull lay in the ground. It's big enough to put three or four of your fingers into, a massive wound that would have required considerable force to inflict – Woosnam-Savage and Sarah Hainsworth (who, as part of her research into imaging and materials, works with the Forensic Pathology Unit in understanding stabbing and dismemberment) think a halberd is a likely candidate.

Wielded by two hands, this was a pole with pitiless Swiss-army-knife aspirations: the heavy steel tip combined a thrusting spear point, an angled spike that could be swung at victims or hooked around armour to dismount or fell the wearer, and a razor-sharp axe blade. So a halberd, or perhaps a heavy sword, had sliced into Skeleton 1's skull, leaving two flaps of bone embedded in the brain that found their way into the grave, but taking more with it, almost entirely removing the base's right side. 'There's going to be a lot of blood coming from those injuries', said Stuart Hamilton, Deputy Chief Forensic Pathologist at the Forensic Pathology Unit, on the second Channel 4 TV film. 'There is going to be brain visible. You don't walk away from something like that, not even today with modern neurosurgery.'[9]

The Battle of Shrewsbury (1403) illustrated in 1485 in the Pageants of Richard Beauchamp; in the foreground a standing man in armour strikes an opponent on the head with a halberd.

The other basal wound is smaller, but no less vicious or potentially fatal. In fact, on available evidence, while the larger could have caused rapid death (it's not possible to tell exactly how far the blade penetrated the brain), the second undoubtedly would have done so, had the man still been alive. The micro-CT scan shows a clear impact mark on the top of the skull opposite the wound at the back. The blade penetrated 10.5 cm (4 in.) of brain before the inner wall of the skull stopped it short. Also apparently linked to this thrusting blow, is a cut on the back of the atlas vertebra, the bone in the spine that connects with the skull. It lines up with the penetrating wound.

These two injuries, which avoided marking any other bone apart from the nick to the vertebra, were almost certainly delivered when the man's head was flexed downwards, his bare neck and the underside of his skull exposed. The blows were clean and efficient, almost like an execution. A simple explanation for the angle of Skeleton 1's head is that he was kneeling.

Anything else might seem superfluous, but the other wounds are informative. The first of three on the face is a small knife or dagger cut on the right side of his mandible (lower jaw) near the base. Further back on the jaw is an injury from a sharp weapon whose nature could not be determined. Finally, higher up, is a 10 mm hole (0.4 in.) where a dagger with a stiff, square section blade – perhaps the same rondel that burst through the top of his skull – penetrated his right cheek; its tip emerged close by, breaking the bone.

If Skeleton 1 was alive, these facial wounds would have been bloody – though in the adrenalin-swamped moment perhaps unfelt – but no threat to life. They are slight and subtle compared to the gaping holes and fissures left by cutting and crushing that disfigure many of the Towton faces; the archaeologists there spent considerable time rebuilding skulls from smashed fragments.

Woosnam-Savage wondered if these facial injuries might all have been inflicted from behind: an attacker, or perhaps more than one, grabbed Skeleton 1's head, stabbed him in the cheek and released his helmet (a right-handed man thus attacking the right side of his face) – the cut on the jaw is where the chinstrap on a sallet, the sort of all-enveloping helmet Skeleton 1 might have worn, would have been found.[10]

On the other hand, they might have been inflicted after death. That this could have happened is suggested by the last two wounds, significant for our understanding of Skeleton 1's treatment. Like his skull wounds, and again unlike most of those on the examined Towton victims, they were delivered from behind. They were inflicted on parts of the body where not one of the Towton victims was affected: the back and the buttocks.

The first was caused by a sharp implement, a knife or dagger perhaps, and appears on the tenth rib in his right lower back; the rib did its job, and stopped the blade penetrating any deeper. There are two distinct cuts within the injury, which might, says the scientific report, 'relate to movement of the ribcage, or to the blade becoming stuck as the blow was delivered'.

The buttock wound, however, was altogether more vicious. The forensic team spent some time examining the scans, converted into a highly detailed 3D model of the pelvis, debating exactly what had happened. They decided a sharp blade, again possibly a dagger, had been thrust up into the right buttock, sufficient to penetrate the muscle, cut clean through the bone and perhaps pierce the skin on the opposite side. It was, says Woosnam-Savage, 'a delicate wound in an indelicate place'. Chief Forensic Pathologist Guy Rutty said this too was potentially fatal, though they all agreed, because of its position, that the blow had been delivered after death.

Woosnam-Savage – who followed a path from childhood fascination with castles, to medieval and Renaissance art history, to arms and armour and a museum career – told me that in attempting to understand these wounds, we should recognize that on the battlefield, 'nothing is impossible'. Yet there are a limited number of reasonable explanations, and without evidence to the contrary, we can go with what makes best sense. He is confident that none of these wounds could have been inflicted through armour, including, if Skeleton 1 had been horse-mounted, the protective wood, leather and steel of a defensive saddle.

In just about every detail, the wounds are different from those on the Towton soldiers. Skeleton 1 was attacked from behind, not the front. The face is cut and bloodied, not smashed beyond recognition. Postcranial wounds – below the head – are not on the arms or legs, but on the back and buttocks. It seems to me the contrast can be summed up in one word: narrative. The Towton men succumbed, in Shannon Novak's phrase, to 'frenzied killing', seemingly random rains of blows that achieved their effect through sheer brutality as much as skilled intention. Not so Skeleton 1. Here it is as if we can read a story, of capture, immobilization and efficient dispatch, and finally humiliation.

Most of the Towton men were probably protected by heavy padded jackets called brigandines. 'The common soldiery ... do not wear any metal armour on their breast or any other part of the body,' wrote Dominic Mancini, an Italian traveller-cum-spy in the early 1480s, 'except for the better sort who have breastplates and suits of armour.'[11] Skeleton 1 was of the better sort. He has no defensive wounds, nor any from previous conflict, because – befitting someone treated to burial in a prestigious location in Leicester – he wore the best, all-protecting and expensive steel armour.

This armour could be penetrated by metal-tipped arrows. Experiments by Sarah Hainsworth have convinced her that stories of arrows piercing armour, a knight's leg and a leather saddle, to kill the horse beneath him, are 'entirely realistic'. But Skeleton 1 died at close quarters, his helmet ripped off, exposing his head and neck. He took a few glancing blows as perhaps he struggled and momentarily escaped, before a halberd felled him. Bone took the force of the strike, stopping the blade just short of the neck. Had it made contact a little lower, it might have swung clean through. Perhaps, even, decapitation had been the goal. As he fell mortally wounded to his knees, we might imagine, another man plunged a sword into his head.

His armour was then entirely removed, and his lightly dressed or even naked body was further attacked. The more determined of the blows which we can see was probably delivered, because of its angle, to a buttock raised in the air. How could that have been achieved? In the circumstances, the most likely explanation is that the body had been thrown over a horse to be carried to Leicester. This confirms the impression that the man was important, that he had been recognized and targeted. The treatment of the face conveys the same message: it had apparently been necessary – as it had not for the victims at Towton – to preserve that face, so others could look into its dead eyes, and know.

Of course, no one would have considered it at the time, but saving the face in that way means that we, too, can look. Up in Aberdeen, as the archaeologists, forensic scientists and weapons expert contemplated the bones, Caroline Wilkinson was doing just that.

*

Richard III, Act 3, Scene 4. Men gather to choose a date for the coronation. They try to second guess Richard. You're closest to him, the Bishop of Ely says to the Duke of Buckingham, but the duke protests: we know each other's faces, he says, but what do we know of our hearts? Ask Lord Hastings, he says, he and the king are all but in love. Hastings is flattered. They haven't discussed the date, he says, but he's happy to pass on whatever they decide.

Richard appears, and in an exchange taken directly from Sir Thomas More's *History of King Richard III* (written some 30 years after the real king's death), asks the bishop to bring him strawberries from his garden in Holborn – a short walk from the rose garden where, in Henry VI, Shakespeare pictured Richard's father launching the wars that culminated at Bosworth.[12]

'His grace looks cheerfully and smooth today,' says Hastings when Richard is gone. 'I think there's never a man in Christendom, That can less hide his love or hate than he; For by his face straight shall you know his heart.'

Richard suddenly returns. He is angry. He holds out a withered arm: my enemies have bewitched me! 'Off with his head!', he screams, blaming Hastings, and the despairing man is led straight to the block.

This spectacular facial misreading exposes Hastings' foolishness and Richard's perfidy. Yet it also carries a wider message. We often judge by looks, taking instant – even unconscious – decisions about strangers.

Are they trustworthy, sociable, promiscuous, gay, violent, dominating or aggressive? Psychological research suggests that in such judgments we are more often right than wrong, but not so often that we should rely on first impressions. Faces deceive as well as inform.[13]

Which is part of their eternal draw. Most of the time archaeologists study anonymous people from the past – faceless people. When Jo Appleby was excavating Skeleton 1, part of her saw a man, an individual with a name and an identity, a man with a face. Yet the other, perhaps the bigger part, saw a skeleton, much like the many other remains she had worked with, once a living being but now a relic, which would tell her about aspects of life and death around the time the man had died, but not the intimate details of his unique personality. He had no face.

But what if we could faithfully reconstruct it? There would be historical value in so doing. Critics have questioned the likeness in the many portraits of Richard III, so – on the face of it, we might say – comparing Skeleton 1's appearance with the paintings would not help us assess his identity. Perhaps, however, he really is Richard (it's certainly looking promising), in which case we could then assess the portraits, a distinctly unusual opportunity in historic representation. Yet who among us would stop at historical value? What would we see in the real face of Richard III? Might we do better than Hastings – and perhaps Shakespeare, and generations of leading actors – and know his heart?

A human skull, says Caroline Wilkinson, is as unique as a human face. We are programmed to read only faces, however, so if we wish to recognize an individual from their skull – of obvious use in forensic investigation, from murder cases to war crimes and natural disasters – we need to put a face on the bones. The principle behind this was established by German scientists in the late 19th century: after measuring soft tissue thickness at fixed points on heads in the laboratory, average statistics could be applied to bare skulls to model flesh with clay. In this way were revealed the apparent faces of J. S. Bach, Dante, Schiller and Raphael – and that of an anonymous prehistoric woman.

The idea caught on, but soon lost respectability after different artists working with the same skulls produced entirely different faces, reflecting the then novelty of the technique, but also the inextricable mix of science and artistry behind a complete facial reconstruction. Research continued, however, and craniofacial identification is now a proven, established international practice. Prominent techniques include the Russian method, in which muscles are modelled on to a skull, and the American method, in which soft-tissue thickness is the exclusive guide. Richard Neave, a medical artist, pioneered what became known as the Manchester method when he was working at the university there. This combines the two previous techniques, fixing pegs around the skull cut to the depth of flesh, and then building up the face by layering on muscles and other soft parts. It is a painstaking process that has been revolutionized by digital technology, both in refining facial understanding (particularly important has been clinical imaging on living people) and in creating the faces.[14]

Wilkinson began her career on Neave's team in Manchester, and her distinctive short blond hair and strong jaw became familiar to many through her appearances on archaeological television series such as Meet the Ancestors. She is now an award-winning anthropologist and artist, and Director of the Face Lab at Liverpool John Moores University; in 2012 she was Professor of Craniofacial Identification at the University of Dundee. Skeleton 1's skull could not have been in better hands.

She and Chris Rynn, a Dundee colleague, worked with high-resolution photos and the CT data from Leicester. Because the university was hoping to resolve the skeleton's identity (or not) early in the new year, just four or five months after the bones had been found, she began immediately with the first hospital scans, so that the skull revolving on her computer bore curious flecks of digital dirt; she had to correctly assemble on screen the different skull parts, and replace a missing front tooth. Later she would confirm some of the hidden details with the micro-CT scans.[15]

Her initial analysis was good news for Jo: the skull was undoubtedly male, with a wide palate, square jaw and prominent chin, although with gracile elements such as a more feminine brow. Drawing on an extensive database of soft tissue thicknesses, muscles and facial features, she worked around the bones, adding eyeballs and digital pegs, and layering up the flesh with the aid of a haptic arm, a mechanism that transferred the movements of her right arm and hand into on-screen directions – allowing her to throw digital balls of clay and model them on to the skull, feeling her way as an experienced anatomical artist, a 21st-century George Stubbs of human portraiture.[16]

The creation of every part had its basis in scientific observation, as she chose average statistics for a contemporary white European male aged 30 to 40, selecting the thinner end of the range to reflect a physique likely to be more appropriate to the 1480s than the 1980s. She guided average eyeballs into their correct places in the sockets. She determined eyebrow shape from the character of the eyes, the brow and the upper orbital margin – Skeleton 1's eyebrows were low and straight – and crafted the mouth from key details of the anatomy. As she worked round the skull bit by bit, a flayed, muscled face emerged, on which she could build up virtual skin as she would have done with a clay head.

The chin was very prominent, protruding slightly beyond the mouth, whose corners were turned down a little. The lips were quite thin, the lower a touch more prominent than the upper, with a wide philtrum rising up to the nose. Clinical imaging has particularly improved understanding of noses, which used to be a weak area in this field: 'Noses are our best feature now,' said Wilkinson. Skeleton 1's – as related by exquisite details of bone structure – had a relatively sharp tip, a straight base and a subtle rise along the ridge. Ears, however, remain difficult. All that can be said about Skeleton 1's is that they were quite large, and like most people's, they had lobes. Using standard imagery, Wilkinson then added a neck (adjusted for width as determined by features on the skull), and shoulders, the right one a little higher to match the rest of the skeleton.

It looked like Richard III. At least, it looked uncannily like the portraits, which she remembered seeing as a child, but only now had returned to for a proper viewing. At this point, no one knew how the DNA research was progressing, and she had no idea whether or not Skeleton 1's identity would be confirmed. A little rattled, and, she told me, knowing that she would have to justify her results to a critical audience, she checked the procedures twice. She was happy that the face she had built was 'a scientifically and anatomically accurate' outcome of analysing the skull.

The bald, expressionless bust she had on her screen should closely resemble Skeleton 1's face. Wilkinson had conducted research at Dundee in which she compared reconstructed faces to known originals in blind tests, proving the success and objectivity of the process; on average, 70 per cent of the surface of a recreated face was less than 2 mm out. Yet this was not the end of the story. There is more to a face than shape, and after shape, in Wilkinson's words, 'we're guessing'.

Type of hair and eyebrows; hair, eye and skin colour; facial hair, skin texture, blemishes and wrinkles; and other superficial details so important to individual identity, including 'face fat', are not determined by bone structure, but by a mix of inheritance, lifestyle and cultural choice. In forensics, where Wilkinson does most of her work, recognition is key. Research has shown that a bare head, though correct as far as it goes, is not always recognized – her own 12-year-old daughter did not know the unadorned shape of her mother's face. So adding humanizing details can help.

With nothing to go on, as often happens in forensic work and is clearly the case with Skeleton 1, the best that can be done is to draw on banks of average statistics for the appropriate ethnicity, age and gender. People, though, are unique, and average eyebrows, skin texture and so on can also make a reconstructed face unrecognizable to people who knew the subject well. Between the bust and the person lies a critical gap that can mostly be filled only by art and subjectivity.

Wilkinson presented Janice Aitken, a digital artist at Dundee University, with a life-sized 3D printout of Skeleton 1's head, made in

Richard III in an early portrait (left, see frontispiece) with the face on Skeleton 1's skull (right) built by Caroline Wilkinson and interpreted by artist Janice Aitken.

Cardiff at PDR, the National Centre for Product Design and Development Research. It arrived on Aitken's desk with prosthetic eyes, and – in a chance nod to the skeleton's provenance – sprayed grey with a can of car paint. They knew the skull dated from around 1500, give or take 50 years. Aitken would study relevant contemporary portraits for dress and styling, including those of Richard III, and craft an individual on the plain, acrylic plastic face.

In her forensic work, Wilkinson will sometimes superimpose an image of a skull on a portrait photo, rotating it to the correct angle, to see if it's even possible that the two could be the same person. Now she thought she would try the same approach with Skeleton 1. She selected three portraits of Richard III. One of them, a fine example in the National Portrait Gallery and very similar to one in the Royal Collection – thought to be one of the oldest to survive – gave an astonishing match.[17] 'It's incredible how well the skull fits with this portrait', she said, adding that even in modern cases she very rarely sees such a good fit. It was enough to convince her that Skeleton 1 *was* Richard III.

Which was odd, because historians had been saying that the portraits didn't look like him.

Why might they not? Could it be that at that time portraits were more conventional than real? Or perhaps there was a more sinister reason? Certainly, by the time Richard came to the throne in 1483, there was a growing tradition of European painting which aimed to capture personality as well as physical realism. The Dutch artist Jan van Eyck, who died ten years before Richard was born, had created some stunning portraits; among well-known paintings by Leonardo da Vinci, his Portrait of a Young Man dates from a year or two after Bosworth, and the Mona Lisa from the early 1500s – but for Bosworth, Richard III might have been in his 50s as it was being painted. We have a right to seek the real king in early portraits.

There are plenty of them, too, approaching 20, largely thanks to the popularity of historical series of royal portraits to hang in great halls. Unfortunately none is by a known artist, nor is there proof that any were painted when the king was alive. With one exception (a piece now in the collection of Sir Tim Rice, which is a little fuller) all show just head and shoulders, with arms across the chest. The three oldest are different from each other: one (apparently painted soon after 1510 and in the collection of the London Society of Antiquaries) faces left, another (in the Royal Collection, apparently painted around 1500–20) faces right, and the third (also owned by the Society of Antiquaries and with attributed dates ranging from soon after 1523 to after 1550) faces left and holds a broken sword. In all others he holds a ring on his smallest right finger in his left finger and thumb, and the remaining dozen probably painted before 1620 copy this and other details from the Royal portrait, or a similar missing early version.

As Caroline Wilkinson found, there is a striking similarity between the faces in these portraits and the one she built from the skull of Skeleton 1. Most have the thin mouth with downturned ends, prominent chin, straight nose and relatively thin eyes below the straight, smooth brow of the model. Indeed, a small line drawing in the Beauchamp pageant, an illustrated biography thought to have been made for the Earl

Anne Neville (centre) is admired by her first husband, Edward Prince of Wales (left) and her second, Richard III (right), in the Beauchamp Pageant.

of Warwick's daughter Anne around 1485 when Richard was still alive, shows the same features.[18] There is a strong case for saying that all these portraits show us the real Skeleton 1.

They also show a raised shoulder. This is on the king's right in all but the two Society of Antiquaries' paintings – posing the question whether these might be inverted copies (the Beauchamp sketch, perhaps diplomatically, hides shoulders under a cloak). So the portraits show not just the face of Skeleton 1, but the raised right shoulder too.

These asymmetric shoulders have been much discussed. X-ray images revealed that in two of the earliest paintings (the one with the sword, examined in the 1954 and again in 2007, and the Royal portrait, examined before 1973), the original shoulders appeared even. It was immediately assumed they had been altered after Richard's death to match the view of antagonistic Tudor historians, elaborated by Shakespeare, that Richard III was deformed (albeit Thomas More said it was his left shoulder that was higher).[19]

Here was objective evidence that the histories written after Richard's death could not be trusted, of a Tudor need 'to make Richard physically resemble the nature of his crimes ... crude, if effective propaganda'.[20] Annette Carson goes to some trouble to distinguish between 'commentaries' written when Richard was alive, 'personal reminiscences' of people who knew him writing after his death, and 'Tudor "histories"' – with the last word pointedly in quotation marks.[21] Evidence of later distortion becomes demonstration of earlier truth. The logic is applied to the paintings, too. In her excellent catalogue to an exhibition about Richard III held by the National Portrait Gallery in 1973, Pamela Tudor-Craig argues that the added raised shoulder and 'slit-like' eyes suggest the original painting owned by the Queen dates from Richard's lifetime – or those features would have been put in at the start.[22]

There was always an alternative explanation. Richard III could have had a raised right shoulder, but either successfully concealed it, or – quite reasonably – did not wish it portrayed. Once he was dead, and his naked body had been seen by two armies and everyone in Leicester, there was neither means nor need to hide his real appearance. There is evidence that history portraits were researched for verisimilitude.[23] Perhaps later artists and their clients simply wanted to get it right.

So if, as it seems, the portraits of Richard III illustrate Skeleton 1 so well, what of the written descriptions? How do they compare? The answer is again very well. We can dismiss extremes, such as the notion that Richard was born feet-first with all his teeth after a two-year pregnancy. More's history is imaginative and rhetorical, and can be ignored for this exercise – thus we lose the 'shrivelled, withered and small arm', and the limp, both absent before More.[24]

Richard, says John Rous around the time of the king's death, was 'small of stature', and 'small in body and physically weak'. Nicolas von Poppelau, a visiting German knight, compares Richard to himself (whom he unfortunately does not describe), as 'three fingers taller, but a little slimmer and not as bulky, also very much more lean; he had very fine-boned arms and legs'.

Rous describes 'unequal shoulders, the right higher and the left lower'. Polydore Vergil (who reaches England from Italy in 1502, and pronounces Richard of 'petty stature') says one shoulder was higher than the other.[25]

As we saw in the last chapter, all these features – short, fine-boned and a higher right shoulder – are characteristic of Skeleton 1. We cannot from the paintings tell Richard's height, but otherwise the descriptions fit those too. It all matches so well, it seems reasonable to listen to what the records say about aspects of Richard's appearance we *can't* see in the bones.

On the morning of Bosworth, says the Croyland Chronicle (1486), Richard's 'countenance, which was always attenuated, was ... more livid and ghastly than usual'. Vergil describes a 'short and sour countenance, which seemed to savour of mischief', and a 'little and fierce face'. 'He used constantly to chew his lower lip,' he adds, 'as if the savage nature in that tiny body was raging against itself'. And he fiddled: 'he was wont to be ever with his right hand pulling out of the sheath, and putting in again, the dagger which he did always wear.'[26]

Having come this far, it does not seem too much to see these traits in the portrait faces, which show a 'man of care' old for his age, with 'evident intelligence'. He is 'a not uncomely man, despite the obvious lines of anxiety on his brow', but bearing 'a gaunt, bony, tight-lipped face', and looking 'much older than his true age'.[27] Perhaps here are the clues to filling that gap between Skeleton 1's smooth bust – and suggesting a yet thinner face – and a truly recognizable individual, who bites his projecting bottom lip, and twists his finger ring.

The bones speak eloquently of a specific, brutal death: of a sword thrice slicing the scalp, another driven up through a bared neck, and a sword or halberd swung with such force as nearly to decapitate the man. What of the texts? The record of English kings who died violently does not gloss over brutal details. Harold, for example, supposedly died from an arrow in his eye at the Battle of Hastings; abdominal injuries killed

William I when he fell off his horse; and Richard I was hit by a crossbow bolt in his left shoulder. Are the wounds on Skeleton 1 compatible with descriptions of Richard III's death?

The answer is intriguing. No clear record of that event appears to exist. Yet there are stories, often traditionally regarded more as myth than history, that offer a remarkably supportive narrative. They say the king was unhorsed when he rode into a marsh, and then, declining offers of a new steed, continued on foot. Barely the length of a lance or a sword between him and Henry, he fought 'manfully in the thickest press of his enemies', 'my battle ax in my hand', 'pierced with numerous and deadly wounds'. Soldiers 'hewed the crown down right, That after he was not able to stand... The[y] beat his bassnet [bassinet, a type of helmet] to his head, Untill the braine came out with bloode'. A Welshman 'struck him dead with a halberd'. Sir Rhys ap Tomas 'shaved his head'.[28]

Severely wounded, his head shaved, unable to stand and killed with a halberd so his brain flowed, Richard III's death thus described could equally have come from the study of Skeleton 1. And there is more.

The dead king, say the texts, was 'layd upon a horse back with the armes and leggs hanging down on both sides', 'his head pulled under his feet', a rope around his neck and 'trussed ... like a hog or calf'. His corpse was 'naked of all clothing', 'besprinkled with mire and blood', and 'insults were heaped upon it'. There is no mention of blows, but the body wounds in Skeleton 1 require at least that armour had been removed, and the angle of the hip thrust suggest buttocks raised in the air. Those two cuts, like the slight damage to the face, could be described as 'insults'.

A compelling case is emerging. It starts with the grave, which both archaeology and contemporary record describe as being in the choir of the Greyfriars church in Leicester, and whose stark functionality is consistent with a lack of 'pompe or solemne funeral'. It continues with the scientific evidence of the remains, carbon dated to the right era, identified as a man of the right age and status, who died violently in battle – through targeted assassination rather than random killing – and who matches the portraits and the historical descriptions. Skeleton 1, the sitter in the paintings and Richard III could all be the same man. There remained just one line of evidence to consider, that could prove or demolish the argument: DNA.

*

Philippa Langley was right to be excited, back in 2006, when John Ashdown-Hill announced that he had found Richard III's mitochondrial DNA 'alive and well in Canada'.[29] It meant that if remains were found that might be the king's, there would be the possibility of testing the theory. Archaeologists had found a likely grave. After intensive study, everything seemed to support the idea that it might have been Richard III's. Could DNA now conclude the case?

We are all more or less related, and share a great deal of genetic material. Most of our DNA cannot be used to determine precise ancestry, as it consists of a random combination from each parent (which is why we do not look exactly like either of them). However, two types of DNA are not mixed as they are passed on. During millions of years of evolution, sufficient changes have accumulated in these forms to enable us to distinguish individuals who are not related in a particular way. But for those who are, going back just a few centuries, the DNA is likely to be identical.

One of these forms is passed exclusively down the female line, the mitochondrial DNA, or mtDNA, that Philippa hoped would prove Skeleton 1 to be Richard III. It is not part of the DNA that defines us (so cannot tell us anything about how a person looked), but is found in mitochondria. Billions of years ago these were probably bacteria, but they found safe homes inside cells of other forms of life, and they now reside in our cells, in simplified form with their own DNA, as important sources of energy, like tiny batteries. They are very common, which makes them ideal when looking for ancient DNA to understand ancestry.

Among the DNA molecules that do make us what we are, one is copied with relatively little change. It is packaged in the Y chromosome, and is what makes a human male. Y-chromosome DNA offered the second possibility for testing the identity of Skeleton 1 – which is of course male – as well as the potential to learn a little about him. As all descendants through an unbroken female line to Richard III's mother will have mtDNA that is comparable to his, so anyone on a male line to his father – Richard himself left no descendants – will have a comparable Y chromosome.

Several challenges had to be overcome for this quest to succeed, and it would be expensive – accounting for the greater part of the £94,000 the University of Leicester had given to post-excavation by the end of 2012 alone.[30] By far the hardest task would be to find and describe either of the two forms of DNA – ideally both – in the bones of Skeleton 1. First, however, living people needed to be identified with proven links to Richard III through unbroken male or female lines.

Ashdown-Hill had traced such a person, Joy Ibsen. Mrs Ibsen had died in 2008. But she left a daughter and two sons who possessed copies of her mitochondrial DNA, which should look like the mtDNA Richard III would have inherited as copies from *his* mother. One of her sons, Michael, born in London, Ontario, was now helpfully living in London, England, and had readily agreed to take part in the project. However, if after successful mtDNA extraction it turned out that Skeleton 1's did *not* match Michael Ibsen's, it could have been because of a fault in the family tree; the remains might still have been Richard III's. Ashdown-Hill's attempt to confirm the Ibsen connection by analysing some of Edward IV's hair had unfortunately not been successful.[31] Kevin Schürer, the project's genealogy expert, set out to test the tree.

The first 13 generations from Richard's mother, down to Anne Spooner who died in 1873, had been published in 1909; Ashdown-Hill had brought the line up to date. The links had not been documented, however, so Kevin and his genealogical colleagues searched the archives.

From Anne of York's 15th-century will, to a 17th-century baptismal register, an 1851 census and a passenger list for SS *Mauretania* (which took Joy Brown, as Mrs Ibsen was then, to New York),[32] all told the same story: the lineage was good. Michael Ibsen is a true descendant of Richard III's mother.

In the process they discovered a second maternal line, the search for which Kevin described as 'a long shot, and overly hopeful and ambitious with several blind alleys'. This was critically important. Michael Ibsen's new-found 'distant cousin' agreed to take part, while wishing for the time being to remain anonymous, allowing the team to triangulate two modern mtDNA samples with any retrieved from Skeleton 1. The checks were watertight.

Kevin was even more successful with a continuous male line. This went up from Richard III to his great-great-grandfather Edward III, then down through 15 generations to the 5th Duke of Beaufort, who died in 1803 – an apparently well-documented noble line that can be looked up in Burke's Peerage. They then found nearly 20 living men claiming descent from the duke. They tracked down five, all of whom agreed to take part, again anonymously. The men didn't know each other: among them one lives in England, one in Scotland and two in Australia.[33]

Analysing modern DNA is now a relatively quick and simple process and one that Turi King, leading the genetic study, could do at the University of Leicester. Skeleton 1's DNA, however, was no simple matter. Turi had extracted teeth early in the project, as the skull could not be otherwise handled or studied until this was done, for fear of contamination. She chose teeth because these held the best chances of preserving DNA, protected by the enamel.

As with all parts of the body, survival of ancient DNA depends on burial conditions. Skeleton 1's DNA was bound to be degraded: but was sufficient left to be of any use at all? That damage brought a second problem. To make it possible to study any extracted DNA, it would have to be biochemically amplified. This is a standard procedure, but if there is any contamination, it too will be amplified, and can completely swamp the ancient DNA.[34]

This work could not be done in Leicester. They wanted to have two independent studies in case anything should go wrong, as they had had with the radiocarbon dating. It was December by the time Turi had a slot in the first lab's schedule, in Toulouse.

It is easy to picture Turi returning from the Université Paul Sabatier – where she worked with Patricia Balaresque (whose research focused on male–female interaction in evolution) and Laure Tonasso (studying human migrations) – holding up a long queue at airport customs while she explained in rusty French that her white powder was a ground-up tooth. Turi grew up in Vancouver, and has a relaxed sense of humour and a mane of auburn hair. She came to Leicester to study molecular genetics after obtaining a degree at Cambridge, and now researches the genetic impact of diasporas on Britain, and how genetic genealogy testing can affect a person's perception of their identity – an interest she can now perhaps share with fellow Canadian Michael Ibsen. The powdered tooth is safely back in Leicester.

In January she set off for her second lab, the Ancient DNA Facilities in the University of York. Here she worked with Michael Hofreiter and Gloria González Fortes, who between them had previously studied, among other things, the ancient DNA of woolly mammoths and cave bears.

Early results were promising. Modern DNA proved an exact match between Ibsen and his anonymous 'cousin', confirming the female-line tree. The labs in York and Toulouse had both found sufficient ancient mtDNA for analysis. Y-chromosome DNA proved more elusive, early in 2013 Turi was still working on trying to isolate meaningful quantities. But mitochondrial DNA looked set to provide another strand of evidence in the case for the identity of Skeleton 1. On 9 January the University of Leicester Press Office alerted the media. In the first week of February, it said, the university would reveal what its scientists had been up to. The announcement was headed, The Search for King Richard III.

Act V

'It doesn't look like the face of a tyrant. He's very handsome. It's like you could just talk to him.' Philippa Langley in February 2013 with the model of Richard III's head.

When it came, on 4 February, the conference was something that no one there, whether behind the scenes, in the audience or on stage, would ever forget. This time the event was not down by the cathedral, in a car park or in the medieval Guildhall, but up the hill at the university. It challenged Ather Mirza's Press Office long in advance, as media organizations around the world – some of which you might have imagined would be above such tactics – tried anything they could to get advance information (Mirza trusted one journalist, who for a few days was privileged to witness the genuine up-to-the-hour research: the *Leicester Mercury*'s Peter Warzynski).

But the press team was only one of many concerns making the day. Academics from departments across the university had joined in the research. Now, it seemed, the entire institution was wired up, roped in, briefed, preened and enthused, as Richard Taylor, in his best suit and tie, grasped the lectern in front of banks of TV cameras and rows of blogging and tweeting journalists. Among the audience were Philippa Langley,

Michael Ibsen, David Baldwin (who had predicted in 1986 that Richard III might be found and exhumed), Channel 4 executives (they would broadcast Darlow Smithson Productions' film that evening) and members of the research teams. Others watched a relay in an adjacent room. Outside, satellite vans were ready to broadcast live to the rest of the world.

Round the corner and up four flights of stairs, behind an unmarked door in an obscure small room of the David Wilson Library, a complete human skeleton (minus feet) lay under a clear acrylic case on black velvet. Two security guards and two chaplains watched in silence.

'Today', said Taylor, 'we bear witness to history.'

In his second sentence, he said that what we were about to hear would be published in leading peer-reviewed journals. Suddenly, this was no longer a press event: it was an academic conference. When Taylor had finished his introduction, five specialists in turn talked about their fields, with pictures on a screen – Richard Buckley (showing the world the first images of Skeleton 1), Jo Appleby, Lin Foxhall, Kevin, Turi and finally Buckley again. More than half an hour after the start, without a cough or dropped pen, the ever-silent room knew what was coming. With immaculate theatrical timing, Richard Buckley paused, looked down at his text, breathed deeply, his broad shoulders straining his jacket, and raised his eyes to the audience.

'Ladies and gentlemen,' he said. 'It is the academic conclusion of the University of Leicester that beyond reasonable doubt, the individual exhumed at Greyfriars in September 2012 is indeed Richard III, the last Plantagenet king of England.'

There was a pause. Then we clapped. Journalists smiled and cheered. We were children at the feet of royalty.

'I was working up to the wire,' said Turi later. She recalled seeing a match in the first DNA results. 'I went utterly still,' she said. 'And then I got up and did a little dance around the lab!' She carried on with the work, telling no one – not even her husband, though he might have guessed from seeing her dance in the kitchen. Only by the end of the week before

At the Leicester University press conference on 4 February 2013, left to right: Richard Buckley, Jo Appleby, Lin Foxhall, Kevin Schürer and Turi King.

the press event was she convinced Skeleton 1 was Richard III: his mtDNA precisely matched the two modern samples. It belonged to a relatively rare group (known as J1c2c), making it unlikely the matches could be chance. She told her colleagues on the Sunday. The conference was the next day.[35]

Her father watched the conference from Vancouver. As Turi walked across to the lectern, wearing a plain, long-sleeved black dress and a simple necklace, he knew before anyone else what she would say. They had agreed on a jewelry code.

EPILOGUE

Battlefields and burials

The third of February 2013 had been Super Bowl day, when the Baltimore Ravens beat the San Francisco 49ers to become national football champions. It was a major sports event, but for non-Americans it might help to illustrate what that means by listing a few facts.

Before play began, Alicia Keys sang the national anthem. Beyoncé performed in the interval. TV advertising spots cost $4 million or more (over £2.6 m) for just 30 seconds of air-time. Half-time (when British viewers of an equivalent sports event traditionally leave the room to make a pot of tea) was faithfully watched by 104 million Americans; 164 million were said to have seen at least part of the actual game.

It would be no surprise to hear that people were talking about the Super Bowl the next morning. But what, for hours, was the top trending topic on Twitter? Richard III.[1]

Leicester University had been in no doubt that the announcement of the identity of Skeleton 1 would make a noise. The information itself had been very closely guarded – even the press office found out only the day before, giving them their Super Bowl moment as they shredded release option two, 'Skeleton proven not to be that of famous man'. But journalists had been alerted to the conference nearly a month ahead, and with two weeks to go had been given detailed instructions for attendance. Ather Mirza was going to be ready.

Yet even he was taken aback. He might have spotted a hint of what was to come from the BBC's determination – unrewarded – to get the story ahead of the pack; having dismissed pitches in the early days of the project from both Philippa Langley and Darlow Smithson Productions, the BBC would have known that rival broadcaster Channel 4 was in on the secret. And British interest was bound to be strong. Richard III was a star, prominent on the stage and in school history books. In reports from *The Times* (running two successive leaders on the topic) to the *Stratford Herald* ('Body of ex-Warwick Castle owner found under a car park'), there was a compelling sense of detection and mystery – a lost Agatha Christie plot found buried in the centre of England. But it went much further than that.

'We were on the front page across the globe,' Mirza told me. He bumped into a porter tidying up after the conference. 'I've just had a text from my brother in Columbia,' he said. 'We're on the front page there!'

Among over 500 web comments on *The New York Times'* story, Jay (NYC)'s seemed to speak for many – it was recommended by over 350 readers. 'I grew up as a black kid in the Bronx', he wrote, 'and fell in love with Shakespeare one night... [watching] Kenneth Branagh... on Masterpiece Theater.' He tells how his passion grew. The first book he bought with his first paycheck was about Richard III. Later he read Josephine Tey's novel. 'Perhaps it was the heady days of growing up in a city divided by various power-brokers and seeing that play out in a different time and place,' he mused. 'Perhaps it was an adolescent fascination on the darker aspects of human nature. Whatever it was, this lifelong attraction to this story has not abated and the news today leaves me giddy, breathless and relieved.'[2]

Leicester University and the city were delighted. A global public was enthralled. But there was confusion too. If the world was hungry for information, it was also affected emotionally. A heady mix of history, drama and myth had been given life by a personal quest, concluded almost miraculously by forensic science. This was not just a successful archaeological dig. Philippa Langley, who had begun it all, had spent years of her life overcoming obstacles, persuading doubters and courting mockery. Her own involvement was not purely, or even mostly, scientific.

Media images of the press conference focused on a panel of smiling academics describing their research, introduced by the university's Vice-Chancellor and the Deputy Registrar. Richard Buckley delivered his momentous conclusion, the Deputy Registrar stood up to thank everyone, and journalists rushed to file their copy. But there was more.

Sir Peter Soulsby, the City Mayor, addressed practical issues, including the news that a visitor centre would be opening at the reburial in 2014. 'It has been agreed by all concerned', he announced, 'that the king's body will be reinterred, here, in Leicester Cathedral.' David Monteith, the cathedral's Canon Chancellor, confirmed the point. Following best archaeological practice, he said, 'human remains are interred as near to their site of discovery as possible ... The licence from the Ministry of Justice specifically names Leicester Cathedral.'

Ralph Lee said a few words for Channel 4, Mary Ann Lund and Sarah Knight, from the university's School of English, pondered Richard III's withered arm, and finally, out of the dissipating audience, Philippa Langley rose to take the lectern.

'Today', she said, 'marks the culmination of an extraordinary journey of discovery. Everyone thought that I was mad.' She didn't talk about the dig, or the science. 'We have searched for Richard, and we have found him,' she said. 'It is now time to honour him. The two-dimensional caricature promoted by the Tudors will be no more.'[3]

As I have already noted (page 125), when the dig began the intention had been to rebury Richard III's remains within four weeks, though few expected to find them. That had already become five months, and now the mayor was saying the reburial would be in 2014 – probably at least another year (to allow time for a visitor centre to be built, perhaps).

In the excitement I suspect only a few of us were aware that while the exhumation licence did indeed name the cathedral as a reburial site, it was only an option – others were keeping the bones in a museum or burying them elsewhere – and one proposed by Leicester's archaeologists. Even fewer knew that Philippa believed a contract existed between her and the archaeologists, which gave her, as she saw it, authority over the king's remains. And none of us knew that over the coming months, powerful disagreements would emerge over such apparently simple issues. Nor did we know that people who had had nothing to do with any part of the project would join the fray, delaying reburial yet another year and costing the council, the university and the Ministry of Justice far more than had been spent to dig up the grave.

King Richard III probably arranged for the death of his nephews, Edward and Richard, in the Tower of London. He survived a rebellion. He beheaded men he saw as threats to his power. He established a form of regional government for the north of England, strengthened laws regulating trade and social justice, founded the College of Arms, endowed two colleges at Cambridge University and planned a large chapel in York Minster. With a better wind, and without the treasonable action of Thomas and William Stanley, he might have won a glorious victory in a historic battle at Bosworth.[4]

The king reigned for a little over two years – five months less than it took for his bones to be excavated and reburied. A judge was to warn that an 'unseemly, undignified and unedifying ... legal tussle over these royal remains' could result in 'the (legal) Wars of the Roses Part Two'.[5] That did not seem an unreasonable comment. The arguments were underway even as the press conference was being reported in February. In March came war.

*

I am sitting in the Royal Courts of Justice in England, in central London, at the back of a court presided over by no less than three judges – among them one deemed by the BBC to be the eighth most powerful woman in the kingdom. The room seems carved from dark oak. A huge royal coat of arms watches, its gilded lions glistening indifferently.

There is a shout behind me. I recognize Philippa Langley's voice.

'I have to say something,' she exclaims. 'So much of the information here is being misrepresented.'

Lady Justice Hallett, perhaps accustomed to the occasional outburst from the public benches, gently moves things on. But a little later she does something quite unusual. She invites Langley to submit a written statement.

'After all,' she says, 'we wouldn't be here if it wasn't for Miss Langley.'

Poor Miss Langley. Her quest to find Richard's grave had been testing but successful, if not entirely flawless (scoliosis was not part of the vision). But there she was, complaining in court. She had hoped for a private, royal burial in a handmade coffin (£970 plus tax), but a year and a half later she was still waiting. To add to her woes, pending reburial the bones were secreted somewhere in Leicester University – not, as she had asked the archaeologists, in *her* custody and enjoying 'continual prayer and worship' in a nearby abbey.[6]

The delay was bad enough, but its prime cause was a huge distraction in itself, and one that had, perhaps more than anything, dragged aspects of public debate into a disrespectful shambles. Philippa had anticipated giving Richard the proper burial he had been denied at his death, after a brief scientific study designed to prove the remains' identity. Leicester Cathedral was the obvious site for the new grave. But not everyone thought so.

By the time Leicester had revealed that Skeleton 1 really was the king's, a petition to re-inter Richard III in York Minster had already garnered over 24,000 votes. Leicester had launched its counter measure a few weeks later, but by early February 2013 was struggling with a mere 7,600 votes.[7]

Over the next few days the question of where the burial should take place was asked several times in Parliament, and on 12 March it was debated, airing several canards that would feature strongly in what was to come. 'Historians widely believe that Richard III expressed his desire to be buried in York,' went one. This was supported by 17 'living descendants', another. A third, 'It is the responsibility of the state to decide where, how and when King Richard … is buried … [not] a group of academics at Leicester University' – although the voices of 'the royal family, the Church of England and the Catholic Church' should also be heard. Unfortunately, 'there had been little public consultation'.[8]

On other parliamentary occasions, several ministers, including the Prime Minister, were asked about the possibility of a state funeral – to which the common answer was, 'We have no such plans'. This was an issue easily dealt with: as Pete Hobson, Acting Canon Missioner, Leicester Cathedral, pointed out repeatedly, the reburial was 'not a funeral (that happened in 1485)'.[9]

More complex was the notion that Richard III's remains should be treated to Catholic ceremonies, befitting a 'Catholic monarch'.[10] The university held that because the king died before the Reformation, which saw 'the separation of what we now call the Church of England from what we now call the Roman Catholic Church', such a view was anachronistic.[11] Yet the Looking for Richard team were determined that the skeleton should benefit from 'Catholic sanctity with the prayers and rites of his own religion', launching a petition to that effect in advance of the reburial. The Catholic diocese was forced to say such concerns had nothing to do with Catholic tradition, and were 'fundamentally misplaced'.[12]

So too the idea could be dismissed that the king had said where he wanted to be buried. Immediately after the February press conference, a motion was tabled in Parliament asking that the king's remains should be reinterred in York, 'in accordance with his last-known wishes'.[13] Throughout the protracted arguments, most academic historians would insist that this was a fiction, that no one knew what Richard III's 'last wishes' were – not least, it was said, the 32-year-old king himself, who had not planned to die at Bosworth. Certainly no one supplied any evidence.[14]

Yet more easily ignored was the apparently common popular belief that as a member of the House of York, Richard III's natural home and resting place was the City of York. Comparable logic might suggest, for example, that the late singer Michael Jackson should have been buried in Jackson, Wyoming, or Winston Churchill in the eponymous Somerset village (where mourners, perhaps, could have retired to the Churchill Inn). York, as in house, was about property, status and power; it was not the name of the king's nursery school.

Richard III has no 'living descendants'; he is not known to have had any grandchildren. The gang of 17 noted in Parliament were collateral descendants, whose apparent claimed ancestors were Richard's siblings (no evidence for those relationships was ever proffered). Calculations, however, soon show that there are likely to be over a million such collateral descendants alive today. As Rob Eastaway, a mathematician, put it, 'Since there's a chance that anyone with English ancestry is related to Richard III, we should all be able to vote on where he should be buried.' Yet even that is not the end. Who is this 'we'? Kevin Schürer noted that many collateral descendants live around the world outside the UK – and few, if any, would be aware of their connections, each of which would take extensive research to prove. Consultation limited by such relationships would be impossible.[15]

Yet in the 18 months between exhumation and the High Court, niceties of fact or sense were not always paramount in debate about the king's bones. In particular, notions of kinship and consultation, and a desire by some to bury the remains in York, proved powerful, frequently defying logic or science, and occasionally – as the Dean of York found out, leading her to refer correspondence to the police – leading to public abuse.[16]

It was easy, at first, to miss what was happening in the midst of all the clamour. One of many proclamations on the future of Richard III's remains, following the February press conference, was a letter to Her Majesty the Queen and the Ministry of Justice, putting forward the case for a York reburial. Signed by leading York officials, it was backed by 'senior politicians, civic leaders and academics across the whole country', including one Stephen Nicolay, 'an archaeologist and 13th generation descendant of Richard's wife'.[17]

A few weeks later Nicolay sent his first tweet: 'The living family of King Richard III demand that his mortal remains be re-interred in his beloved Yorkshire.' Soon his name was among nine who signed an open letter 'demanding' the remains be 'returned' to York. All claimed a distant relationship with the king – Nicolay as Richard's '16th great nephew'.[18]

Before anyone noticed, Nicolay and his remote relatives had formed the Plantagenet Alliance, a limited company, and were threatening legal action against the Ministry of Justice and the University of Leicester. A Yorkshire law firm called Gordons provided Matthew Howarth to fight their corner, arguing that his clients' human right to be consulted on the reburial had been broken. The ministry and the university were minded to laugh it off, but this proved a mistake. In August Mr Justice Haddon-Cave granted the application for a judicial review on all grounds.[19]

Further good news for the Alliance was that even if it lost the case, its costs would be protected; ultimately the British taxpayer would foot the bill. The judge had hoped an independent advisory panel could settle the matter, but no one wished to discuss it. It got murkier still in November, when for mysterious reasons Leicester City Council was dragged into the dispute and the review was adjourned. Symptomatic of the confusion was a leader in *The Times*, calling for the king to be buried in Leicester: earlier the same paper had insisted that 'he must be reburied in Westminster Abbey'.[20]

When the review finally opened the following March, it seemed everyone was there. Of course the Alliance and the defendants – the Secretary of State for Justice, the University of Leicester, and Leicester City Council – had turned up with their lawyers, but around the court were all manner of supporters and observers. Among these were Phil Stone and John Ashdown-Hill, Peter Warzynski from the *Leicester Mercury*, a BBC journalist who tweeted throughout, a crew from Darlow Smithson Productions scripting their next Channel 4 film, Richard Buckley and friends, and representatives of Leicester Cathedral. A historian might have looked down from high above through the ornate, oak-framed roof lantern, and drawn a battle plan.

None of them, not least the heady presence of King Richard III, would have been there without Philippa Langley. Yet no one was expecting her to stand up and shout. The incident was the odder still in that it wasn't clear whose side she was on, or exactly what had upset her. But then again, perhaps, it was an appropriately eccentric moment in a hearing in the highest court in the land, that throughout its two days never quite seemed to be in the real world. It originated with Mr Haddon-Cave's belief that a matter such as the reburial of an English king was too important to the people of Britain to be decided by closeted bureaucrats. In the hands of counsels, the issue lurched from obscurity to farce and back. The Plantagenet Alliance's case became increasingly unclear, and when, finally, in late May the judges rejected its claim, few informed observers could have been surprised.[21]

The review was dismissed essentially for two reasons. First, there was no legal requirement for the Secretary of State for Justice to consult about the reburial. Secondly, he knew enough about what everyone thought – including the fact that both Henry VII and the present Queen were happy for Richard III to be buried in Leicester – that consultation would not have achieved anything useful. That left the exhumation licence, as issued by the Ministry of Justice and specifying reburial in Leicester, a valid document.[22]

The Plantagenet Alliance did not appeal, and its website disappeared. An angry Justice Secretary Chris Grayling, already unhappy with the system of judicial review, complained that the Alliance was 'a shell company set up ... to avoid paying legal costs'. Defence set back his ministry £82,000, the university £70,100, the cathedral £7,000 and Leicester City Council £85,900 – a total of nearly a quarter of a million pounds (over $375,000). Leicester Cathedral, to its obvious delight and relief, could continue with its reburial preparations. But the business had fostered animosity and the spread of misinformation, and consumed much time and money. There were few winners.[23]

It could all have been settled at little cost by e-petitions on Her Majesty's Government's website. There were at least 37, including those rejected, such as 'Richard III – stick him back under the carpark'. Among accepted proposals for reburial sites were Westminster Abbey, Arundel Roman Catholic Cathedral in Sussex, Fotheringhay in Northamptonshire, and Priory Street Centre car park, York. Only two received many votes.

York Minster closed with a strong 31,349. After a late start, however, Leicester, encouraged by a local paper campaign, took advantage of its remaining 18 days, and soared to victory with 34,479 votes. The people had spoken.[24]

*

Shakespeare's play ends on Bosworth field, after the battle. The victorious Earl of Richmond is handed Richard's crown, 'pluck'd off the dead temples of this bloody wretch'. Now Henry VII, he anticipates an England of peace and prosperity. He looks around at the fallen. 'Inter their bodies', he says, 'as becomes their births.'

Tradition says that many of the lower born were buried at Dadlington. One man, however, waited nearly 530 years for an interment that became his status. On a bright, fresh Sunday, a little before eleven o'clock on 22 March 2015, Richard III's remains began their final, extraordinary journey.

Since September 2012, when Mathew Morris had driven the bones the few minutes from the excavation up to the ULAS offices, apart from a few small samples sent out for scientific analysis, they had never left the care of the university. Now the academics were to pass the remains into the guardianship of Leicester Cathedral. This was a legal transaction, and the skeleton had to return to close to where it had been found. The reburial ceremony, due in four days, was not a state event. But none of this was reason to hold back on celebration and ritual; it was time to have fun.

Indeed, the absence of the state and the Crown, combined with the dignity and imagination of the cathedral and city authorities, meant we were treated to a spectacular, varied and often eccentric mix of events, the like of which has surely never been seen before. In her poem for the reburial, read in the cathedral by the actor Benedict Cumberbatch, Carol Ann Duffy wrote how Richard III 'once dreamed of this, your future breath in prayer for me'.[25] But he could not possibly have foreseen what happened in the days leading up to that moment.

Preparations had begun before the court judgment on the Plantagenet Alliance's claim the previous May – the excavation licence had stipulated that reburial should occur before September 2014. The burden fell on the cathedral. By chance already busy with a landscaping and building project outside the church, it now faced major interior alterations as well.

The city also had much to attend to, as did Channel 4, which announced on the day of the court judgment that it was the reinterment's 'official broadcast partner'. The BBC, also approached by the cathedral, was apparently unsure whether anyone would be interested, and five and a half hours of programming fell into the waiting lap of Darlow Smithson Productions.[26]

So there we were, once again, at Leicester University's Fielding Johnson Building, satellite vans round the corner, journalists, TV and radio crews from around the world (not least DSP and the BBC), squeezed into our pen with inquisitive crowds flowing by on the lawn. Ahead of the ceremony, Richard Buckley, Turi King, Philippa Langley, John Ashdown-Hill and others mingled with the press. I asked Kevin Schürer – a key member of the research team, but also a Pro-Vice Chancellor at the university, helping to look after their side of affairs – what he most feared? 'Students on the roof setting off fire alarms,' he said. 'And rain.' But it was to be a favoured day, unseasonably warm and sunny, with no disruptions.

Two years ago we were inside, eager to hear whether or not a skeleton was Richard III's. The presentations were serious and restrained, though electrified by an unspoken expectation of the announcement to come. Now we knew that Richard III was there, his bones laid out in the coffin they never had. This was our journey too, from discovery and excavation, through scientific research, debate, argument and all the preparations for this day. In handing the remains to the cathedral, the university was releasing them for everyone.

Before us, on the stone slabs in front of the Fielding Johnson's three-storied, Georgian-style brick façade, stands a pair of decorative oak trestles. A clear temporary cover – redundant in the intermittent sunshine – shelters the invited guests. The orator asks the seated to stand, and the big white doors behind swing inwards. The funeral director – whom I suppose we should call the reburial director – steps out, followed by the fresh, golden, English oak coffin on the shoulders of six pallbearers.

The coffin is beautifully simple, a rectangular box whose only ornament is a rose and 'Richard III 1452–1485' – carved on the lid by Anna Louise Parker – and protruding bevels at top and base. It was made by Michael Ibsen, one of the four living female-line collateral descendants of Richard III found and proven by Kevin Schürer and Turi King (all four – Michael and his siblings Jeff and Leslie, and Wendy Duldig – are among the guests).[27] Remarkably, while Michael is a Canadian living in London, Wendy Duldig, though born in Australia, also lives in London. A tall, elegant man, Michael has a gentle, measured voice, and his work reflects his personality. He made the coffin plain, he has said, so as not to show off; there are no dovetail joints, which would be about him, not the king.[28]

A distant helicopter thrums. Birds sing. The coffin seems to weigh heavily on the bearers. It holds a 60 kg lead lining, inside which Richard's bones are laid anatomically, from his head to lower legs (his feet not having survived). Small fragments are in linen bags, made by children at Leicester's King Richard III Infant School; even the powdered residues from scientific tests are in the coffin. Every last part of the king is packed safely in natural, British materials – washed woollen fleece, wadding and unbleached linen. Over it all, including a rosary supplied by John Ashdown-Hill, lies a piece of Irish linen, embroidered by Elizabeth Nokes of the Richard III Society.[29]

The lead ossuary, made in Leicester by Jonathan Castleman, was soldered shut during a small, private ceremony the previous Sunday, in a former chapel at the university. Ibsen sealed the lid. This is intended to be a definitive closure, with no further study of the original remains expected. Jo Appleby, who perhaps has spent more time with the bones than anyone else, would later say, 'I actually feel the time is right for him

to be laid to rest in the cathedral – it is exactly what should be happening.'
A reflection partly of the intensity of scientific studies in the previous two
years, this unusual attitude for an archaeologist to historically interesting
remains – shared by her colleagues – is also indicative of their emotive
impact, of the national cultural weight that Mr Justice Haddon-Cave had
recognized.[30]

While the bearers circle and lower the box onto the trestles, further
guests emerge and stand at the back. Many of the faces are by now
familiar; archaeologists, scientists, historians, the descendants of
Richard's sister, and senior representatives of the Richard III Society, the
university, cathedral, city and county. The ceremony begins.

With the university mace shining from a table to one side, the
Chancellor, President and Vice-Chancellor address the crowd, and the
Revd Canon Dr Stephen Foster leads a ceremony of reflection. Sarah
Hainsworth reads passages from Khalil Gibran, the Diamond Sutra, Soto
Zen Buddhist scripture and Hindu ancient Sanskrit. Later Turi King reads
from Robert Frost ('I took the one less travelled by...'), and Father David
Rocks from Hebrew Psalm 22, a Sikh Shabad and the Qur'an, closing
with Eid Mubarak, a Muslim festival greeting – all interpreted by a signer.

It would be easy to parody this, if, like some vociferous objectors to
reburial in Leicester, you are dismissive of the city's multiculturalism. In
February, Philippa Langley, who had wanted Richard's remains to be
placed in a Catholic 'holy place' pending their reburial, had complained
that the university was treating the king 'as a scientific specimen right up
to and including the point at which he is laid in his coffin'. Why can't they,
she asked, 'put their secular narrative to one side?'

The narrative is certainly now no longer entirely secular. It's difficult
to know Philippa's feelings, as she sits at the front, smartly dressed in
dark blue, her face partly concealed by a wide-brimmed hat (throughout
the week she sets a sombre, stylish tone matched by few). 'If King Richard
were a Jew or a Muslim', she had said, 'the appropriate rites and
ceremonies would be observed without question.'[31]

For most of us, at least, the words are good. The presence of the coffin, and what it contains, is powerful. Already there is a sense that the day, and the week to come, will at last overwhelm the squabbles and ill-informed sniping. Set in Leicester, this is a landmark moment of universal significance.

Twenty people take it in turns to lay a white rose over the king's remains. They approach in groups: three archaeologists, three scientists, two further groups from the university, two groups from the Richard III Society and three royal descendants. When the bearers come to move the coffin to the waiting black hearse, Richard Buckley holds the rose-laden cushion before it is placed in the car. And off they go. The cortege – hearse, limousines and suite cars carrying Buckley, the Ibsens, the Bishop of Leicester, the University Chancellor and others – edges out to its first allotted stop in the Leicestershire countryside: the place where Richard III met his death.

In August 2013 I went to Bosworth to witness a battle. It was a sunny day. Glare flashed from curved and riveted steel, as men sweating in layers of bright-coloured leggings, undergarments, chain mail and plate armour laughed and joked. Decorated flags caught the breeze. Explosions interrupted the commentary, dutifully speaking up for 'good king Richard'.

Jo Appleby, Sarah Hainsworth and Turi King place roses on Richard III's coffin at the start of a day in which the University of Leicester passed the king's remains over to the Cathedral.

Musketeers in 2013 at the annual Bosworth Battlefield Anniversary Re-enactment on Ambion Hill. Gunshots fired in 1485 proved critical to locating the actual battlefield.

The effort and enthusiasm of thousands made this event. If it was entertainment and escapism, a hobby, a laugh and a get-together, it was also more than that: it would have had little meaning had not real armies met here over five centuries before, and men died; one in particular whose story caught Shakespeare's imagination. But where exactly had they fought?

The Battlefield Visitor Centre opened in 1976 there on Ambion Hill, because that was then the favoured location, fixed by an 18th-century antiquarian called William Hutton. Most had followed his reading of history and landscape, yet there were rival sites. By 2003 there were three, while Ambion had its new champion. The others were down by the Roman road in what would then have been flat, open country. The County Council, planning to refurbish its visitor centre, launched a hunt for the true field.

It took six years. Six years of lonely, intermittent searching across the cold mud, men patiently finding heaps of old iron with their metal detectors, but not the evidence they sought. Until, at ten o'clock in the morning on 1 March 2009, when the money had run out and the quest was to be abandoned, they found a lead ball. It was the size that convinced them: 3 cm, or a little over an inch across, it could only have been fired at Bosworth. The next week they found another one, and then another, which brought in a final year's grant. By the end of 2010 they had mapped the place where Bosworth was fought, even picking up a silver-gilt heraldic badge shaped like a boar with an arched back, lost by a man 'at least of knightly status'. That place was Fenn Lane.[32]

Six years later, some of those now waiting at Fenn Lane Farm have been active before dawn, posting photos of themselves online in medieval dress and armour, tending a ground beacon. The city is already several

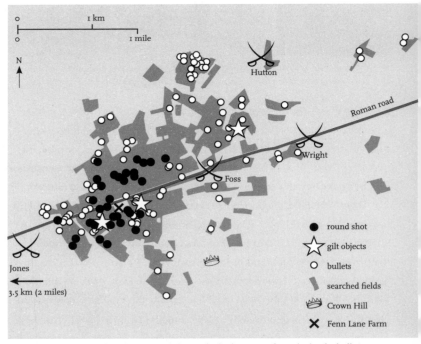

Bosworth revealed by archaeology. Round shot and gilt objects are from the battle, bullets are more recent; the area of 1485 combat is away from sites proposed by historians (further fields were surveyed to the east, and no round shot found). Data from Foard and Curry.

Silver-gilt boar from the Bosworth battle site; thousands of Richard III's followers owned heraldic badges, but only the highest status would have displayed precious metal (27 mm long).

hours into its preparations. Reporters, traffic wardens, the cathedral (whose early morning service was broadcast live by BBC Radio) and locals and visitors busy themselves and take up places. 'It's 7am', tweet the police with photos of four horses, 'and breakfast for Ariel, Lionheart, Bowron and Temple'; the officers and their mounts come from London.[33] The world watches. 'Never thought I'd say this but I wish I was in Leicester instead of Adelaide!' tweets Michele Walter.

When the cortege arrives at the farm, the serried formality of the university ceremony has dissipated. The farm has been tidied up, a screen hides parked vehicles and a bright temporary surface leads to two wooden trestles on the edge of a flat, green field. The cortege party is led out by a pair of men shouldering pikes, the sun glaring from their helmets and armour. A small crowd watches from a grassy bank as the coffin is shouldered onto its next station.

A breeze thins the Revd Hilary Surridge's voice. 'We are gathered here at Fenn Lane Farm,' she says, 'overlooking the area where archaeologists believe Richard III fell.' Rooks caw from bare trees. Heads of people out on the lane move behind trimmed hedges. Returned to the hearse, the king is now accompanied by a new, small box, made and engraved like the coffin, that holds three glass Kilner jars. They contain soil from Fotheringhay, Middleham and, freshly dug from his farm by Alf Oliver, Fenn Lane.

Back on the winding country roads the cortege is now led by two spectacular mounted knights, Tobias Capwell, originally from California, and now Curator of Arms and Armour at the London Wallace Collection, and Dominic Sewell, director of Historic Equitation Ltd. Both are active jousters. They will accompany the coffin up to the cathedral doors.

The mix of religion, ceremony, symbolism intentional and accidental, myth-making and myth-telling, continues and builds. The parade stops at Dadlington for a short service on the village green, watched by thousands (the relevance of Morris dancers is not immediately clear). Twenty minutes later it has reached Sutton Cheney, outside the church adopted by the Richard III Society, where their king is said to have prayed before Bosworth. The Revd Julia Hargreaves leads a short ceremony.[34]

The crowd swells. The cortege climbs Ambion Hill for another ceremony, led by the Bishop of Leicester at the Bosworth Battlefield Heritage Centre. This is a popular event: the ticket website had repeatedly crashed under international pressure as soon as it opened. Removed from the hearse, for the final ascent the coffin is pulled on a bier by members of the Leicestershire, Northamptonshire and Rutland army cadet corps. It is difficult to tell plans from spontaneity. People in black robes bearing flaming torches look like extras from a cheap horror movie. Medieval music is played. The Duke of Gloucester lights a beacon, which will be extinguished when Richard is buried. The Kyng's Guns – the artillery wing of the Wars of the Roses Federation, a re-enactment group – fire a 21-cannon salute. White roses are laid.

There is a short service in Market Bosworth, watched by 5,000 people. Thousands more cheer and throw roses as the cortege passes through Desford, site of perhaps the strangest tribute of the week, blankets of white roses made from recycled plastic bottles; there are said to be 5,929 blooms, the number of people reported missing in Leicestershire in a year.[35]

So, at about 4.30 in the afternoon, to Bow Bridge. The route through Leicester's streets is packed with expectant people, pushing against barriers: later the County Council estimates that more than 35,000 had lined the lanes and roads between the university and the cathedral. Where Richard III's body is said once to have entered the city in shame, naked and bloodied, his remains now are greeted by the City Mayor, the Lord Mayor and the Guild of Freemen. Every accessible space on St Augustine Road and its strimmed and tidied banks is filled with people. Shadows are lengthening, but it's still warm. There is laughter and cheer. More roses are thrown. To escape the crush, you need to go back along St Augustine where it continues from King Richards Road. There, off to the right, curves a silent backwater utterly free of people and traffic – Tudor Road.

The last stop before the cathedral is St Nicholas Church, said to be the oldest in Leicester and rising behind a large chunk of Roman city wall. After yet another short service, the coffin is transferred to a black gun carriage drawn by four dark horses. For the street parade they follow the black and the white horses of Capwell and Sewell, led and trailed by pairs of police horses, and police on luminous yellow motorbikes beyond. It does, now, have all the appearance and solemnity of a state funeral.

As the cathedral comes into view, the carriage passes between the new King Richard III Visitor Centre and Butler's restored statue. Moved by the City Council, the bronze king now looks out to Bosworth, his old grave to one side, his new to the other; for just a few days, both are empty. The cortege finally stops close to the end of New Street and its infamous car park.[36] Clumps of roses slip onto the pedestrianized street. Capwell and Sewell guard the cathedral doors. The Dean, David Monteith, and the Bishop of Leicester, the Rt Revd Tim Stevens, come out to greet the Duke of Gloucester. Then in their respectively secular and religious black and red robes, Richard Buckley and Stephen Foster, the university's Co-ordinating Chaplain, walk forward towards the waiting clerics. Buckley holds a black tube with gold detailing, like a smart Pringles packet. He shakes hands with the Dean.

They address each other, reading short speeches from scraps of paper. Mr Dean, says Buckley. We excavated the remains of Richard III 'not far from this spot', and it is now my duty, representing the University of Leicester, to transfer them into your custody, 'so that they may be buried with honour and dignity in Leicester Cathedral as befits a former king of England'.

The cathedral receives these remains for reburial, replies Monteith, taking the proffered licence. 'It is with a due sense of honour and responsibility, acting on behalf of the nation, that we provide this place of lasting sanctuary for the remains of the last English king to die in battle.'

And it is done. They bow, and move to enter the cathedral.

By now most of the congregation are in place. I have been watching the parade on a screen in St George's Chapel, filled with memorials to the men of the Royal Leicestershire Regiment; when the video feed first came on, the gun carriage was passing a McDonald's. The Dean and the Bishop enter and stand just to our right. 'We receive the remains of our brother Richard', says Monteith. 'We brought nothing into this world,' says Stevens, 'and we can carry nothing out.' The coffin enters. Outside, the crowd claps and cheers.

While the choir sing the Introit in Latin (this is a traditional Compline service, gentle, thoughtful and beautiful), the coffin is placed at the western end of the nave. The world watches. Thanks to the alterations, the church feels bigger inside, more open. These changes will serve more than the reburial.

For decades the authorities had struggled to overcome the impact of 1920s modifications to the building's 900-year-old layout. It was difficult to achieve a sense of people coming together in worship and prayer – 'particularly challenging in a city which is among the most diverse in the country'.[37] Richard III, and the growing number of visitors he was inspiring, unleashed the necessary funds for a radical re-ordering; with days to go, Leicester City Football Club announced a gift of £100,000 (nearly $150,000) towards the cathedral's successful £2.5 million appeal ($3.6 m).

Richard III's sarcophagus-like tomb, in the enclosed ambulatory beneath the cathedral spire, consists of Swaledale limestone from Yorkshire on a Kilkenny marble plinth.

The works were designed and managed by architects van Heyningen and Haward. They opened up the main space by moving modern seats and a screen, putting a new high altar in the sanctuary (made in alabaster by James Elliott), and siting a new royal tomb – where currently an empty, brick-lined vault awaits – immediately beyond in the ambulatory, under the spire. Kindersley's memorial stone has been moved to the visitor centre (which opened in July 2014, after £4.5 million of work), close to Richard's original grave. This has been preserved intact beneath the floor of its own chapel-like room. As you step on the glass cover, Mathew Morris's field drawing of the skeleton lights up, projected onto the dirt – in Duffy's words, 'My bones, scripted in light, upon cold soil, a human braille'.

At the cathedral's far east end is a new Chapel of Christ the King – 'Divine kingship speaking to earthly kingship', as David Monteith has put it. In addition there is new flooring, a new cathedra (the bishop's seat, a soaring thing in walnut and leather designed by Draisci Studio, London), new furniture and interpretation units, and new stained glass windows telling emotive stories in swathes of colour (by Tom Denny).

Jacquie Binns's pall, embroidered with figures from the University, the Council and the Cathedral, and the Richard III Society, concealed the coffin before burial.

I watch Jacquie Binns's black pall being lowered onto the coffin by four men, descendants of Peers of the Realm who fought in the Wars of the Roses. This playful embroidery captures the moment, with its parade of angels and 18 figures around the sides – a medieval knight, Queen Anne Neville, Appleby holding Richard's skull and Ashdown-Hill holding his own book – and a coat of arms on top. Foster places a 15th-century Bible from the university library on one end, and on the other Emma Chamberlain, a young Leicester Brownie dripping with badges, lowers a crown, supplied by Ashdown-Hill, within an embroidered ring of roses. Outside, the setting sun turns the sky red; I can hear horses' hooves scrape on stone. No British cathedral, I think, can have undergone such rapid and dramatic a transformation in modern times, architecturally and, separately, emotively.[38]

*

It was, you might say, the most successful six hours and 34 minutes in the history of archaeology. That, Mathew Morris told me, is how long – including a lunch break – it took to find Richard III.[39]

Proving his identity, however, demanded more time. The team used the delayed reburial to full advantage, publishing research about Richard III's diet, his appearance (probably blue eyes and fair hair), where he lived at different times, his scoliosis and how he died.[40]

Some of this might seem to tell us things we already knew; few were surprised to learn that late in life, the king had dined on luxury foods and enjoyed a lot of wine. However, different types of corroborative evidence are always valuable. For the archaeologists these discoveries were especially important. Well tried but continually developing techniques were, for the first time, being applied to a historical person whose identity and lifestyle are known. The chance to explore the sciences in this way was of great value.

Turi King and Kevin Schürer's research into the identity of Skeleton 1 was completed less than four months before the reburial. The large team concluded, conservatively, that the probability that the remains were *not* the king's was between less than 1 in 100,000 and 'much less' than 1 in a million. However, five men who, according to genealogy, should have shared the same Y-chromosome haplotype as Skeleton 1, turned out not to: somewhere in their ancestry at least two male births had been attributed to the wrong father. This was a useful reminder that, as Josephine Tey might have written, we should take nothing for granted.[41]

Yet one question remains. As presenter Jon Snow asked at the end of Channel 4's reburial coverage: 'Have the bones changed anything?'

This had been commonly asked by historians. 'But does it have any HISTORICAL significance?' tweeted Mary Beard, Professor of Classics at Cambridge University, on the day of the 2012 press conference. Paul Lay, editor of the magazine *History Today*, felt that 'this episode tells us little new about the past'. Michael Hicks, biographer of Richard III, can't even bring himself to accept that the king's grave has been found.[42]

In one important sense, the bones have changed a great deal. They have affected people's lives. Every organization involved, from the Richard III Society to the printer who freely supplied the Orders of Service to the cathedral, continue to benefit from the publicity – as did many who had no hand in it, such as the Midland Belles agency, offering 'scantily-clad escorts' for the reburial, or Soks4U, commemorating 'the events in 1487' (sic) with designer hosiery. The boost to the city and the university is almost incalculable.[43]

Many individuals, too, have been deeply affected, not least the Ricardians, archaeologists and scientists on the project. It will attract new students to history and archaeology, and stimulate new lines of research.[44] Especially, it has inspired a huge public.

After the grave's discovery was announced, annual visitors to Leicester Cathedral rose from 30,000 to 160,000. The cathedral had anticipated strong interest between the Reception of the Remains on the Sunday, and the Reinterment the following Thursday morning. Yet they were overwhelmed by the queues circling the city's streets – echoing those famously seen for the British Museum's Tutankhamun exhibition in 1972. They extended their opening hours. In two and a half days, over 20,000 people from around the world saw the pall-draped coffin.[45]

Richard's tomb will be a place of international concern and of continuing controversy. It will be a draw for modern pilgrimages, encouraging people to reflect on Shakespeare and history, on the nature of absolute power and the indignities of personal pain. Lucy Worsley, Chief Curator of Historic Royal Palaces, found 'something admirable, indeed noble, about the people arguing over Richard III. They're doers rather than naysayers, romantics rather than realists.'[46]

It was in this sense that Jon Snow answered his own question: yes, the bones *have* changed things. The reburial 'captured imaginations'.[47]

But there is another meaning to the question. This is the one that Snow's interviewees responded to, as they sat on a red sofa in a live studio tent in front of the cathedral, immediately after the coffin had been lowered into its grave. Has the discovery changed the way we read history?

Not really, said the resident historian, Helen Castor. And then a remarkable thing happened. After all the interviews, with Ricardians, archaeologists, historians, artists, people from the Church, the king's descendants and many others, it was an actor and storyteller – and screenwriter of dramas including Downton Abbey – who saw the point.

Something has changed, said Julian Fellowes. 'The whole idea that the hunchback, Richard the villain, was invented by the Tudors – we do [now] at least know he *was* hunch backed, and so there is some truth in that version.'

'We know he wasn't hunchbacked,' objected Castor, 'he had scoliosis and could fight extraordinarily well ...'

Fellowes: 'He was a very brave man ...'

Castor: '... despite that condition.'

Fellowes: '... but Shakespeare didn't make it up, that's the point. Nor did [Thomas] More.'[48]

We saw, in the Inquest (Act V), that wounds on Richard III's skeleton are atypical for medieval battle, but remarkably consistent with near-contemporary texts describing his death. These are colourful records traditionally regarded as unreliable witnesses. Ardent revisionists of Richard's dark reputation like to dismiss the texts' suggestions of humiliation. Yet here, surely, we see the ultimate achievement of Philippa Langley's quest. She brought in archaeology, and she changed history.

Over 25 years ago, Rosemary Horrox, a historian at the University of Cambridge, wrote a book about Richard III. It was praised for the insights she drew from previously obscure historical sources. She was troubled by More's simplistic portrayal of a hated, deformed king – the caricature that inspired Shakespeare's compelling stage tyrant, without which (as Gregory Doran, artistic director of the Royal Shakespeare Company, emailed Julian Fellowes as he sat on the cathedral sofa), 'The Richard III Society would not exist.'[49]

Just before the reburial, the British Academy in London hosted three lectures about 'the skeleton in the car park'. Horrox was one of the speakers. Most of the stuff from the dig, she said, relates to the king's appearance, which 'will not force a rethink of political history'. We knew Shakespeare exaggerated. But there was something else – the post-mortem mutilation.

She found this 'very negative, and very difficult to put into context'. Stabbing the corpse of a king was not something you would expect people to do. But if it was true, 'Richard III's desecration was a sign of anger, disgust and hatred, and needs to be taken seriously.' A censorious view of the king was *not* a subsequent Tudor creation.

Further insights came shortly after the reburial, in an article about Richard's scoliosis by Mary Ann Lund, a lecturer at the School of English in Leicester University.[50] She describes an extraordinary premonition of a scene during the Reception service in the cathedral. When Richard was crowned, his body, 'unarayed and unclothed' for anointing by the Archbishop, was hidden from the congregation by four Knights of the Garter, holding a pall. Lund writes how the king's physician would have both treated his spinal condition, and, along with his tailors and other attendants, forever concealed it from a wider public. Only at his death did it become known. At that very moment, an ogre may have been born.

When a typical scoliosis sufferer reaches to touch their toes, ribs attached to the spine rise up on one side of the back and create a bulge. The phenomenon is so clear, it is used as a medical diagnostic tool – the Adam's Forward Bend Test. With Richard's naked body doubled over a horse for the journey into Leicester, his 'rib hump', as it is known, would have been displayed for all to see. A hunched back, literally, may not have been a fabrication.[51]

We do not today connect physical conditions with states of mind or character. Philippa's project has gone some way to demystifying scoliosis – an important achievement in its own right. Channel 4 tracked down Dominic Smee, who suffers from the same form and degree of scolios as Richard III did. No one who saw the TV film, where Smee learnt to swing a sword and joust in full armour on horseback, can be in any doubt about the condition.[52] Scoliosis can result in uneven shoulders and hips, but it does not disable people. It does not make monsters.

Things were different in 1485. Almost certainly Richard would have expected to have been judged for his condition. It makes sense that only at his death did the secret get out. It also makes sense, in the culture of the times, that people who wished to besmirch his reputation would exploit the knowledge. It would play, too, to those who already disliked him. The post-mortem wounds and the texts, now strengthened by the full range of archaeological evidence, imply intended humiliation of an unpopular king.

Fellowes commended Philippa Langley for her 'extraordinary achievement, I mean almost mythical achievement, in persisting in what she believed to be true'. The new mixture of archaeology, science, history, art and more offers rich material for debate, research and understanding. Philippa's project changed, and promises to change, history. And she has done this not in a closeted academic library, but in full view of the world, followed by millions.

Yet the outcome, as I have described it here, is loss. In seeking to clear Richard's reputation, and to show him devoid of deformity, Philippa realized the opposite. Here is the ultimate test of the Ricardian boast to reject propaganda and myth. Who now will attempt to read history as it happened?[53]

Why are we all so pleased about finding a king, asked writer Hilary Mantel? 'Perhaps because the present', she answered herself, 'is paying some of the debt it owes to the past, and science has come to the aid of history. The king stripped by the victors has been reclothed in his true identity.'[54]

We should thank Shakespeare, said Doran and Fellowes, for animating Richard III's memory; for provoking debates which centuries later led to the rediscovery of his body and his proper burial.

We should thank Philippa Langley, and the archaeologists and scientists. And we should thank everyone in Leicester, who, when it came to it, gave a former king of England a spectacular, eccentric, polished, why-not-have-a-go and very modern British send off.

Richard III will not be forgotten.

NOTES

Prologue, pp. 6–8

1 P. Langley, 'This dig is not normal.'
   British Archaeology 131 (2013), 12.

Act I, pp. 9–32

1 Siemon 2009.
2 Such are the genealogical and political
   complexities of these times (to say nothing of the
   disagreements of interpretation), they can barely
   be contained within a single book, let alone a
   chapter. For what follows I found especially
   helpful Ross 1981, Hipshon 2011, Hicks 2010,
   Baldwin 2013 and Skidmore 2013. Wikipedia is
   useful for charting genealogies, though like any
   analytical source it needs to be read with caution
   and checked against others. The complexities are
   doubtless part of the reason why so many
   incidents appear different whenever they are
   described, sometimes significantly so.
3 And Hilary Mantel's Cromwell trilogy opens with
   Wolf Hall just 15 years after Bosworth: Cromwell
   was born in the year of the battle.
4 Ross 1981, 63.
5 Hipshon 2011, 3.
6 According to the Ordnance Survey, the centre of
   mainland England is at Lindley Hall Farm, 1.5 km
   east of Fenny Drayton.
7 The film is widely recognized as one of British
   cinema's great comic creations.
8 Gairdner 1878, 4–6.
9 Hipshon 2011, 10.
10 Wheatley 1891, 353–54.
11 First Battle of St Albans, 22 May 1455.
12 Skidmore 2013, 26.
13 Battle of Blore Heath, 23 September 1459. Most
   (but not all) of the battles and their locations
   are well documented in the English Heritage
   Register of Historic Battlefields, and the
   Battlefields Resource Centre maintained by
   the Battlefields Trust. As both organizations
   maintain websites with many relevant
   downloads, it seems appropriate to refer only to
   their main online sites, from which details of
   specific battles are easily found. The Battle of
   Blore Heath is described at English Heritage 2013
   and Battlefields Trust 2013.
14 Battle of Ludford Bridge, 12 October 1459.
   Battlefields Trust 2013; English Heritage 2013.
15 Hipshon 2011, 30. There is an appealing story
   that the king found Cecily and her children
   standing bravely at Ludlow's market cross, like
   figureheads on a storm-tossed ship. Sadly, a
   historian made this up (Kendall 1955, 37 and
   footnote 15, 517).
16 Battle of Northampton, 10 July 1460. Battlefields
   Trust 2013; English Heritage 2013.
17 Battle of Wakefield, 30 December 1460.
18 Henry VI part 3, act 1, scene 2, set in
   Sandal Castle.
19 Battle of Mortimer's Cross, 2 February 1461.
   Battlefields Trust 2013.
20 Second Battle of St Albans, 17 February 1461.
21 Battle of Towton, 29 March 1461. Battlefields Trust
   2013; English Heritage 2013; Fiorato *et al.* 2007.
22 Battle of Hedgeley Moor, 25 April 1464; Battle of
   Hexham, 15 May 1464.
23 Battle of Edgecote, 26 July 1469. Battlefields Trust
   2013.
24 Battle of Losecoat Field, 12 March 1470.
25 Battle of Barnet, 14 April 1471. Battlefields Trust
   2013; English Heritage 2013.
26 Battle of Tewkesbury, 4 May 1471. Battlefields
   Trust 2013; English Heritage 2013.
27 Clarence's death by wine was recorded by
   contemporary historians, but they do not
   implicate Richard, an addition by later writers
   adopted by Shakespeare in the opening act of
   Richard III.
28 The story that the boys' bodies were concealed by
   a heap of stones under a staircase inside the
   Tower (like all such details, first written down
   some time after the event) encouraged people to
   imagine that two child skeletons found in such a
   location in 1674 were those of the princes. The
   urn in which the bones were reinterred was
   opened in 1933 (Tanner and Wright 1935), and the
   evidence then published reconsidered by
   Molleson (1987). Molleson (perforce like almost
   all commentators, using secondhand
   observations) judged the remains to be consistent
   with what we might expect to see if they were of
   the two princes: the individuals both seem to be
   male, there are indications that they were related,
   and their approximate ages were such that if they
   were the princes (with known birth dates), they
   would most likely have both died in 1484. She
   also noted that the younger boy was unusually tall
   for his age, as would befit a son of Edward IV;
   and that they were related to Anne Mowbray
   (whose known remains had recently been
   analysed: Warwick 1986; Watson 2013), the
   young, related wife of Prince Richard.
29 Ross 1981, 128–32; Hipshon 2011, 167.

30 Hipshon 2011, 155.

31 Not the Fosse Way (*pace* Hammond 2010, 72), a major Roman route driving southeast from Leicester that follows the current Narborough Road out of the city (not Fosse Road).

Act II, Scene 1, pp. 34–55

1 The 18th-century Watt's Causeway was renamed King Richard's Road around this time, a grammatically punctilious if descriptively optimistic appellation for a route over a branching river which regularly flooded into an area downhill of the town's open sewers (an ambitious sewerage scheme was proposed by Joseph Bazalgette, saviour of London's far worse situation, in the 1850s, but rejected by Leicester's leaders); the road was described as a 'disgraceful ... quagmire' in December 1869 (Correspondence: King Richard's-Road, *Leicester Chronicle* 1 January 1870).

2 The Old Bow Bridge, Leicester, *Illustrated London News* 5 February 1861; Johnson 1906, 148; Billson 1920, 182. A visitor to Leicester around 1675 noted, 'Here is also an old bridge over the river which they call Richard III's bridge by which some say he is buried' (McKinley 1958, 153).

3 Some historians (e.g. Baldwin 2013, 225; Hammond 2010, 71) guess that Richard in fact probably stayed at the castle, but this may have been a case of more room at the inn (for Richard's large entourage). On the inn and the bed, see also Billson 1920, chapter 12; Ashdown-Hill 2013, chapter 7; and Baldwin 2013, 224–26.

4 In 1611 the coffin was in use as a horse trough, and was later spotted by pioneering travel writer Celia Fiennes at the (non-existent) Greyhound Inn; soon it was at the White Horse, and by 1758 it had gone, reportedly broken up (Baldwin 1986, 22–23). In the 1980s a new candidate was found in Earl Shilton, where it had been set up as a garden feature in 1903, improving on its former use as another drinking trough in Leicester. It was given to the Bosworth Battlefield Centre in 2009. 'Has Reg [Colver] found the discarded coffin of Richard III?', asked BBC-TV's One Show. 'The archaeologists can't be sure.' (bbc.co.uk/blogs/theoneshow/onepassions/2008/11/is-this-the-coffin-of-richard.html). The tradition continues. In October 2013 a scrap of weathered fabric said to have come from Henry VII's battle standard at Bosworth was auctioned for £3,800; curiously, an inscription in the 19th-century frame describes it as having come from Richard's standard.

5 Local History: The old Bow Bridge, *Leicester Chronicle* 12 January 1861.

6 The original is Old French (in modern French, *loyauté me lie*), and often written '*Loyaulte me lie*'; but not here – at least, not until the reburial ceremony in 2015, when the bridge was spruced up and a careful hand outlined the lettering in black, squeezing 'UL' over the embossed 'U'. York's Lendal Bridge, which features a similar painted cast iron parapet with white roses and gold lions, is exactly contemporary.

7 Correspondence: The new Bow Bridge, *Leicester Chronicle* 2 May 1863; Correspondence: The proposed inscription on the new Bow Bridge, *Leicester Chronicle* 16 May 1863.

8 Discovery of a skeleton near the Bow Bridge, *Leicester Chronicle* 31 May 1862.

9 Correspondence: On the human skeleton in the bed of the Soar, near Bow Bridge, *Leicester Chronicle* 7 June 1862.

10 The four friaries were Franciscan (Grey Friars, founded before 1230), Dominican (Black Friars, founded before 1284), Augustinian (White Friars, founded before 1304) and the Penitence of Jesus Christ (Friars of the Sack), founded before 1283. The latter had disappeared before 1295, but the others all survived to be seized and destroyed by Henry VIII in 1538. See Hoskins and McKinley 1954, 33–35.

11 One skull is still in the possession of Henry Goddard's descendants, and said to have been found by this Victorian Leicester architect while he was working on Bow Bridge; it was radiocarbon dated in 1983, and found to be 9th century or Anglo-Saxon – six hundred years older than Richard III (A. Wakelin, Is there a king under this bridge? *Leicester Mercury* 8 October 2002). The county heritage environment record notes two skulls, one found during the construction of the Great Central Railway in 1895, the other near Bath Lane in 1896, that could have come from the Dominican or Augustinian friaries. Throughout the next century Leicester hung on to the idea that the king's remains might be found. In one account a lead coffin and a skeleton were dug up when the School of Art and Technology was extended at the site of the church of St Mary of the Blessed Annunciation, in the Newarke; the skull exhibited 'a receding forehead and projecting jaw,' said the college principal, 'attributes of King Richard' (King Richard III, supposed discovery of his skeleton, *Bath Weekly Chronicle & Herald* 7 September 1935). Thanks to Chris Wardle, City

Archaeologist, for help with these stories.

12 Cawthorne 2007.

13 'It is a relaxed book, and though it does contain a lot of miscellaneous information, its function is simply to entertain.' Cottrell 1957.

14 Derrick 2005.

15 Mellor and Pearce 1981, 4.

16 The society conducts research into the world of Richard III, publishes a journal, the *Ricardian*, organizes conferences and has an impressive website, at http://www.richardiii.net.

17 In my old Penguin copy (Tey 1951), Cecily Neville's name seems to be spelled randomly Cicely or Cecily, suggesting perhaps a knowing wink from the author, whose real name was Elizabeth Mackintosh. Peter Hitchens has described the book as 'one of the most important ... ever written', having read which 'you will never again believe anything that you are told until you have checked it personally' (A Good Read, BBC Radio 4, 30 October 2012). Who could argue with such a sentiment?

18 The curiously unforgettable tambourine suggestion is Colin Hyde's, in a video that tours Leicester's Richard III-associated sites: http://www.le.ac.uk/richardiii/multimedia/videos/lookatleicester.html.

19 Plans to celebrate Richard III at the cathedral began in the 1960s; a statue was designed but never made. The eventual memorial slab was made in 1980 by David Kindersley, who had been apprenticed to Eric Gill and died in 1995. His son Peter co-founded the publisher Dorling Kindersley.

20 Try searching Richard III in Google trends; for possibly obvious reasons, before that date there had been hardly any news searches at all.

21 Kendall 1955, 428–29.

22 J. McManaway, In defense of a king, *New York Times Book Review* 26 August 1956; Kendall 1955, 11.

23 Jones 2002. In a famous incident at Bosworth field, the victorious Henry dons Richard's lost crown, retrieved from a thorn bush. Richard is described as wearing a crown in several historical sources, and Henry is given it. From these simple observations, Jones conjures three separate scenes: one before the battlefield, in which the king sports his coronation crown in a symbolically laden ceremony, which Jones uses to support a case that Richard had plenty of time and was thus well organized (2002, 23–24); one when Richard leaves Leicester, and a third when he actually fights, in both of which he wears 'a

gold circlet welded to his helmet', a practical badge of royalty in battle – this was 'leadership from the front' (2002, 163–64). See also Hammond 2010, 134–36. Joining in the spirit perhaps a little too enthusiastically, the publisher boasts a quote on the back of my 2010 paperback edition that is not quite what it seems. In 'an extraordinary shift ... puts this key English battle over the county line THE GUARDIAN' (full quote), the first three words are the book's author's, and the rest is an altered extract from the paper's headline – to a news story, not a review.

Act II, Scene 2, pp. 56–76

1 The official website of the British monarchy (http://www.royal.gov.uk) later removed that statement, but as of October 2013 nothing had replaced it (J. Russell, Rewriting history through DNA, 2013, *The Legal Genealogist*). Although, as we shall see, evidence had long been in print suggesting Richard III's grave lay undisturbed inside the city walls, many historians repeated contrary stories. For example, Ross (1981, 226) says, 'the bones were thrown out and the coffin became a horse-trough outside the White Horse Inn'; Seward (1997, 256) that 'during the Dissolution of the Monasteries ... Richard's bones were dug up and thrown into the River Soar. For many years a coffin said to have been his was used as a horses' drinking trough'; Jones (2002, 206) that 'At the dissolution of the monasteries Richard's body disappeared. No-one knows its final resting place'; and Hammond (2010, 106) that 'The tomb was destroyed and the body perhaps thrown into the river Soar during the Reformation. All trace of the tomb has vanished'.

2 Interview with Ashdown-Hill by A. Fox, March 2013, at http://www.lostincastles.com, since deleted.

3 The rather confused history of the remains and their excavations was described by Paul de Win in 2003, published in English as De Win 2005.

4 C. Mills, Canadian family's DNA helps identify King Richard III's remains, *Toronto Star* 4 February 2013; J. Ashdown-Hill, The search for Richard III, talk at a conference organized by the Richard III Society, 2 March 2013 (http://www.richardiii.net/leicester_conference.php#).

5 Ashdown-Hill 2006. See also Ashdown-Hill 2013, chapters 14–15.

6 Soon after this, he helped the Richard III Society

fix its counter-plaque on the wall beside the stone one pictured prominently on the BBC web page. J. Ashdown-Hill, The fate of Richard III's body, 2004, BBC website.

7 John Tate, lead author of the dig report, seems to have found it quite interesting: Tate 2007.

8 Ashdown-Hill, The search for Richard III, March 2013, https://www.youtube.com/watch?v=6YGCT kvyr9K. It could not have helped that Time Team presenter Sir Tony Robinson had made a film in which he said Richard's body had been dug up and thrown into the River Soar. *Fact or Fiction: Richard III*, a Spire Films production for Channel 4, first broadcast 3 January 2004.

9 Ashdown-Hill, as note above. ULAS says it has no record of communications from him at this date.

10 Ashdown-Hill 2010, 128 and plate 29.

11 Carson *et al.* 2014, 44.

12 Buckley *et al.* 2013, 521.

13 Billson 1920, 180; Buckley *et al.* 2013, 521; Foard and Curry 2013, 66.

14 Baldwin 1986, 21.

15 Ashdown-Hill (2013, chapter 11) details the tomb's manufacture in Nottingham. An apparent transcription of a Latin epitaph shows it commemorated Henry's generosity and, depending on whose translation you prefer, said Richard 'held the British Kingdoms in trust' (Ashdown-Hill 2013, 102) or 'By trust betray'd ... to the Kingdom came' (Hackett 1757, 92).

16 Buckley *et al.* 2013, 530.

17 Billson 1920, 185–86; the transcript of Speed's text is from Ashdown-Hill 2013, Appendix 4.

18 Throsby 1791, 288–89; his name is spoken today as Throwsby. Strange (1975, 6) noted that John Wycliffe's bones really had been disinterred and thrown into a river (after burning), in Lutterworth, 13 miles south of Leicester, in 1425.

19 Billson 1920, 182–83; Baldwin 1986, 22. Herrick was born very shortly after the Dissolution; as Billson notes, one might have expected his parents to have passed on a story as dramatic as that of Richard's exhumation if it had occurred, even if he himself had not witnessed it. David Baldwin made the same point more recently (King's body 'lying under city centre', *Daily Telegraph* 4 October 1993).

20 Billson 1920, 183; http://gawainsmum. wordpress.com/page/2 and Strange 1975; J. Hughes, A king's bones lie beneath a city car park, *Leicester Mercury* 16 July 1965; Baldwin 1986, 24, where he made a remarkably successful stab at predicting the actual location of the grave (and see Baldwin 2013, 221–24); Foss 1998, 52.

Baldwin, again, in 2002: 'It is my opinion that [Richard III] is still there, somewhere under those well trodden streets towards St Martins' (Is there a king under this bridge? *Leicester Mercury* 8 October 2002).

21 Google Street View photographed this route on a bright day in October 2012. I recommend starting at the cathedral this year, and following round as I describe in the text – search for Peacock Lane Leicester in Google Map. As New Street bends to the right, you leave the shade of the narrow passage to see the cathedral spire framed ahead of you in the sun. A car park opens up on the left. Continue to the end of that, then face round to the right. You can now see a smaller car park, at the back of which are some temporary wire barriers and, if you look closely, a camera crew. They are filming beside the site of Richard III's grave. Most of the excavation trench has been refilled, but is there still open; the grave itself is down below the kink in the near side of the trench. Continue back to St Martins, turn right and then round to the right where the sun shines across the street. New black tarmac in the school playground marks the entirely backfilled and last of the three 2012 excavation trenches. The Council was even then negotiating to buy the old school for its new visitor centre. Google Street View 2014, looking down St Martins from the end of New Street, shows you the newly installed statue of Richard III, under a tree.

22 See Billson 1920, 183–84.

23 Throsby 1789, 51.

24 Throsby 1791, 291.

25 Morris and Buckley 2013, 31.

26 The Record Office for Leicestershire, Leicester & Rutland. Holding priceless archives in towns and cities across the country, curated by people familiar with the places they document and available to be consulted by anyone, record offices, along with heritage and environment records which collate archaeological evidence, are the heart and lungs of Britain's history. Occasionally it is necessary to remind cash-starved authorities how much these records, like museums, matter to their citizens.

27 Leicestershire County Council set up there in custom-built offices in 1936; in 1967 the staff moved out into a futuristic and lovely County Hall built on former farmland west of the city (with a fine concrete mural by Anthony Holloway depicting the River Soar), and Leicester City Council moved in, with what is now their Health and Social Care department.

Notes

Act II, Scene 3, pp. 77–98

1 The words are Allison Pearson's (Me, a sex god? Spooks star Richard Armitage on his army of female fans, *Daily Mail* 25 January 2010). In 2009 he beat Johnny Depp to top place as the Romantic Novelists' Association's 'Sexiest thing on two legs'.

2 The proposed tomb for King Richard III, http://www.richardiii.net/whats_new.php#team.

3 Carson 2013. Her publisher comments that she examines 'the events of [Richard III's] reign as they actually happened, based on reports in the original sources ... In the process Carson dares to investigate areas where historians fear to tread, and raises many controversial questions.'

4 A. Carson and P. Langley, The Greyfriars Dig – A new Richard III, March 2013, http://www.youtube.com/watch?v=f6oCyRdCXls#at=11.

5 For the quotation and details of all the references, see Hipshon 2011, 217–27. Alternative histories of Richard III are well reviewed by Pollard (1991, chapter 8) and Hipshon (2011, chapter 9), the former with good illustrations, noting how dozens of modern novels have taken up the cause of a goodly king.

6 R. Dallek, The medical ordeals of JFK, *The Atlantic* December 2002. To accommodate the pain Kennedy wore 'a "corset-type thing" and [slept] with a plywood board under his mattress'; out of public sight, he would sometimes walk with crutches. He suffered from osteoporosis and degeneration of his lower back, to counter which a metal plate was inserted but later removed in a second operation. Dallek even suggests that it was the back brace that held Kennedy erect and in the path of the fatal bullet.

7 R. Dallek, Why do we admire a president who did so little? *Salon* 20 January 2011.

8 Curiously, after I had written the above, I discovered that Richard Armitage had tweeted from the *Hobbit* movie set in March 2013 (responding to the question, if you could have dinner with any three people, real or fictional, who would they be?), 'Richard III, John F. Kennedy, and Ian McKellen.' McKellen may have been invited as a fellow actor playing Gandalf or as a performer of a famous Shakespearean Richard III – or perhaps both. One theory about Lee Harvey Oswald, JFK's killer, was that he was a substituted Russian spy, leading to the excavation of his grave in 1981 and the demonstration, largely on the basis of the teeth, that Oswald was Oswald. He was a model traitor, a US Marine who had defected to the Soviet Union, bringing to mind Richard III's

battlefield cry of 'Treason, treason, treason!'

9 R. A. Griffiths in Ross 1981, xi–xxviii.

10 Ashdown-Hill 2013, 22.

11 See Hunt 2011 (DBA) and Carson *et al.* 2014, Appendix 5 (WSI).

12 Morris *et al.* 2011.

13 See note 4 above.

14 Austrums 2011.

15 See note 4 above.

16 Leicester City Council plans to close museums as part of cutbacks, *Leicester Mercury* 26 January 2011.

17 Langley 2012a.

18 Langley 2012b.

19 K. Catcheside, Communication, reputation and fees: Q&A with Leicester's Richard Taylor, *Guardian Professional*, 14 March 2011.

20 Ashdown-Hill is not happy with the commemorative service at Sutton Cheney. The notion that Richard III attended mass there is, he says, an 'unfortunate and quite incredible 20th-century invention ... There is certainly no contemporary authority for this nonsense', which, following Foss (1998, 40 and footnote 67), he ascribes to the early days of the Richard III Society in the 1920s (2010, 76).

Act III, Scene 1, pp. 100–121

1 There is in fact a good view from the Holiday Inn – 'Henry Tudor's camp' in the original – from high bedrooms on the south side of which you can see St Augustine Road and the park where Richard's statue was, sweep round across town where Richard's body would have been carried and displayed, and find the car park backed by the distinctive Victorian roof-line of the old school, site of the new visitor centre.

2 It was slight wonder that some journalists left a little confused. The *Daily Telegraph* reported (Is Richard III 'buried under council car park'? 24 August 2013) that the story that the king's body had been thrown in the River Soar could be traced back to a 17th-century map maker called 'John Speedie'; perhaps he should have left his car in the parking lot.

3 Alderman Newton's Boys' School was opened in 1784 with money left by Gabriel Newton (who, 'in spite of the many unpaid debts of his clients and relations ... died an extremely prosperous man'). It moved to St Martins in 1864 and was enlarged in the 1880s and 1890s. It was taken over by the Local Education Authority in 1907, becoming Leicester Grammar School. See Place 1960.

1   For a comprehensive introduction to this field, covering the nature of the evidence, cross-cultural approaches to death, and the ethics and politics of burial archaeology, see Tarlow and Stutz 2013; useful in a specifically British context is Giesen 2013. Sarah Tarlow is a professor of archaeology at the University of Leicester. As I was writing this book, she and Matthew Beamish, an archaeologist with ULAS who did not work at the Greyfriars site, wrote to the *Independent* on their concerns about the display of a photo of a severed human head in an art exhibition (Hirst photo betrays the dead, 13 July 2013). Picked up by art critic Jonathan Jones, the issue was debated at length online (Don't lose your head over Hirst, *Guardian* 17 July 2013); see also S. Tarlow, Damien Hirst insults the dignity of the dead, *The Conversation*.

2   See Parker Pearson, M., Pitts, M. and Sayer, D. 2013. Changes in policy for excavating human remains in England and Wales, in Giesen 2013, 148–57.

3   St George's Chapel, Windsor (Berkshire), is the burial place of Richard III's older brother Edward IV, and of Edward's predecessor Henry VI, whom Richard himself arranged to be reburied there in 1484. Henry's vault was opened in 1910, revealing the fragmentary remains of 'a fairly strong man, aged between 45 and 55' (T. Tatton-Brown, Letters: What Richard did with Henry's bones, *Times* 23 March 2013).

4   Horrible Histories is an award-winning comedy series made for the BBC that plays with history in a sometimes penetratingly informative way. One of Farnaby's best known characters is Death, who checks historical figures into the afterlife after hearing the strange ways in which they died, among them Richard I (but not III). My daughter frequently complains how boring archaeology is, but she loves Horrible Histories.

5   *Richard III: The King in the Car Park*, Darlow Smithson Productions for Channel 4, first broadcast 4 February 2013. The DSP scenes described in this chapter come from this film, though sequences in the second film also helped to reconstruct events: *Richard III: The Unseen Story*, DSP for More 4, first broadcast 27 February 2013. Film shot by Carl Vivian for the University of Leicester also proved critical to understanding, with, of course, discussions with people who were there.

6   *Richard III: The King in the Car Park.*

7   S. McGinty, How Richard III was discovered by an ex-Scotsman employee, *Scotsman* 6 February 2013.

8   In the Channel 4 films *Richard III: The King in the Car Park*, and *Richard III: The Unseen Story*, it might look as if the public were watching and filming the excavation of Trench 1. That is an illusion of editing.

9   DSP's Simon Young later gave as one of his three 'tricks of the trade' – a few days before the public announcement of Skeleton 1's identity and the first broadcast of the film he executive produced – 'Never give up – but never guarantee a commissioner that you'll find the bones of Richard III' (Richard III: The King in the Car Park, C4, *Broadcast* 31 January 2013).

10 Carter and Mace 1923, 95–96.

11 T. G. H. James, Howard Carter: The Path to Tutankhamun, Kegan Paul, London 1992 (reprinted 2001 Tauris Parke, London), 478.

12 That was certainly Thomas Hoving's view. The one-time head of the New York Metropolitan Museum of Art (who described his own collecting style as 'piracy') found 'discrepancies' between Carter's text and the many photos taken at the time, leading him to call Carter's entire published account 'a lie' (*Tutankhamun: The Untold Story*, New York: Simon and Schuster 1978, 89). Another theory has it that Carter entered the tomb years before he said he had found it, and 'unearthed a secret so potentially damaging to world order that a string of murders were instigated to ensure the truth never saw the light of day' (G. O'Farrell, The Tutankhamun Deception, London: Sidgwick and Jackson 2001, 93). For the proper record see *Tutankhamun: Anatomy of an Excavation. Howard Carter's Diaries and Journals*, Griffith Institute, Oxford, at http://www.griffith.ox.ac.uk/gri/4sea1not.html. I have no doubt that Skeleton 1's excavation will inspire conspiracy theorists to elaborate heights, but the site record will make it hard for them to be taken seriously.

13 These words are transcribed mainly from Carl Vivian's unedited sequence, from which we realize, even listening to what was truly said, that the exchanges were being skilfully manipulated.

14 Not least DSP. Executive producer Simon Young, then in France, received a text from the location director: 'You're not going to believe this folks, but the skeleton in Trench 1 is a male hunchback with head injuries ... you couldn't make this up!' (Richard III: The King in the Car Park, C4, *Broadcast* 31 January 2013). Channel 4 finally commissioned the film after a press conference a week later, when it became obvious that if *they* didn't buy it, somebody else would. Persuading

broadcasters to be adventurous with archaeology has never been easy.

15 A. Carson and P. Langley, The Greyfriars Dig – A new Richard III, The 'Looking for Richard Project', March 2013.

Act IV, pp. 149–72

1 When the dig began, the budget had been £33,000, of which the Richard III Society had contributed a little over half. By 31 December costs stood at £142,000, the additional funding coming from the university, which by then was supporting 80% of the entire project. See http://www2.le.ac.uk/news/blog/2013/february/the-search-for-richard-iii-statement-of-costs-up-to-31.12.12.

2 Press Conference 12 September 2012, http://www.youtube.com/watch?v=k8mk1Kcgyho.

3 Toulmin Smith 1907, 17. From the context, it seems likely that Leland did not see their tombs, either because he failed to visit the Greyfriars site, or because they were no longer there.

4 State Funeral for Richard III, Early Day Motion 527 tabled 13 September 2012 by Chris Skidmore, M.P.; Burial of King Richard the III at a Catholic Burial Site, e-petition created 13 September 2012 by Thomas McLean; Ben Macintyre, Queen rejects royal place of rest for Richard III's troubled spirit, Times 15 September 2012; Richard III to be Re-interred at York Minster, e-petition created 24 September 2012 by Mark Cousins.

5 P. Warzynski, Richard III dig: What Leicester pupils think about the Greyfriars discovery, Leicester Mercury 19 September 2012; M. Biddle, Times 9 September 2013; P. Turnbull, Guardian 17 September 2012.

6 A month later, Lin Foxhall felt she had to ask for 'restraint in discussions about ... where the remains ought to be buried ... As archaeologists we go where the evidence takes us, but we have not yet proven that these remains are Richard III, because we do not yet have the evidence to do so' (University of Leicester press release, 26 October 2012). The day before, 'Richard III' was the name given to a debate in Parliament. Arguing in the House of Commons over the king's 'mortal remains', said Hugh Bayley, Labour MP for York Central, 'is more like medieval cathedrals fighting over saints' relics. I do not think it is appropriate'.

7 Stirland 2000.

8 The figure of 206 is a conventional number that relies on counting in a particular way; we might, for example, think of the skull as one big bone, but it figures as 21, including six curving plates which protect the brain, and in older life more or less fuse together. For general archaeological study of human remains see Mays 2010 and Roberts 2009.

9 The R was about 5 m (15 ft) north of the grave. Its origins had seemed mysterious to some, so I can exclusively reveal that it was painted for Age Concern. The whole park was marked out for cars for council staff and for others renting spaces, including – as it was then – Leicester Age Concern, which had offices facing St Martins at the north end. AGE CONCERN was painted across the corner, and one of the spaces was singled out with an R (for this information I thank Liza Kozlowski, Admin Manager and PA to the Executive Director of Age UK Leicester Shire & Rutland).

10 A huge backfilled pit, whose excavation at some time in the past had removed the northwest corner of the choir and what might have been the church walking-place, reached close to Richard III's head, leaving the grave isolated and suggesting that something was in the way; even a wall of the outbuilding above came down to within 9 cm of the knees. This is a topic of continuing research. News, British Archaeology 133 (2013), 6–7.

11 Shona Campbell, Consultant Radiologist at the UHL Trust, on Inside Health, BBC Radio 4, 6 February 2013.

12 When I first wrote this chapter, the information in what follows about Skeleton 1 came mostly from Buckley et al. 2013, and conversations with members of the Leicester team. The paperback benefits also from Appleby et al. 2014, which allowed me to update a few details. For more on the other graves, see British Archaeology 142 (2015), 9.

13 It was medieval practice to bury priests with their feet to the west (continuing, perhaps, the privileged relationship with God they had in life).

14 Medieval European adults were only a little shorter than their modern counterparts. A study of 2,800 skeletons ranging from the 10th to 19th centuries from a redundant church in Barton-upon-Humber, Lincolnshire, revealed that typical medieval men were 5 ft 7 in. (171 cm) and women 5 ft 2 in. (158 cm) tall, both 2 in. (5 cm) shorter than today. S. Mays, A community united in church, British Archaeology 96 (2007), 40–41.

15 M. H. Young, Richard III doubts, Times 14 September 2013. I quote this as an illustration, from a man with a scientific training, of something commonly expressed with less logic and courtesy: that the archaeologists and other scientists researching Richard III's burial and

remains did not consult with each other or anyone else, and generally had no idea what they were doing. Many people seem to lack a basic understanding of how academic research works, making it difficult for them to follow debates about everything from where we park our cars to climate change, which must be seen as a failing in our education system.

16 New Richard III 3D printed skull presented to Guildhall exhibition, http://www.lboro.ac.uk/news-events/news/2013/june/114newskull.html.

17 Tobias Capwell has described how Richard III's personal armourer (whom he calls a 'biomechanic') could have fitted armour to accommodate the asymmetric torso while minimizing visual signs of this, which would have been further concealed by a loose surcoat bearing the royal arms – thus his back condition could have been entirely hidden on the battlefield. T. Capwell, Adapting Richard III's armour, talk at a conference organized by the Richard III Society, 2 March 2013, http://www.youtube.com/watch?v=8Sn9FoVHTjY.

18 Mitchell *et al.* 2013.

19 Things get a little more complex in Europe once tropical foods become commonplace, but that was not, quite, an issue in 1485. Renfrew and Bahn 2012, 302–04.

20 Hamilton and Bronk Ramsey 2013; this 95% probability result supersedes that published in Buckley *et al.* 2013.

Act V, pp. 173–200

1 See Act I and Hicks 2010.

2 Ross 1981, 140.

3 Foard and Curry 2013, 60–61, 100–01.

4 The Towton grave is described in Fiorato *et al.* 2007, the wounds in particular by S. Novak, Battle-related trauma, 90–102.

5 Hipshon 2011, 52; A. Boardman 2007, The historical background to the battle and the documentary evidence, in Fiorato *et al.* 2007, 15–28.

6 Foard and Curry 2013, 148.

7 In the descriptions that follow, bodies are described from the perspective of the individual not the viewer, so, for example, 'right arm' might refer to Skeleton 1's right arm, 'on the left', his left side, etc.

8 I have been able to update details in what follows with the paper on perimortem trauma, published online in September 2014: Appleby *et al.* 2015.

9 *Richard III: The Unseen Story*, DSP 2013.

10 Langley and Jones 2013, 175, 272.

11 Mancini 1969, 99.

12 Ackroyd 1998, 155–59. See Act I.

13 J. Pincott, What's in a face? *Psychology Today* 5 November 2012.

14 Prag and Neave 1997; Wilkinson 2004; Wilkinson and Rynn 2012.

15 C. Wilkinson, Craniofacial analysis of Richard III, talk at a conference organized by the Richard III Society, 2 March 2013, http://www.youtube.com/watch?v=1uwsBvebPP0. Wilkinson 2013.

16 The 18th-century British artist began by studying human anatomy, but moved to horses after 18 months of intensive dissection and recording.

17 As part of a continuing major project at the National Portrait Gallery, Making Art in Tudor Britain, Catherine Daunt and Sally Marriott have analysed the gallery's Richard III portrait, which they ascribe to the late 1580s or 90s; the tree that supplied the wooden boards is estimated to have been felled after 1577. The king's outlines are 'more or less identical' to those in the Royal Collection portrait, the effect, they suggest, of copying from a standard pattern. See http://www.npg.org.uk/research/programmes/making-art-in-tudor-britain.php and http://www.youtube.com/watch?v=rjoXsvbI578.

18 Tudor-Craig 1973, 80.

19 More left two unfinished versions of his history, one in English, one in Latin; in the latter he does not specify which is the higher shoulder (Knight and Lund 2013). It may be, as most believe, that the older Society of Antiquaries portrait's shoulders are also even (Gaimster *et al.* 2007, 84–85). Full analyses of these paintings have yet to be published, so it is difficult to know what to make of reported dendrochronological studies (attempts to age them by looking at growth rings in the wood) or X-rays. To my uneducated eye, the X-ray images of the Antiquaries portrait (preserved with reports in the Society's archives) do not prove a consciously altered shoulder. The 1954 X-ray shows nothing. The 2007 X-ray shows an apparently augmented shoulder, but all the images (including a UV image made in 2007) reveal a painting that has been badly damaged, and unskilfully restored and overpainted. It seems quite possible that a raised shoulder resulted from a restorer's attempt to make a botched arm have some semblance of being attached to the body (if so, success was elusive). See J. Fletcher, 1974, Tree ring dates for some panel paintings in England, *The Burlington*

Notes

Magazine 854 (May 1974), 250–58.

20 Jones 2002, 37.

21 Carson 2013, 330ff. Of course, if a writer is swayed by one monarch to say unpleasant things about his predecessor, there is no reason why he should not have been similarly encouraged to flatter the other king when he was alive. If we really seek a 'balanced view', we need to treat all sources as if they were in quotation marks, not just those we don't like.

22 Tudor-Craig 1973, 93. Catherine Daunt tells me that in their unpublished study of the Royal Collection picture, she and Marriott found that while 'it is clear that the shoulder line has been altered at an early stage [becoming the prototype for later portraits], there was no evidence that any other changes, such as a narrowing of the eyes, had been made'.

23 Tudor-Craig 1973, 80.

24 For the arm, Ross 1981, 81–2, and the leg, Knight and Lund 2013, who suggest Shakespeare got the idea from More's reference to 'unequal and unformed limbs'. 'As far as I know,' says Siemon (2009, 3), 'the limp begins with Shakespeare'; as most did until now, Siemon traced Richard's 'spinal curvature' to More (2009, 5).

25 Baldwin 1986, 120; Knight and Lund 2013. The dog in the ditch reference noted earlier, quoted at a court case in York in 1491, also contains the first known mention of Richard III's 'crookback'; the speaker was accused of slander, and retracted the description of an ignominious burial, but 'crookback' seems to have gone unchallenged (Tudor-Craig 1973, 80). Knight and Lund (2013) argue that Shakespeare's introduction of 'bunch-backed', indicating a hump rather than just a raised shoulder, derived from a linguistic misunderstanding of 'crookback', a crooked or twisted back. But see Epilogue.

26 Baldwin 1986, 123–24; Knight and Lund 2013.

27 Tudor-Craig 1973, 80; Ross 1981, 140.

28 Ashdown-Hill 2010, 83–85; Baldwin 2013, 212–13, 234; Heywood 1829, 47; Hipshon 2011, 183; Morris and Buckley 2013, 54–55; Ross 1981, 224–25; Seward 1997, 253; Skidmore 2013, 307–10, 317–18; Ruth E Richardson (2014) at http://kingrichardinleicester.com/killed-king-richard-iii.

29 Ashdown-Hill 2006; see Act II Scene 2. For Richard III's DNA to be 'alive and well' in the 21st century would in fact require a miracle of medieval proportions – even the most ardent Ricardian accepts, I think, that the king (and his DNA) died in 1485. His mtDNA is not, in Ashdown-Hill's words, 'still to be found today': Joy Ibsen's mtDNA was a copy of her mother's, which had been copied from her mother's, and so on back to Richard III's sister, whose mtDNA had been copied from her mother's, as had Richard III's. A long sequence of copies may be remarkably precise, but that does not make the DNA at either end the same thing.

30 See note 1, page 234.

31 Ashdown-Hill 2010, 123.

32 This was the 'new' *Mauretania*, launched in 1939; film on board in the year of Joy Ibsen's journey can be seen at http://www.youtube.com/watch?v=MeUCbBjkOtE.

33 Most of the genealogical information is taken from Kevin Schürer's presentation at the February 2013 press conference, and a public talk at the University of Leicester on 29 June 2013. See http://www.le.ac.uk/richardiii/science/genealogy.html and Kennedy and Foxhall 2015.

34 The mtDNA was amplified using conventional PCR, and sequenced using the Sanger method: C. Cole, The discovery of King Richard III: SelectScience interviews Dr Turi King, 12 February 2013, http://www.selectscience.net.

35 Writing about Joy Ibsen's mtDNA, Ashdown-Hill (2013, 118–19) describes 'the seven clan mothers of Europe' referred to by some genetic genealogists. These derive from simplifying complex statistics, and whatever they mean, there is little evidence that they would have been apparent to people living in ancient times. For related reasons, 'mitochondrial Eve', the most recent theoretical person to whom we can all trace a female line, while a useful research construct today, had no known genetic significance at the time she was alive; the attribution will shift to different women as generations continue to breed and die.

Epilogue, pp. 201–27

1 https://speakerscorneratx.wordpress.com/2013/02/04/richard-iii-and-bodies-why-are-we-so-interested-in-this-news.

2 Loser's justice: As Richard III is exhumed a piece of Tudor propaganda could be buried, *The Times* 4 February 2013; Dead chuffed: The great and good of Leicester are brimming with civic pride over their royal link, *The Times* 5 February 2013; S. Woodings, Body of ex-Warwick Castle owner found under a car park 527 years on, *Stratford-upon-Avon Herald* 4 February 2013; J. Burns, Bones under parking lot belonged to Richard III, *The New York Times* 4 February 2013. Nearly 14,000 people 'liked' the story on the *New York*

Times Facebook page, and over 1,300 commented.

3   You can see different takes on this press conference, including the entire academic presentation, at https://www.youtube.com/watch?v=91R-LkW2x3s and https://www.youtube.com/watch?v=VT86ZAgO9Ro. The latter shows a clip from Langley's speech.

4   Baldwin 2013, 215–19.

5   S. Jones, Son of York! Richard III relatives' descendants allowed to challenge Leicester burial, *Guardian* 16 August 2013.

6   Documents including Langley's requirements of a TV broadcaster, and early excavation budget, the Written Scheme of Investigation and the exhumation licence are helpfully reproduced in Carson *et al.* 2014. Paragraph 5.7 of the WSI says any remains which might be the king's would be handed to the client, who would transfer them to the Abbey of Mount St Bernard in a suitable coffin for prayer and worship (who by is not specified), until private reburial in the cathedral, which was not to be 'filmed or photographed at any time'. In Carson *et al.* 2014 and elsewhere, the Looking for Richard team made much of this reburial 'contract', but they misunderstood the situation. By the time the dig occurred, their relationship with the archaeologists (who paid for the WSI) was as partners, not clients, the Richard III Society (at £18,083) and Leicester University (£19,935) together paying the bulk of immediate excavation costs in approximately equal part; the university subsequently covered all the much higher post-excavation costs. The exhumation licence named the archaeologists as legal guardians of any human remains. All this made redundant paragraph 5.7 of the WSI. Paragraphs 4.3–5.8 could also be ignored. These describe the client's desire for severe restrictions on photography, including a requirement that only legitimate scientists could see photos of Richard III's remains 'in a secured archive'. If this had been adhered to, Channel 4 would never had got its films, and Langley could not have reproduced photos of the skeleton in her book. With hindsight it was unfortunate that in the late rush to get the dig underway, such unworkable details, inserted into the WSI in earlier circumstances at Langley's request, were not adjusted.

Langley also misunderstands the excavation of Skeleton 1. Langley and Jones (2013, 100) describe how she had to persuade Buckley to excavate the remains, which were 'of no interest to him'. Having quizzed Buckley and others about this, and from my own knowledge of how excavations work

– and how archaeologists think – I am confident that this did not happen as she remembers it; it is absurd to suggest that an excavation looking for human remains would ignore any found. Langley's memory of the original discovery is also at odds with the archaeologists', and with basic archaeological practice (Langley and Jones 2013, 64–65; compare Act III Scenes 1 and 2).

When the *Essex County Standard* printed a story in which Ashdown-Hill asked for the king's remains to be taken from the university 'and put in some prayerful environment', the paper was obliged to publish a revised piece allowing the university to say the bones were 'in a secure and controlled environment' while research continued: Leading historian says Richard III's bones should be given a proper burial, 10 January 2014.

7   Keep Richard III remains in Leicester, e-petition created 12 October 2012 by Roy Shakespeare.

8   Daily Hansard – Westminster Hall, 12 March 2013, Column 23WH–31WH.

9   Debate over King Richard III simply cannot be buried, *Leicester Mercury* 19 November 2014. Father Cole, spokesman for the Catholic Diocese of Nottingham, which includes Leicester, said, 'A Christian ceremony was held [in 1485] and his body was given back to God'; B. Truslove, Richard III: Does it matter where he is buried? http://bbc.co.uk/news.

10 C. Skidmore, Richard III: a ceremony fit for a king? http://blogs.spectator.co.uk, 19 September 2012.

11 Questions about the re-interment, http://www.le.ac.uk/richardiii/faq/reinterment.html

12 Petition calls for King Richard III to be given Catholic observances when placed in his coffin, http://looking-for-richard.webs.com. 'If King Richard were a Jew or a Muslim', complained Langley, 'the appropriate rites and ceremonies would be observed without question.' Petition calls for Catholic ceremony for Richard III, http://www.bbc.co.uk/news, 23 January 2015.

13 King Richard III and his Return to Yorkshire, Early Day Motion 1046 tabled 6 February 2013 by George Galloway, M.P.

14 Notwithstanding celebrity support (strong among actors, including Judi Dench, Edward Fox and Mark Rylance), and press reports (e.g. J. Groves, Revealed: King Richard III planned to be buried in York not Leicester, according to extraordinary 529 year old letter, *Daily Mail* 18 June 2014, in which the source, Chris Skidmore, said, 'It doesn't prove that Richard wished to be buried at York'; others found the whole issue 'absurd': C. Howse, A sordid song and dance

Notes

over Richard III's bones, *Telegraph* 24 September 2013. A valuable resource on this issue, as well as others, is Richard III: Rumour & Reality (http://richardiii-ipup.org.uk). Supporters of a northern reburial quoted (frequently, in the absence of much else to support their cause) a York document made at the time of the king's death that refers to 'his merciful reign', and how he was 'piteously slain and murdered to the great heaviness of this city'. They did not quote, as the website does among similar texts, a record of a man saying of the Duke of Gloucester, as Richard was then, 'What might he do for the city? Nothing...' See also M. Ormrod, A burial fit for a King, http://www.york.ac.uk.

15 http://www.robeastaway.com/blog/great-uncle-richard; M. Pitts, Richard III update: a coffin, walls and reburial, *British Archaeology*, 133 (2013), 6–7. See also http://www2.le.ac.uk/projects/greyfriars/R3timelineV9.pdf.

16 L. Dixon, Dean is sent hate mail over Richard III, *The Times* 13 March 2013. As Tim Tatton-Brown, a senior medieval archaeologist, wrote in a letter to *The Times* (23 March 2013), 'It is extraordinary how much muddled and ill-informed comment has been aired since the so-called "king in the car park" was summarily excavated in Leicester'.

17 Letters Submitted for Richard III to be Buried in York, 6 February 2013, http://minsterfm.com/news/local/888195/letters-submitted-for-richard-iii-to-be-buried-in-york.

18 Which sounds better than 'descendant of Richard's wife', which implies no blood relationship at all; the queen, like the king, had no direct descendants. Tweet: https://twitter.com/StephenNicolay, 20 February 2013. Letter: R. Alleyne, Bury him in York, say Richard III's descendants, *Telegraph* 24 February 2013.

19 M. Kennedy and O. Bowcott, Richard III's distant relatives threaten legal challenge over burial, *Guardian* 26 March 2013; J. Harris, Gordons secures judicial review for Richard III's descendants, *Lawyer* 16 August 2013.

20 Royal Rumpus: The last Plantagenet King should be laid to rest in Leicester, near where he fell, *The Times* 27 November 2013.

21 J. Harris, High Court rules that Richard III must be buried in Leicester Cathedral, *Lawyer* 23 May 2014.

22 The Judgment, a fascinating read, is available at http://www.11kbw.com/uploads/files/RichardIIIJudgment.pdf. I wrote at length about the review immediately after the hearing, one of the more curious experiences of my archaeological

career: M. Pitts, Richard III in court, https://mikepitts.wordpress.com/2014/03/16/richard-iii-in-court, 16 March 2014.

23 Only when the judgment had been issued did it become clear why the City Council had become involved. It transpired that it saw itself as 'the official owner of [the king's] remains' (a misconception, as English law does not recognize a right of ownership in human bodies). It had also proposed a consultation over their future – raising the possibility that the entire circus might have been avoided if it had kept out of it. Detailing Sarah Levitt's actions, the Judgment found 'The Council's intervention ... was unnecessary, unhelpful and misconceived'. See M. Pitts, Leicester celebrates its king, http://mikepitts.wordpress.com/2014/05/29/leicester-celebrates-its-king, 29 May 2014.

24 According to H. M. Government, e-petitions 'are an easy, personal way for you to influence government and Parliament in the UK' (http://epetitions.direct.gov.uk). The House of Commons promises to hold a debate on a subject if it attracts 100,000 signatures. Most e-petitions are less successful, and none has any constitutional power. With 10,000 votes, the relevant government department responds with a brief comment. In the case of the two Richard III e-petitions that achieved that target, the position of the Ministry of Justice was already clear. The *Leicester Mercury* delivered a paper petition to the Prime Minister's front door, supporting its 'campaign for Richard III to be buried here in the city' (Leicester's 40,000-signature Richard III petition handed over in Downing Street, 15 October 2013).

25 Watch Cumberbatch's arresting reading of the poem in a Channel 4 clip at https://www.youtube.com/watch?v=38nodTfpro4. Dame Carol Ann Duffy is Britain's current Poet Laureate, a ten-year honorary appointment by the reigning monarch.

26 B. Dowell, BBC left scratching its head after C4 snaps up Richard III burial show, *Radio Times* 7 March 2015.

27 T. King and K. Schürer's story of how Richard III's female-line collateral descendants were found and proven is told in Chapter 6, Kennedy and Foxhall 2015.

28 P. Treble, Canada's connection to King Richard III: the inside story, *Maclean's* 22 March 2015.

29 R. Parris, Bones of Richard III sealed in his coffin ahead of funeral, *Hinckley Times* 17 March 2015. Ashdown-Hill had also hoped to put in the coffin 'a relic of the True Cross, and a relic of St Francis', but these were too much for the

cathedral to allow (M. Kennedy and C. Davies, Richard III reburial: 'May you rest in peace in Leicester', *Guardian* 22 March 2015).

30 G. Watson, Richard III burial: Should his remains stay on display? *BBC News* 26 March 2015.

31 B. Donnelly, Cardinal urged to intervene over rites for King Richard III, *Herald* 23 January 2015, http://looking-for-richard.webs.com.

32 Foard and Curry 2013. The most closely argued and nearest alternative location had been proposed by Peter Foss in 1985 (Foss 1998). Not everyone accepts the archaeological evidence (Skidmore 2013, 379–89; P. Foss, A battlefield queried, 13-page privately circulated pamphlet, 2014). Slight though they are, properly understood, the physical data are the best we have.

33 A. Ruck, City of London Police horses to lead Richard III cortege during reburial service tomorrow, *Evening Standard* 21 March 2015.

34 The Society held a candlelit communion service in the church the evening before, complete with armoured knights and medieval woodwind music.

35 R. Parrish, White roses tribute to rain down on Richard III, *Hinckley Times* 8 February 2015.

36 The County Council commissioned a new sculpture, an installation of steel panels called Towards Stillness sited near the cathedral's west end, from architects Dallas Pierce Quintero. P. Warzynski, £75,000 Richard III sculpture is chosen to stand outside Leicester Cathedral, *Leicester Mercury* 28 January 2014; http://dp-q.com/Towards-Stillness.

37 Van Heyningen and Haward Architects, Leicester Cathedral: Proposed Works for the Reinterment of Richard III and Re-ordering Master Plan, CFCE Application 23 September 2013. See also http://www.vhh.co.uk/our-work/leicester.

38 The pall is now a cathedral exhibit; see http://www.jacquiebinns.com for details of the design. The works at Leicester Cathedral are described in a series of blogs at http://kingrichardinleicester.com/topics/blogs and by the Revd Pete Hobson, Acting Canon Missioner, at http://www.leicestercathedralkingrichardiii.org/category/cathedralblog. I have told the events of 22 March in detail because of their interest and, from a narrative and archaeological perspective, symbolic importance. Five days of services and celebrations followed, attended by thousands. The cathedral hosted a Service of Reinterment on 26 March, and a Service of Reveal on 27 March. At the latter, the wonderfully medieval-modern new stone tomb was unveiled in the last of three modern dramas by members of Leicester's Curve Theatre. Bible readings and players enacted a story of conflict, resolution, diversity and peace. Cathedral seats were allotted mostly by invitation, with others made available through a public ballot; 5,000 people applied on the first day, five times the spaces at all three services (Richard III reburial ballot sees thousands apply for public seats, *BBC News* 31 December 2014).

39 From time-stamps on Carl Vivian's photos, the archaeologists ascertained that the mechanical digger broke ground on 25 August 2012 at 8.31 a.m. Morris established at 3.05 p.m. that a human bone was part of an articulated skeleton.

40 Appleby *et al.* 2014; Appleby *et al.* 2015; King *et al.* 2014; Lamb *et al.* 2014. Richard III's head in the Leicester visitor centre was promptly given a striking blond wig. The DNA study noted a 77% probability of blond hair, but added that current DNA predictions 'resemble childhood hair colour, and it is important to note that ... colour can darken during adolescence. It is therefore possible that Skeleton 1 had brown hair' (King *et al.* 2014, 4; see also http://nerdalicious.com.au/history/king-richard-iiis-plastic-head).

41 King *et al.* 2014; Kennedy and Foxhall 2015, Chapter 6 and appendices.

42 P. Lay, Digging up Richard III will not bury old arguments, *Guardian* 4 February 2013. M. Hicks, letter to *The Times*, 4 December 2014. Dominic Selwood, historian, barrister and journalist, takes the same incredible view: Richard III: We're burying the wrong body, *Telegraph* 21 March 2015.

43 But not totally. In May 2015 the *Leicester Mercury* reported that consultants had estimated increased visitor spend in Leicester due to Richard III of nearly £60 million – a good return on £8.9 million (the reported cost of the dig, judicial review, visitor centre, new sculpture, cathedral alterations and reburial) – and the creation of 1,000 full-time equivalent jobs. Phil Stone has described the discovery of the king's grave as 'truly the greatest thing to happen in 500 years of Ricardian history'. The society acquired 450 new members in the month after the February 2013 press event, and nearly 1.5 million hits a day on its website – impressive figures for a small independent organization. P Warzynski, Richard III: [Print] publicity is equivalent of £2m of advertising for Leicester University, *Leicester Mercury* 24 February 2013; if print was worth that much, one can only marvel at the value of broadcast and online coverage, then and since. The Times Higher Education Awards named the discovery of Richard III's remains the 2013

Research Project of the Year, across all UK institutions and subjects; among other awards, the university won a Queen's Anniversary Prize for Higher and Further Education in 2014.

44 For examples of new research, Lansdale and Boon 2013 (psychology); http://www2.le.ac.uk/ offices/press/press-releases/2013/february/ how-did-richard-iii-sound (voice); Knight and Lund 2013 (literature); http://www.youtube.com/ watch?v=hnyYLIdR3bc (Blue Boar Inn). The 2012 excavation is described in a peer-reviewed article, with free online access, in the international journal *Antiquity* (Buckley et al. 2013); within a week the website received twice its normal monthly activity, and two years later the paper was still the most downloaded, at nearly three times the next most popular.

45 The cathedral could see at once that 'this was going to be far, far bigger than we had ever imagined', blogged the Revd Pete Hobson, http:// kingrichardinleicester.com/richardreburied-he-is-now. Tutankhamun drew 7,000 visitors a day; admittedly over a much shorter period, Richard III's score was 8,000.

46 L. Worsley, Why Richard III's final resting place matters, *Guardian* 30 March 2013.

47 J. Snow, Richard III find has changed the course of history: why the King's burial is so important, *Sun* 22 March 2015.

48 This was in the last of the reburial week programmes made for Channel 4 by DSP, *Richard III: The King Laid to Rest* (first broadcast 26 March 2015). The others were *Richard III: The Return of the King* (the reception, 22 March 2015) and *Richard III: The Burial of the King* (the reburial, 26 March 2015).

49 Horrox 1989.

50 Lund 2015.

51 Bupa, a British-based healthcare company, illustrates the bend test wth a self-diagnosis animation: https://www.youtube.com/watch? t=117&v=-iGULOq10ac. D. Singer, Letter to *The Times Literary Supplement*, 15 March 2013, 6; Lund 2015, 2.

52 *Richard III: The New Evidence*, DSP for Channel 4, first broadcast 17 August 2014.

53 Not Langley, perhaps, for whom the same evidence apparently confirms what a nasty lot the Tudors were (P. Langley and M. Jones, 2014, *The King's Grave* [paperback edition of Langley and Jones, 2013], 239–40).

54 H. Mantel, Royal Bodies, *London Review of Books* 35.4 (21 February 2013), 3–7.

FURTHER READING

The Richard III Society's informative website is building a free archive of the *Ricardian*; the society's newsletter, *Ricardian Bulletin*, is also online. Many useful articles can be found on the website of the Leicestershire Archaeological and Historical Society, where its entire *Transactions* since 1855 are freely available. The Bosworth Battlefield Project has a free archive, with substantial reviews of historical sources, at the Archaeology Data Service (ADS, http://archaeologydataservice.ac.uk/archives). The ADS's Grey Literature Library archives all field reports from the University of Leicester Archaeological Services (the Grey Friars project code for both seasons is A11.2012; as I write, the reports have yet to be uploaded). The cathedral's King Richard in Leicester website carries informative blogs about the reburial and other matters, with handy links to other city websites.

Ackroyd, P., 1998. *The Life of Thomas More*. London: Chatto & Windus. New York: Nan A. Talese.

Appleby, J., P. Mitchell, C. Robinson, A. Brough, G. Rutty, R. Harris, D. Thompson and B. Morgan, 2014. 'The scoliosis of Richard III, last Plantagenet King of England: diagnosis and clinical significance.' *The Lancet* 383, 1944.

Appleby, J., G. Rutty, S. Hainsworth, R. Woosnam-Savage, B. Morgan, A. Brough, R. Earp, C. Robinson, T. King, M. Morris and R. Buckley, 2015. 'Perimortem trauma in King Richard III: a skeletal analysis.' *The Lancet* 385, 253–59.

Ashdown-Hill, J., 2006. 'Alive and well in Canada – the mitochondrial DNA of Richard III.' *The Ricardian* 16, 1–9.

Ashdown-Hill, J., 2010. *The Last Days of Richard III*. Stroud: The History Press.

Ashdown-Hill, J., 2013. *The Last Days of Richard III and the Fate of his DNA: The Book that Inspired the Dig*. Stroud: The History Press.

Austrums, R., 2011. *Geophysical Survey Report: Greyfriars Church, Leicester*. Upton-upon-Severn: Stratascan.

Baldwin, D., 1986. 'King Richard's grave in Leicester.' *Transactions Leicestershire Archaeological and Historical Society* 60, 21–24.

Baldwin, D., 2013. *Richard III* (2nd edn). Stroud: Amberley.

Battlefields Trust, 2013. *UK Battlefields Resource Centre*. http://www.battlefieldstrust.com/ resource-centre.

Billson, C., 1920. *Mediaeval Leicester*. Leicester.

Buckley, R., M. Morris, J. Appleby, T. King, D. O'Sullivan and L. Foxhall, 2013. '"The king in the car park": new light on the death and burial of Richard III in the Grey Friars church, Leicester, in 1485.' *Antiquity* 87, 519–38.

Carson, A., 2013. *Richard III: The Maligned King* (2nd edn). Stroud: The History Press.

Carson, A., J. Ashdown-Hill, D. Johnson, W. Johnson and P. Langley, 2014. *Finding Richard III: The Official Account of Research by the Retrieval and Reburial Project*. Horstead: Imprimis Imprimatur.

Carter, H., and A. Mace, 1923. *The Discovery of the Tomb of Tutankhamen*. Mineola, NY: Dover Publications. Reprinted 1977.

Cawthorne, D., 2007. 'The Leicester Arch and the Temple of Janus.' *Leicestershire and Rutland Life*, December 2007, 16–17.

Cottrell, L., 1957. *Lost Cities*. London: Robert Hale. New York: Rinehart.

De Win, P., 2005. '*Danse macabre* around the tomb and bones of Margaret of York.' *The Ricardian* 15, 53–69.

Derrick, M., 2005. *An Archaeological Evaluation of Land at Highcross Street and Vaughan Way, Abbey Ward, Leicester*. Leicester: University of Leicester Archaeological Services.

English Heritage, 2013. *Registered Battlefields*. http://www.english-heritage.org.uk/caring/listing/battlefields.

Fiorato, V., A. Boylston and C. Knüsel, 2007. *Blood Red Roses: The Archaeology of a Mass Grave from the Battle of Towton AD 1461* (2nd edn). Oxford and Oakville: Oxbow Books.

Foard, G., and A. Curry, 2013. *Bosworth 1485: A Battlefield Rediscovered*. Oxford: Oxbow Books.

Foss, P., 1998. *The Field of Redemore: The Battle of Bosworth, 1485* (2nd edn). Newtown Linford: Kairos.

Gaimster, D., S. McCarthy and B. Nurse (eds), 2007. *Making History: Antiquaries in Britain 1707–2007*. London: Royal Academy of Arts.

Gairdner, J., 1878. *History of the Life and Reign of Richard the Third: To which is Added the Story of Perkin Warbeck from Original Documents*. London: Longmans, Green and Co.

Giesen, M., (ed.), 2013. *Curating Human Remains: Caring for the Dead in the United Kingdom*. Woodbridge: Boydell Press.

Hackett, J., 1757. *Select and Remarkable Epitaphs on Illustrious and Other Persons*. Vol. 2. London: Osborne and Shipton.

Hamilton, D., and C. Bronk Ramsey, 2013. *Grey Friars, Leicester 2012: Radiocarbon dating of human bone from Skeleton 1, the, since confirmed, remains of Richard III*, http://www.le.ac.uk/richardiii/science/carbondating.html.

Hammond, P., 2010. *Richard III and the Bosworth Campaign*. Barnsley: Pen and Sword.

Heywood, T., 1829. *The Most Pleasant Song of Lady Bessy*. Manchester: Richard Taylor.

Hicks, M., 2010. *The Wars of the Roses*. Newhaven and London: Yale University Press.

Hipshon, D., 2011. *Richard III*. Abingdon and New York: Routledge.

Horrox, R., 1989. *Richard III: A Study of Service*. Cambridge and New York: Cambridge University Press.

Hoskins, W., and R. McKinley, 1954. *A History of the County of Leicester*. Vol. 2. London: Victoria County History.

Hunt, L., 2011. *An Archaeological Desk-Based Assessment for Land at Greyfriars, St Martin's, Leicester*. Leicester: University of Leicester Archaeological Services.

Johnson, A., 1906. *Glimpses of Ancient Leicester, in Six Periods* (2nd edn). Leicester: Clarke and Satchell.

Jones, M., 2002. *Bosworth 1485: Psychology of a Battle*. Stroud: The History Press. Charleston: Tempus.

Kendall, P., 1955. *Richard the Third*. London: Allen & Unwin. Reprinted 2002 by W. W. Norton.

Kennedy, M., and L. Foxhall, 2015. *The Bones of a King*. Chichester: Wiley Blackwell.

King, T., G. Fortes, P. Balaresque, M. Thomas, D. Balding, P. Delser, R. Neumann, W. Parson, M. Knapp, S. Walsh, L. Tonasso, J. Holt, M. Kayser, J. Appleby, P. Forster, D. Ekserdjian, M. Hofreiter and K. Schürer, 2014. 'Identification of the remains of King Richard III.' *Nature Communications* 5, article 5631, 1–8.

Knight, S., and M. A. Lund, 2013. 'Richard Crookback.' *Times Literary Supplement*, 6 February 2013, 14–15.

Lamb, A., J. Evans, R. Buckley and J. Appleby, 2014. 'Multi-isotope analysis demonstrates significant lifestyle changes in King Richard III.' *Journal of Archaeological Science* 50, 559–65.

Langley, P., 2012a. 'The Man Himself: Looking for Richard: in search of a king.' *Ricardian Bulletin*, June 2012, 26–28.

Langley, P., 2012b. 'Update: Looking for Richard: in search of a king.' *Ricardian Bulletin*, September 2012, 14–15.

Langley, P., and M. Jones, 2013. *The King's Grave: The Search for Richard III*. London: John Murray. New York: St Martin's.

Lansdale, M., and J. Boon, 2013. 'The Man Himself. Richard III – a psychological portrait.' *Ricardian Bulletin*, March 2013. 46–56.

Lund, M. A., 2015. 'Richard's back: death, scoliosis

and myth making.' *Medical Humanities* 8 April 2015, doi:10.1136/medhum-2014-010647

Mancini, D., transl. C. Armstrong, 1969. *The Usurpation of Richard the Third*. Stroud: Alan Sutton.

Mays, S., 2010. *The Archaeology of Human Bones* (2nd edn). Abingdon and New York: Routledge.

McKinley, R., 1958. *A History of the County of Leicester*. Vol. 4: *The City of Leicester*. London: Victoria County History.

Mellor, J., and T. Pearce, 1981. *The Austin Friars, Leicester*. London: Leicestershire County Council and Council for British Archaeology.

Mitchell, P., H.-Y. Yeh, J. Appleby and R. Buckley, 2013. 'The intestinal parasites of King Richard III.' *The Lancet* 382 (7 September), 888.

Molleson, T., 1987. 'Anne Mowbray and the Princes in the Tower: a study in identity.' *London Archaeologist* 5, 258–62.

Morris, M., R. Buckley and M. Codd, 2011. *Visions of Ancient Leicester: Reconstructing Life in the Roman and Medieval Town from the Archaeology of Highcross Leicester Excavations*. Leicester: University of Leicester Archaeological Services.

Morris, M., and R. Buckley, 2013. *Richard III: The King Under the Car Park*. Leicester: University of Leicester Archaeological Services.

Place, I., 1960. 'The history of Alderman Newton's Boys' School, Leicester, 1836–1914.' *Transactions of the Leicestershire Archaeological and Historical Society* 36, 22–44.

Pollard, A., 1991. *Richard III and the Princes in the Tower*. Stroud: Alan Sutton. New York: St Martin's.

Prag, J., and R. Neave, 1997. *Making Faces: Using Forensic and Archaeological Evidence*. London: British Museum Press. College Station: Texas A & M University Press.

Renfrew, C., and P. Bahn, 2012. *Archaeology: Theories, Methods and Practice* (6th edn). London and New York: Thames and Hudson.

Roberts, C., 2009. *Human Remains in Archaeology: A Handbook*. York: Council for British Archaeology.

Ross, C., 1981. *Richard III*. London: Methuen. Berkeley: University of California Press. Reprinted 1999 by Yale University Press.

Seward, D., 1997. *Richard III: England's Black Legend* (2nd edn). London and New York: Penguin Books.

Siemon, J., (ed.), 2009. *King Richard III (Arden Shakespeare, Third Series)*. London: Methuen Drama.

Skidmore, C., 2013. *Bosworth: The Birth of the Tudors*. London: Weidenfeld and Nicolson.

Stirland, A. J., 2000. *Raising the Dead: The Skeleton Crew of King Henry VIII's Great Ship, the Mary Rose*. Chichester and New York: Wiley and Sons.

Strange, A., 1975. 'The Grey Friars, Leicester.' *The Ricardian* 3/50, 3–7.

Tanner, L., and W. Wright, 1935. 'Recent investigations regarding the fate of the Princes in the Tower.' *Archaeologia* 84, 1–26.

Tarlow, S., and N. Stutz, 2013. *The Oxford Handbook of the Archaeology of Death and Burial*. Oxford: Oxford University Press.

Tate, J., 2007. *An Archaeological Field Evaluation on Land Adjacent to the Former Nat West Bank, Grey Friars, Leicester*. Leicester: University of Leicester Archaeological Services.

Tey, J., 1951. *The Daughter of Time*. London: Peter Davies. Reprinted 2002 by Arrow and 2009 by ImPress.

Throsby, J., 1789. *Select Views in Leicestershire, from Original Drawings*. Leicester: J. Throsby.

Throsby, J., 1791. *The History and Antiquities of the Ancient Town of Leicester*. Leicester: J. Throsby.

Toulmin Smith, L., (ed.), 1907. *The Itinerary of John Leland in or about the Years 1535–1543*. Vol. 1. London: George Bell and Sons.

Tudor-Craig, P., 1973. *Richard III*. London: National Portrait Gallery.

Warwick, R., 1986. 'Anne Mowbray: skeletal remains of a medieval child.' *London Archaeologist* 5, 176–79.

Watson, B., 2013. 'The princess in the police station.' *British Archaeology* 130, 20–23.

Wheatley, H., 1891. *London Past and Present: Its History, Associations, and Traditions*. Vol. 3. London: John Murray. 1968, Detroit: Singing Tree.

Wilkinson, C., 2004. *Forensic Facial Reconstruction*. Cambridge and New York: Cambridge University Press.

Wilkinson, C., 2013. 'The man himself: the face of Richard III.' *The Ricardian* 23, 50–55.

Wilkinson, C., and C. Rynn (eds), 2012. *Craniofacial Identification*. Cambridge and New York: Cambridge University Press.

ACKNOWLEDGMENTS

I thank the many people who helped me in the research for this book, especially those Leicester University archaeologists and scientists whose work was greatly disrupted by the arrival of Richard III into their lives, but yet found time to tell their stories and answer my questions: Richard Buckley, Turi King, Mathew Morris and Kevin Schürer in particular, as well as Jo Appleby, Jon Coward, Tony Gnanaratnam, Sarah Hainsworth, Leon Hunt and Deirdre O'Sullivan. Also at the university Ather Mirza, Peter Thorley (Press Office) and Carl Vivian were very helpful, and I am most grateful for the help and encouragement I received from Lin Foxhall and Richard Taylor. Other thanks go to David Baldwin, Glenn Foard, Sir Peter Soulsby, Phil Stone, Chris Wardle, Peter Warzynski, Caroline Wilkinson and Bob Woosnam-Savage, and Catherine Daunt (Assistant Curator, National Portrait Gallery), Bryony Millan (Archivist, National Portrait Gallery), Theya Molleson (Natural History Museum), Heather Rowland (Head of Library and Collections, Society of Antiquaries) and staff at the Record Office for Leicestershire, Leicester & Rutland. I was delighted to be invited by Leicester Cathedral to the Service for the Reception of the Remains on 22 March. I thank Philippa Langley, without whom none of this would have begun. I interviewed her before I knew I was to write the book, which itself would not have happened had Colin Ridler not suggested it: working with Thames & Hudson has been a pleasure, not least with Colin and Alice Reid as editors, Jennifer Moore as editor for the paperback edition, Louise Thomas as picture researcher and Karolina Prymaka as designer. The University of Leicester acknowledges over 100 named people in its search for Richard III (http://www2.le.ac.uk/offices/press/media-centre/richard-iii/press-conference-4-february/), as well as unnamed individuals who include 'the staff of the "secret location" where the bones [were] retained'.

In February 2013 I left a press conference in Leicester with great excitement. I was impressed with the research and the presentation, and pleased that the archaeologists had agreed to write about the excavation for the magazine I edit, *British Archaeology*. Later I found much cynicism, especially among academics. 'All they can see', I wrote in my diary, 'is PR and fluff, I get quite angry.' Working on the book allowed me to confirm that this really was a well managed, cooperative project in which extraordinary talents wished no more than to establish what truths they could. In November 2013 I watched Mathew Morris (wearing jeans and a T-shirt featuring a Dalek and the word 'Excavate!'), Jo Appleby and Turi King address an audience in the Royal Institution's Faraday Theatre in London. Between them they had personally found and excavated Richard III's remains, and established their identity – yet none of them once said, 'I did it', preferring to talk about the larger team. It has been some achievement of all involved to remain so focused in the whirlwind of global attention.

SOURCES OF ILLUSTRATIONS

2 National Portrait Gallery, London 11 Nigel Norrington/ArenaPAL/TopFoto 14 Lambeth Palace Library, London 18 Bristol Record Office 22 Courtesy of the Duke of Buccleuch 31 Mike Pitts/Drazen Tomic 35 Mike Pitts 37 Album/Quintlox/SuperStock 38, 48, 49, 54, 57 Mike Pitts 65 Mike Pitts/Drazen Tomic 72 Blom UK/Getty Images 81 By permission of the Society of Antiquaries of London (LDSAL 321) 86 Mike Pitts 92 Gavin Fogg/AFP/Getty Images 97 Mike Pitts 103 Rui Vieira/Press Association Images 105 Mike Pitts/Drazen Tomic after ULAS 111 Mike Pitts 117 Mike Pitts/Drazen Tomic after ULAS 125 Gavin Fogg/AFP/Getty Images 132 Mike Pitts 136 Aman Phull 143 Dan Kitwood/Getty Images 162 Aman Phull 163, 175 Mike Pitts 179 British Library, London/Robana/Getty Images 188 left National Portrait Gallery, London 188 right Mike Pitts 190 British Library, London 198 Andrew Winning/Reuters/Corbis 200, 214, 215 Mike Pitts 216 Mike Pitts/Drazen Tomic 217 Courtesy of Dr. Glenn Foard FSA 221 Joe Giddens/PA Wire/Press Association Images 222 Mike Pitts

INDEX

Addison, Heidi 160
Aitken, Janice 187–8
Ambion Hill 218
Anne of York 59–60
Appleby, Jo excavates Skeleton 1
126–45; excavates Skeleton 2
127; career 129; 2012 press
conference 143, 154; unease
with graveside ceremony
146–7; takes Skeleton 1 from
site 148, 150; post-excavation
meeting 156–7; analysis of
Skeleton 1 157, 160, 165–71;
2013 press conference 199,
200; remains passed to
Cathedral 212–3, 214
Armitage, Richard 77, 94
armour 143, 181, 182, 235n17(L)
arrowhead, iron 145, 152, 165
Arundel Roman Catholic
Cathedral 209
Ashdown-Hill, John 58–62,
64–5, 70, 87, 89, 102, 110, 145,
147, 163, 194, 195, 208, 211,
212
Austin Friars 40, 42–3, 46,
49–50, 65, 69, 87

Balaresque, Patricia 197
Baldwin, David 70, 199,
231n19(L), 231n20(L)
Barnet, Battle of 26, 27, 31
Battles, Wars of the Roses: see
Barnet; Blore Heath;
Bosworth; Edgcote; Hedgeley
Moor; Hexham; Losecoat Field;
Ludford Bridge; Mortimer's
Cross; Northampton; St
Albans; Tewkesbury; Towton;
Wakefield
BBC 60, 201–2, 211, 217
BBC Radio Leicester 96, 100, 101
Beard, Mary 223
Beaufort, Margaret 16, 21–2
Billson, Charles 70–1
Binns, Jacquie 222, 222
Black Friars 65, 69, 87
Blore Heath, Battle of 22–3, 31
Blue Boar Inn, Leicester 36–7, 46
bone, behaviour of 132, 158

Book of Hours 13–14, 14, 98
Bosworth, Battle of 10, 11, 13, 17,
21, 22, 31, 32, 34, 41, 47, 52, 53,
54, 91, 96, 100, 160, 174, 175,
176, 183, 189, 192, 204, 210,
218; archaeology 11, 215–16,
216, 217; re-enactment 96–8,
215–16, 215
Bosworth Battlefield Heritage
Centre 96, 215, 218
Bow Bridge: see Leicester: Bow
Bridge
Bow Bridge skeleton 39–40
British Academy 225–6
British Museum 224
Broadbent, Benjamin 34–5, 39, 49
Bronk Ramsey, Christopher 172
Buckingham, Henry Duke of 17,
27, 28–30, 183
Buckley, Richard: doubts about
finding Richard III 7, 63, 78,
115; director of ULAS 41; with
Leicester Archaeological Unit
41, 45; first dig 41–4, 46–7;
school 42–3; university 44;
Langley contacts 50, 63–6; no
interest in finding Richard III
56; search for friary 63, 153;
plans 2012 dig 64; works
with Langley 76–8, 83–4, 88;
agrees to join search 84; WSI
85, 93; Guildhall book launch
86; GPR survey 88–90;
costing 90; university grant
95; excavation launch 101–2;
Skeleton 1 found 113–14;
walls found 115–16; delegates
121; applies for exhumation
licence 122, 124; plans for
reburial 124–5; invites
Appleby 128–9; discusses
with O'Sullivan 134; Richard
III found 137–142, 151, 154;
press briefing 138; Langley
asks to drape flag 145; press
conference 154; post-
excavation meeting 156–7;
skeletal analysis 166; public
talks 170; 2013 press
conference 6, 199, 200, 203;
remains passed to Cathedral
211, 214; reinterment 219–20
Butler, James 47–8, 48, 79, 219

Cambridge University 223
Capwell, Tobias 218–19
car parks: New Street 51, 54, 60–1,
73, 74, 106, 117, 195; R on
tarmac 55, 107, 110, 133, 145,
159, 234n9(R); Social Services
55, 58, 61–2, 64, 73, 74–6, 84,
87–91, 94, 101–2, 105, 106, 110,
111, 117, 118–19, 121, 156, 231n21
Carson, Annette 78–9, 79, 89,
91, 92, 94, 146, 191
Cassiman, Jean-Jacques 59
Castillon, Battle of 20
Castleman, Jonathan 212
Castor, Helen 224, 225
Channel 4 50, 61, 62, 89, 96,
108, 126, 140, 146–7, 148, 178,
199, 202, 211, 223, 226
Clarence, George, Duke of 15, 17,
26, 27–8
Clay, Patrick 41, 43, 44, 45–6
clinical imaging 184–5, 186
Codd, Mike 86–7, 93
Cooper, Nick 156–7
Coppack, Glyn 134–5, 139, 151
Croyland Chronicle, the 192
Cumberbatch, Benedict 210

Dadlington 175, 175, 210, 218
Darlow Smithson Productions 62,
88–9, 108, 112, 114–15, 125–6,
130–31, 133, 139–40, 145, 199,
202, 208, 211, 233n5, 233n9,
233n14, 240n48, 240n52
death, archaeology of 122–3, 233n1
desk based assessment 66–8,
70–1, 84, 89, 124
DNA analysis 59–61, 102, 113,
144, 148, 150, 154, 160, 163,
165, 196–7, 199–200, 223
Doran, Gregory 225, 227
Duffy, Carol Ann 210, 221
Duldig, Wendy 212
Dundee, University of 161, 185,
187

East Midlands Forensic Pathology
Unit (EMFPU) 161, 167, 178
Eastaway, Rob 207
Edgcote, Battle of 26, 31
Edmund, brother of Richard III
17, 23–5, 27
Edmund, son of Richard III 17, 18

Index

247